American and European D
of
William the Conqueror

Volume 2
Generations 19 to 23

researched by North East Genealogical Research

compiled by Ronald W. Collins

Hebron, NH

© Copyright 2019 Ronald W. Collins All Rights Reserved

First Edition

ISBN-13: 9781089948018

Other books by Ronald W. Collins

Histories and Genealogies

The McLanes – A New Hampshire Clan

The McLanes - Origin of the Clan

The Genealogy of the Clan MacLean

The Collins Family History

Klingler and Walbolt Family Histories

Sergeant John Ordway, A History with his Genealogy

A History of Newfound Lake

The History of Hebron, NH

The Genealogies of Hebron, NH

Literary Works

Found There

Acknowledgements

The database needed to create these two volumes contains nearly 35,000 genealogical entries. The compilation of the database has taken decades and would not have been possible without the software called Family Tree Maker.

Among the people who have contributed greatly to the desire to build this database are:

My wife Janice Collins, who not only puts up with me on my data collecting hunts, but actually helps me research and make sense of the data.

My parents, for whom this collection was started in 1979.

My good friend P. Andrews McLane whose family research project turned into a multi-year, multi-county adventure.

To the many people who have requested my help in researching their families.

Book Organization

This book follows the nomenclature of the New England Historical Genealogical Register. Below is an example of how to use that nomenclature.

In this example, this family is number 76 in a report (not necessarily in this book, this is just an example), indicated by the "76" in the far-left margin. The main subject, Maud Marshall, was the daughter of William Marshall and Isabel De Clare (61). Notice William does not have a number after his name indicating that he does not appear elsewhere in the book as a direct descendant. Isabel De Clare, Maud's mother, has a 61 after her name indicating that she is a descendant given in this report as entry number 61.

After the details of Maud's life her children by each of her marriages are listed. If the child, for example,

"+   94   i.   Lady Isabel^{16} Bigod"

has a number to the left, in this example 94, that indicated that she had a family and that the family appears as entry 94. If a child does not have a number to the left, then that child does not appear again in this report.

The roman numeral "i" indicates that she was the first child born to Maud. and finally, the superscript "16" indicates that she is in the 16th generation given in this book.

Example - The Family of Maud Marshall and William De Warenne

76.   Maud^{15} Marshall was born in September 1192 in Pembroke, Pembrokeshire, Wales. She was the daughter of William Marshall and Isabel De Clare (61).

Maud was known by the title of Countess of Surrey. She died in Tintern Abbey, Chapel Hill, Monmouthshire, England, on March 27, 1248, at the age of 55.

Maud married Hugh Bigod about 1212. Hugh Bigod was born in Norfolk, England, in 1186. He was the son of Roger Bigod (80) and Isabel.

Hugh was known by the title of 3rd Earl of Norfolk. Hugh reached 39 years of age and died in Norfolk, England, on February 18, 1225. He was a signer of the Magna Carta.

Maud Marshall next married William De Warenne on October 13, 1225, in Surrey, England. William De Warenne was born in Reigate Castle, Reigate, Surrey, England, in 1166. He was the son of Hamelin de Anjou and Isabel DeWarenne. William was known by the title of 5th Earl of Surrey, and the of 6th Earl of Warren. William reached 74 years of age and died at Age: 73 in London, Middlesex, England, on May 27, 1240. He was buried in Lewes, East Sussex, England.

Children of Maud Marshall and Hugh Bigod:

+ 94   i.   Lady Isabel[16] Bigod was born in Thetford, Norfolk, England, in 1210.

+ 95   ii.   Hugh Bigod was born in Thetford, Norfolk, England, in 1215.

+ 96   iii.   Roger Bigod.

Son of Maud Marshall and William De Warenne:

+ 97   iv.   John de Warenne was born in Warren, Sussex, England, on August 7, 1231.

Contents

Acknowledgements 2
Book Organization 4
Contents 6
Introduction 22
William The Conqueror and Matilda of Flanders 29
Families of the Descendants of William the Conqueror and Matilda of Flanders. ... 29
   19th Generation 29
      Family of Jane Bulkeley and Maurice Wynne 29
      Family of Robert Needham and Frances Ashton 30
      Family of Thomas Howard and Mary of Arundel 31
      Family of John Allen and Elizabeth Alabaster 31
      Family of George Allen and Katherine Starkes 32
      Family of Lady Mary Katherine Cary and Sir Francis Knollys 32
      Family of Walter Hungerford and Ann Dormer 33
      Family of Thomas Yorke and Mary Sutton 33
      Family of Humphrey Styles and Elizabeth ? 33
      Family of Elizabeth Yorke and Edmund Perceval 34
      Family of John Gray and Barbara Sanderson 34
      Family of Sarah Winter and Robert Jordan 35
      Family of John Conger and Mary Kelly 35
      Family of John Thompson and Alice Freeman 36
      Family of Ann Totteshurst and John Thomas 37
      Family of James Burges and Margaret Marsh 37
      Family of Richard Bennett and Elizabeth Tisdale 37
      Family of Hezekiah Usher and Mary ? 38
      Family of John Harrington and Isabella Markham 38
      Family of Agnes Crosse and John Wolcott 39
      Family of Alice Molyneux and James Prescott 39
      Family of Robert Hyde and Jane Davenport 40
      Family of George Gardiner and Margaret Neville 40
      Family of Hervey Bagot and Catherine Adderley 40
      Family of John Walker and Mary Jowet 41
      Family of Jean Baptiste Amiot and Genevieve Guyon 41
      Family of John Townsend and Elizabeth Montgomery 42
      Family of John Crubach McLean and Anne Campbell 42
      Family of Ewen the elder MacLean and Sarah MacLaine 43

Family of Charles Maclean and Margaret Horner 43
Family of Mary MacLean and Charles MacLean 43
Archibald Maclean 44
Family of Marion MacLean and John Roy MacLean 45
Family of Lachalan Og MacLean and Flora MacLean 45
Ewen MacLean 45
Family of Beathag MacLean and Hector Odhar MacLaine 46
Family of Hector Og MacLean and Janet Mackenzie 46
Family of Gillean Maclean and Mary the elder Maclean 47
Family of Lachlan Og MacLean and Marian Campbell 47
Family of Allan Maclean and Mary the younger Maclean 48
Family of Charles Maclean and Margaret MacLaine 48
Family of Janet MacLean and John Garbh MacLean 48
Family of Lachlan MacLean and Florence Macleod 49
Family of John MacLean and Jannet Stuart 49
Family of Mary the elder Maclean and Gillean Maclean 49
Family of Julian MacLean and Hector MacLean 50
Family of Charles Maclean and Mary MacLean 50
Family of Hector Maclean and Jannet MacLean 51
Family of Jannet MacLean and Hector Maclean 51
Family of Mary the younger Maclean and Allan Maclean 51
Family of Lachlan Maclean and first wife unknown 52
Family of John Diurach MacLean and Elizabeth MacLean 52
Family of Lachlan MacLean and Catherine Macdonald 52
Charles MacLean 53
Family of Charles MacLean and Flora MacNeil 53
Charles McLean 53
Family of Duncan McLean and Christian Nikeich 53
Donald Og MacLean 53
Family of Hector MacLean and Marion MacQuarrie 54
Family of John MacLean and ? Campbell 54
Family of Donald MacLean and Isabel Campbell 54
Family of Charles MacLean and Florence MacLean 55
Ewen MacLean 55
Allan MacLean 55
Rory MacLean 56
Family of Roderick MacLean and Marion MacLean 56
Family of John MacLean and Margaret Mauchline 56
Family of John MacLean and Elizabeth Matthews 57
John MacLean 57
John MacLean 57

Donald MacLean 57
Family of John MacLean and Catherine MacLean... 57
Family of Alexander MacLean and Agnes Chisholm 58
Family of John Og MacLean and Margaret Fowler 58
Donald MacLean 59
Family of Bridget MacLean and Angus MacQueen... 59
Family of Margaret MacLean and Donald Campbell 59
Family of Jannet MacLean and Malcolm MacIntosh 59
Family of Alexander MacLean and Agnes Chisolm 59
Hector MacLean 60
Hector MacLean 60
Family of James Borthwick and Margaret Hay 60
Family of William Warren and Catherine Gookin 60
Family of Richard Hardy and Alice Wilson 61
Family of John Dudley and Elizabeth Leighton 61
Family of John Dudley and Elizabeth Leighton 61
Family of Judith Birdsall and Henry Cook... 62
Family of Nathan Birdsall and Temperance Fowler Baldwin 63
Family of Elizabeth St. John and Samuel Whiting.. 63
Family of Olive Welby and Henry Farwell 64
Family of Elizabeth Barker and William Freethy... 64

20th Generation 64
Family of George Wynne and Margaret Green 64
Family of Dorothy Needham and Richard Chetwood 65
Family of Phillip Howard and Anne Dacre 65
Family of Thomas Allen and Mary Fairclough 66
Family of Ralph Allen and Esther Susanna Swift 66
Family of William Knowles and Dorothy Braye 66
Family of Lucy and John St John 67
Family of Mary Yorke and Thomas Randes.. 67
Family of Humphrey Stiles and Bridget Baudrey 68
Family of Christian Perceval and Richard Lowell 68
Family of James Gray and Alison Gifert... 69
Family of Samuel Silas Jordan and Frances Baker 69
Family of John Conger and Mary Tuttle 69
Family of John Thompson and Ellen Harrison 70
Family of Benjamin Thomas and Mirable Fitch... 70
Family of Sarah Burges and William Merriam 71
Family of William Bennett and Joan Hodgson.. 71
Family of John Bennett and Ann Weeks 71
Family of Dorothy Elizabeth Usher and John Harwood 72

Family of John Harrington and Mary Rogers ... 73
Family of Henry Wolcott and Elizabeth Saunders ... 73
Family of John Prescott and Elizabeth Manby ... 74
Family of Robert Hydeand Annie Ardene ... 74
Family of George Gardiner and Dorothy Constable ... 75
Family of Edward Bagot and Mary Lambard ... 75
Family of William Walker and Elizabeth Brigg ... 75
Family of Marie Anne Amiot and Francois Michel Messier ... 76
Family of John Townsend and Susanna Harcourt ... 76
Family of Ewen MacLean and Mary MacLaine ... 77
Family of Lachlan McLean and Mary MacLean ... 77
Family of Jannet McLean and John Diuriach Maclean ... 77
Family of Donald McLean and Janet MacLean ... 78
Family of Allan McLean and Janet MacLean ... 78
Family of Mary McLean and John Maclean ... 78
Family of Lachlan Maclean and Florence Fraser ... 78
Family of Allan the elder Maclean and Mary Cameron ... 79
Family of Allan the younger Maclean and Una MacQuarrie ... 79
Family of Donald MacLean and Catherime MacQuarrie ... 80
Family of Hector Maclean and Jannet MacLean ... 80
Family of Ewen Maclean and Marion MacLean ... 81
Family of Marion MacLean and Ewen Maclean ... 81
Family of Ann MacLean and Lachlan Maclean ... 81
Family of Allan MacLean and Catherine MacLeod ... 81
Hector MacLean ... 82
Allan MacLean ... 82
Family of Murdock Mor MacLaine and Julian Campbell ... 82
Family of Lachlan Mor MacLaine and Margaret MacLean ... 82
Family of Margaret MacLaine and Charles Maclean ... 83
Family of Janet MacLaine and John Cambell ... 83
Family of Mary MacLaine and Neil Maclean ... 83
Family of Sarah MacLaine and Hector McLean ... 83
Family of Hector Mor Maclean and Margaret MacLeod ... 84
Family of Lachlan MacLean and Mary MacLeod ... 84
Family of Finvola (Florence) MacLean and John Garbh MacLean ... 84
Family of Donald MacLean and Finvole (Florence) MacLean ... 85
Family of Hector Maclean and Catherine Campbell ... 85
Family of Jannet MacLean and Hector Maclean ... 86
Family of Mary MacLean and John Garbh MacLean ... 86
Lachlan Og Maclean ... 87
Family of John Diuriach Maclean and Jannet McLean ... 87

Family of Julian MacLean and Allan MacLaine 88
Family of Neil Maclean and Mary MacLaine 88
Family of Margaret MacLean and Hector McLean 88
Family of John Garbh MacLean and Florence Campbell.. 88
Family of Hector MacLean and Julian MacLean 89
Family of Neil MacLean and Florence MacDonald 90
Family of Jannet MacLean and Farquhar Fraser 90
Patrick MacLean 91
Family of Allan Maclean and Una... 91
Family of Hector MacLean and Mary MacLean 91
Family of Donald MacLean and Isabella MacAdam 91
Family of Margaret MacLean and John McLean 92
John Ban McLean... 92
Family of Duncan McLean and Janet McMalvay 92
Lachlan MacLean 93
Allan MacLean 93
Neil MacLean 93
Ewen MacLean 93
Family of Archibald MacLean and a daughter of Samual MacDonald............................... 93
John MacLean... 94
Family of Neil MacLean and a daughter of Lachlan MacLean 94
Family of John MacLean and Florence MacLean 94
Family of Donald MacLean and Isabella Campbell 95
Family of Ann MacLean and Hector MacLean... 95
Family of Archibald MacLean and Susan Campbell... 95
Family of Mary MacLean and John MacLean 96
Family of Neil MacLean and Florence MacLean 96
Family of Lachlan MacLean and Maria Fatmangle 96
Family of Isabel MacLean and John MacLean.. 96
Donald MacLean 97
Lachlan MacLean 97
John MacLean... 97
Neil MacLean 97
Family of John McLean and Marritje DeWitt 97
Family of Lachlan MacLean and Catherine Campbell.. 98
Family of John MacLean and Christina MacLean 98
Hector MacLean 98
Family of John MacLean and Jannet Dallas.. 99
Family of Janet MacLean and William MacIntosh 99
Family of Annie MacLean and James Ross 99
Family of John Og MacLean and Margaret Fowler 99

    Laclhlan MacLean 100
    Family of John Borthwick and Lilias Ker.. 100
    Family of Thomas Warren Warren and Jane Allen King 101
    Family of John Hardy and Olive Council 101
    Family of Roger Dudley and Susannah Thorne.. 102
    Family of Isaac Cook and Elizabeth Barton 102
    Family of Henry Birdsall and Mary ? 103
    Family of Samuel Whiting and Dorcas Chester 104
    Family of Samuel Whiting and Dorcas Chester 104
    Family of Olive Farwell and Benjamin Spalding 104
    Family of James Freethy and Mary Milbury 104

21st Generation 105
    Family of Edward Wynne and Mary Dorothy Berkeley...................................... 105
    Family of Grace Chetwood and Peter Bulkeley 105
    Family of Thomas Howard and Alethea Talbot 106
    Family of Jane Allen and Peter Bulkeley 106
    Family of Ebenezer Allen and Abigail Hill 107
    Family of William Knowles and Grace Clavell.. 107
    Family of Elizabeth Lucy St. John and Allen Apsley 108
    Family of Mary Randes and George Merriton... 108
    Family of Edmond Stiles and Mary Berney 109
    Family of Percival Lowell and Rebecca Alice Goodale 109
    Family of George Gray and Sarah Cooper 109
    Family of Thomas Fleming Jordan and Lucy Corker.. 110
    Family of John Conger and Zipporah Moores.. 110
    Family of Joseph Thompson and Elizabeth Smith 111
    Family of Rebecca Thompson and Daniel Thomas... 111
    Family of John Thomas and Tabitha Charles 112
    Family of Joseph Merriam and Sarah Goldstone.. 112
    Family of William Bennett and Mary ? 113
    Family of Thomas Bennett and Alice Pierce 113
    Family of Peter Harwood and Elizabeth Garey 113
    Family of James Harrington and Ann Clinton... 114
    Family of Anna Wolcott and Matthew Griswold 114
    Family of James Prescott and Mary Copeland 115
    Family of Maria Hyde and George Tomlinson.. 115
    Family of Thomas Gardner and Elizabeth White 116
    Family of Walter Bagot and Jane Salesbury.. 116
    Family of Thomas Walker and Anne Peele 116
    Family of Francois Michel Messier and Marie Josephe Guyon 117
    Family of Solomon Townsend and Catherine Almy 117

Family of Allan MacLean and Anne Cameron.. 118
Family of Donald MacLean and Janet MacLean... 118
Family of Margaret MacLean and Allan MacLachlan 119
Allan MacLean 119
Family of Hector Maclean and Mary MacLean 119
Family of Charles Maclean and Isabella Cameron 119
Family of Donald Maclean and Susanna Campbell 120
Family of Florence MacLean and Hector MacLean 120
Family of Marian Maclean and Hector MacLean.. 121
Family of Margaret MacLean and Allan Maclean 121
Family of John Maclean and Mary McLean.. 121
Family of Donald Maclean and Florence MacLean 122
Family of Lachlan Maclean and Janet MacLeod... 122
Family of Charles Maclean and Marian MacLean 122
Family of John MacLean and Isabella Campbell 123
Family of Margaret Maclean and Hector MacLean 123
Family of Jannet Maclean and John Campbell.. 124
Alexander MacLean... 124
Family of Angus MacLean and Anna MacLean.. 124
Family of Charles MacLean and Jean Campbell 124
Family of Hector MacLean and Julian MacLachlan 124
Allan MacLean 125
Family of Charles MacLean and a daughter of Donald Cameron 125
Allan MacLean 125
Family of Hector MacLaine and Margaret Campbell.. 125
Family of Murdock Og MacLaine and Anne Campbell 126
Family of John MacLaine and Isabel MacDougal... 126
Family of Mary MacLaine and Ewen MacLean 126
Family of Allan Maclean and Julian Macleod... 127
Family of Catherine MacLean and Lachlan MacQuarrie 127
Family of Hector Og MacLean and Janet McNeil... 128
Family of Lachlan MacLean and Isabella Maclean... 128
Family of Marion MacLean and John Crubach McLean... 128
Family of Margaret MacLean and Lachlan Mor MacLaine 129
Family of Lachlan MacLean and Barbara MacDonald 130
Family of John Maclean and Catherine Campbell 130
Family of Isabella Maclean and Lachlan MacLean... 131
Family of Jannet MacLean and Hector Maclean... 131
Family of John Maclean and Mary Campbell 131
Family of Charles MacLean and Marian MacLean 132
Family of Catherine McLean and Hector McLean.. 132

Family of Hector MacLean and Florence McLean 133
Family of Jannet MacLean and Malcolm MacDuffie 133
Family of Catherine MacLean and Ewen MacLean 134
Family of Donald Maclean and a daughter of MacGillvray 134
Family of Ewen McLean and Margaret MacLean 134
Family of Hector Roy MacLean and Marion MacLean 135
Family of Finvole (Florence) MacLean and Donald MacLean 135
Family of John Roy MacLean and an unknown woman 136
Family of Una MacLean and John Maclean 136
Lachlan MacLean 136
Family of Hector MacLean and Catherine MacLean 137
Family of Margaret MacLean and Ewen McLean 137
Family of Marian MacLean and Charles MacLean 137
Family of Allan MacLean and Catherine MacLean 138
Family of Janet MacLean and Charles MacLean 138
Family of Hector MacLean and Florence MacLean 139
Family of Margaret MacLean and Donald MacLean 139
Family of Florence Fraser and Lachlan Maclean 139
Duncan MacLean 139
Family of Charles Maclean and Marianna ? 140
Family of John MacLean and Marion MacQueen 140
Family of Donald MacLean and Anne MacLean 140
Family of Ewen McLean and Catherine MacLean 140
Farquhar McLean 141
Family of Donald McLean and Catherine Stewart 141
Charles MacLean 142
Charles MacLean 142
Family of John MacLean and Deborah Adams 142
Family of Catherine MacLean and Allan MacLean 142
Family of Mary MacLean and Hector Maclean 142
Family of Neil Ban MacLean and a daughter of William MacDonald 143
Alexander MacLean 143
Family of John MacLean and Florence MacLean 143
Neil Ban MacLean 144
Family of Charles MacLean and Catherine MacLean 144
Family of Barbara MacLean and Hugh McLean 144
Family of Florence MacLean and Donald MacLean 144
Family of Ann MacLean and Hugh MacLean 144
Angus MacLean 144
Family of Margaret MacLean and John MacLean 145
Family of John MacLean and Margaret MacLean 145

Charles MacLean 145
Family of Cornelius McLean and Sarah Schoonmaker 145
Family of John MacLean and Finvola MacLean 146
Family of Donald MacLean and Susan Haney 146
Family of Charles MacLean and Marjory MacIntosh 146
Family of John MacLean and Christina Dallas 147
Family of Alexander MacLean and Mary Campbell 148
Family of David MacLean and Anna Gordon 148
Family of Donald MacLean and ? Campbell 148
Family of Jannet MacLean and William MacIntosh 149
Family of Annie MacLean and James Ross 149
Donald MacLean 149
Family of Baron John Borthwick and Lady Mary Elizabeth Kerr 149
Family of Robert Warren and Anne ? 150
Joseph Hardy 150
Family of Elizabeth Hardy and Roger Haskell 150
Family of Thomas Dudley and Dorothy Yorke 151
Family of Hannah Cook and William King 151
Family of Sarah Cook and Isaac Merrill 152
Family of Mary Birdsall and John Gerret Dorlandt 153
Family of Samuel Whiting and Elizabeth Read 153
Family of Samuel Whiting and Elizabeth Read 153
Family of Edward Spalding and Mary Adams 154
Family of Elizabeth Freethy and Robert Gray 154

22nd Generation 154
Family of Edward Winn and Joanna Sargent 154
Family of Gershom Bulkeley and Sarah Chauncey 155
Family of Mary Anne Howard and Jeffery Ferris 155
Family of Edward Bulkeley and Lucien ? 156
Family of James B Allen and Mary Akin 156
Family of John Knowles and Jemima Aster 157
Family of Lucy Apsley and John Hutchinson 157
Family of Anne Merriton and Francis Wright 158
Family of Thomas Stiles and Maria ? 158
Family of Joanna Percival Lowell and William Gerrish 158
Family of Robert Gray and Elizabeth Freethy 159
Family of Thomas Jordan and Margaret Brasseur 159
Family of Phoebe Conger and Benjamin Coddington 160
Family of Ebenezer Thompson and Esther Stevens 161
Family of John Thomas and Mary Ford 161
Family of Israel Thomas and Sarah Humphreville 162

Family of Daniel Thomas and Rebecca Thompson 163
Family of William Merriam and Elizabeth Breed 163
Family of John Bennett and Anne Quaint.. 163
Family of Richard Bennett and Anne Barham.. 164
Family of Peter Harwood and Elizabeth Taylor 164
Family of Robert Harrington and Susanna George... 165
Family of Anna Griswold and Abraham Bronson 166
Family of James Prescott Sr and Mary Boulter 167
Family of Henry Tomlinson and Alice Johnson 168
Family of Rachel Gardner and Thomas Noble 168
Family of Edward Bagot and Frances Wagstaffe 169
Family of George Walker and Mary Brown... 169
Family of Marie Judith Messier and Joseph Bousquet 169
Family of Solomon Townsend and Lydia Tillinghast 170
Family of Isabella MacLean and Donald MacLean... 170
Family of John MacLean and Margery MacLachlan... 171
Family of Margaret MacLean and Angus Maclean 171
Family of Mary MacLean and John MacLean.. 171
Family of Margery MacLachlan and John MacLean 172
Family of Anna MacLean and Angus MacLean 172
Family of Marjory MacLean and Allan McLean 172
Lachlan Maclean.. 172
Family of Allan MacLean and Anne MacLean 172
Family of John Maclean and Margaret Campbell... 173
Family of Alexander Maclean and Mary MacLean 174
Family of Donald Maclean and Anne MacLean 174
Family of Hector Maclean and Catherine MacLean.. 174
Family of Una Maclean and Alexander MacGillvray.. 175
Family of Allan the elder Maclean and Isabella Campbell.................................... 175
Family of Hector Maclean and Julian MacLean 175
Family of Donald Maclean and Mary Mean... 176
Family of Alexander Maclean and Una MacGillivray 176
Family of Donald MacLean and Ann MacLean.. 176
Family of Una MacLean and Allan MacLean 177
Family of Janet MacLean and Duncan MacArthur.. 177
Family of Catherine MacLean and Donald MacDonald.. 177
Family of Hector MacLean and Marion MacQuarrie 177
Hector MacLean... 178
Family of Allan MacLean and Margory MacLean 178
Family of John MacLean and Mary MacLean.. 178
Family of Murdock MacLaine and Anne Campbell 178

Family of John MacLaine and Isabelle MacDougall 179
Family of Allan MacLaine and Julian MacLean 179
Family of Margaret MacLaine and Lachlan McQuarrie 179
Family of Mary MacLaine and Lachlan MacLean 180
Family of Lachlan MacLaine and Flora MacQuarrie 180
Family of John MacLean 4th. Baronet and Mary MacPherson 180
Family of Flora MacQuarrie and Lachlan MacLaine 181
Family of John Hector Og MacLean and Finvola MacLaine 181
Family of Donald MacLean and Isabella MacLean 182
Allan MacLean 182
Family of Lachlan MacLean and Marian MacDonald 182
Family of Donald MacLean and Isabel MacLeod 183
Family of Catherine MacLean and Hector MacLean 183
Family of Jannet MacLean and Hector Maclean 184
Family of Margaret MacLean and Donald MacLean 184
Family of Una MacLean and John MacLean 184
Family of Donald Maclean and Mary Campbell 185
Family of Marion Maclean and Charles MacLean 185
Family of Angus Maclean and Anne MacDonald 185
Family of Hector Maclean and Jannet MacLean 186
Family of William McLean and Irene 186
Family of Allan MacLean and Catherine Stewart 186
Family of Charles MacLean and a daughter of Hector MacQuarrie 186
Family of Janet MacLean and Lachlan Maclean 187
Family of John MacLean and Florence MacLean 187
Family of Allan Maclean and Margaret MacLean 187
Family of Lachlan Maclean and Janet MacLean 187
Family of John Mclean and Isabel MacLean 188
Family of Lachlan McLean and Mary MacArthur 188
Family of Hector McLean and Jennet MacLean 189
Family of John McLean and Mary MacLean 189
Family of John MacLean and ? Campbell 189
Family of Allan MacLean and Susanna Beauchamp 190
Family of John MacLean and Anne MacLean 190
Family of Florence MacLean and Donald MacLean 190
Family of Mary MacLean and John MacLean 191
Family of Lachlan MacLean and Susanna MacLean 191
Family of Lachlan MacLean and Margaret MacDonald 191
Family of Angus MacLean and Elizabeth Campbell 191
Family of Alexander MacLean and Una MacGillvray 192
Family of Hugh MacLean and Flora MacLean 192

Family of Mary MacLean and John MacLean.. 192
Family of Mary MacLean and John MacLean.. 193
Family of Hector McLean and Margaret MacLean.. 193
Family of Florence McLean and Hector MacLean... 193
Farquhar McLean... 194
Family of Hector McLean and Elizabeth McHutcheon... 194
Family of Lachlan McLean and Margaret Black... 195
Family of Duncan McLean and Agnes McDongal.. 196
John MacLean... 196
Lachlan MacLean.. 196
Charles MacLean.. 196
Rory Mor MacLean.. 197
Family of John Mor MacLean and Marion MacLean.. 197
Donald MacLean... 198
Family of John McLean and Anna Margaretha Crist.. 198
Family of Murdoch MacLean and Christina Maclean... 198
Family of William MacLean and Elizabeth MacLean.. 198
Family of Jannet MacLean and Alexander MacIntosh... 199
Family of Marjory MacLean and Alexander Lee... 199
Family of Charles MacLean and Mary MacIntosh.. 199
Family of William Mclean and Elizabeth Rule.. 200
Family of Robert MacLean and ? Fraser.. 200
Family of William MacLean and ? Fraser... 200
Family of Alexander MacLean and Mary Grant.. 200
John MacLean... 201
Family of Lachlan MacLean and Jane MacLean.. 201
Lachlan MacLean.. 202
Family of Thomas Borthwick and Bessie Notman.. 202
Family of Robert Warren and Judith Anderson.. 202
Family of John Hardy and Mary Frances Jackman.. 203
Family of John Haskell and Patience Soule... 203
Family of Patience Dudley and Daniel Dennison... 204
Family of Mercy Dudley and John Woodbridge.. 204
Family of Samuel Dudley and Mary Winthrop.. 205
Family of Anne Dudley and Simon Bradstreet... 205
Family of Sarah Dudley and Benjamin Keayne.. 206
Family of Joseph Dudley and Rebecca Tyng... 206
Family of Paul Dudley and Mary Leverett.. 206
Family of Mehitable King and Benjamin Marsh.. 206
Family of Noah Merrill and Esther Gillett.. 206
Family of Timothy Merrill and Mary Kellog... 207

Family of Eliakim Merrill and Sarah Watson 208
Family of Joseph Merrill and Mary Jewel 208
Family of Sarah Merrill and Matthew Clark Jr. 209
Family of Esther Merrill and Lot Norton 209
Family of Daniel Durland and Sarah De Motte 209
Family of Katherine Whiting and John Lane 210
Family of Ephraim Spalding and Abigail Bullard 210

23rd Generation 210
    Family of Ann Winn and Moses Cleveland 210
    Family of Catherine Bulkeley and Richard Treat 211
    Family of Dorothy Bulkeley and Thomas Treat 211
    Family of Peter Bukeley and Rachel Talcott 213
    Charles Bulkeley 213
    Family of John Ferris and Mary Jackson 213
    Family of Peter Bulkeley and Rebecca Wheeler 213
    Family of Peter Bulkeley and Rebecca Wheeler 214
    Family of Elizabeth Bulkeley and Joseph Emerson 214
    Family of Prince Allen and Deborah Butler 215
    Family of John Knowles and Jemima Austin (Asten) 215
    Family of Richard Knowles and Ruth Bowers 216
    Family of John Hutchinson and Anne Tow 216
    Family of Richard Whittington Wright and Anne Mottrom 216
    Family of Francis Stiles and Sarah Mary Birdseye 217
    Family of John Gerrish and Elizabeth Waldron 217
    Family of Joshua Gray and Jennat Elliot 218
    Family of James Jordan and Elizabeth Ratcliffe 218
    Family of John Coddington and Mary Ann Robinson 219
    Family of John Thompson and Margaret Cook 220
    Family of Recompense Thomas and Elizabeth ? 220
    Family of Lois Thomas and Joseph Collins 220
    Family of John Merriam and Rebecca Sharp 221
    Family of Elizabeth Benat and William Hobbs 222
    Family of Richard Bennett and Anne Alice Pierce 222
    Family of Elizabeth Harwood and Isaac Dicken 222
    Family of Edward Harrington and Mary Ocington 223
    Family of Elizabeth Bronson and Samuel Stanley 224
    Family of Joshua Prescott and Sarah Clifford 224
    Family of Margaret Tomlinson and Jabez Harger 225
    Family of Thomas Noble and Hannah Warriner 225
    Family of Walter Wagstaffe Bagot and Barbara Legge 226
    Family of Margaret Walker and David Morley 227

Family of Joseph Marie Bousquet and Elisabeth Chenet 228
Family of William Townsend and Hanna Lyon 228
Family of Allan MacLean and Una MacLean 229
Family of Catherine Maclean and Lachlan MacLean 229
Family of Isabel MacLean and John MacLaine... 229
Family of Anne MacLean and Allan MacLean 230
Family of Hugh MacLean and Elizabeth Houston 230
Family of Donald Roy Maclean and Lillias Grant.. 231
Family of Mary MacLean and Hector MacLean 232
Family of Catherine MacLean and John Campbell 232
Family of Colin Maclean and Helen Cameron 232
Family of Donald A McLean and Barbara McLean 232
Family of Hector Maclean and Helen Campbell 232
Family of Marion Maclean and Hugh MacLean.. 233
Family of Anne Maclean and Alexander MacKinnon 233
Family of Mary Maclean and Lachlan Ban MacLean 233
Family of Archibald Maclean and Prudence French 233
Family of Alice Maclean and Archibald Maclean 234
Family of Catherine Maclean and Alexander Sinclair.................................... 235
Family of Archibald Maclean and Alice Maclean... 235
Family of Catherine Maclean and Donald MacLean 236
Lachlan MacLean.. 236
Family of Alexander MacLean and Chriatina MacLean 236
Family of Margaret MacLaine and Donald Campbell..................................... 236
Family of Elizabeth MacLaine and Allan MacLaine.. 237
Family of Isabella MacLaine and John Scroyne.. 237
Family of Lachlan MacLaine and Katherine Macdougall 237
Family of John MacLaine and Isabel MacLean... 237
Family of Julian MacLaine and James Maclean.. 238
Family of Finvola MacLaine and John Hector Og MacLean 238
Family of Murdoch MacLaine and Jane Campbell... 238
Allan MacLaine 239
John MacLaine.. 239
Family of John McLean and Mary Mckinnon 240
Family of James Maclean and Julian MacLaine... 240
Family of Christina MacLean and John MacLean 241
Family of Hector MacLean and Mary Campbell... 241
Family of Hugh MacLean and Jannet MacLeod... 241
Family of Lachlan MacLean and Catherine Maclean..................................... 242
Family of John Ardfinaig MacLean and Catherine McLean 242
Family of Catherine MacLean and Hector Maclean...................................... 243

Family of Lachlan MacLean and Mary MacDonald 243
Family of Hector MacLean and Marian MacLean 243
Family of Anne MacLean and Donald Maclean.. 244
Family of Christianna Maclean and Alexander MacLean 244
Family of Lachlan Maclean and Margaret Smith 244
Family of Allan Maclean and Janet MacLean 244
Archibald Maclean 245
Family of Alicia Maclean and Lachlan MacQuarrie 245
Family of Elizabeth Maclean and Lachlan MacLean 245
Family of William McLean and Della Dolla Pittman 245
Family of Anne Maclean and John MacLean... 246
Family of Mary MacLean and Alexander MacLean 246
Family of Catherine Maclean and John MacLean 246
Family of Alexander Maclean and Christy MacLean 246
Family of Hugh McLean and Catherine Cameron 247
Family of Margaret Mclean and Alexander MacLean 247
Family of Florence Mclean and Lachlan McLean 247
Family of Hugh McLean and Barbara MacLean 247
Family of Alexander MacLean and Eunice Mackinnon 247
Family of Alexander McLean and Johannah Smith 248
Family of Duncan MacLean and Mary MacLean... 249
Family of John MacLean and Mary MacAulay.. 249
Family of Farquhar McLean and Elizabeth McQuarrie 249
Family of Donald McLean and Janet Robertson 250
Family of John McLean and Catherine Blair 250
Family of John McLean and Mary McPherson 251
Family of Allan MacLean and Margaret MacFadyen 252
Charles MacLean 252
John MacLean 252
Family of John MacLean and Ann MacLean 252
Angus MacLean 253
Family of Jonas McLean and Mary Trumpour... 253
Family of Charles Maxwell MacLean and Sarah Amelia Marshall 253
Family of William MacLean and Elizabeth Henderson 254
Family of William MacLean and Mary MacIntosh 254
Family of Moses McLean and Sarah Charlesworth 254
Family of Hugh MacLean and ? Manicol... 255
Family of Hugh MacLean and Mary Stewart... 255
Family of Elizabeth Borthwick and James Tweedie 255
Family of Hinchey Warren and Rachel Anderson.. 256
Family of Joseph Hardy and Mary Burbank... 256

- Family of Josiah Haskell and Sarah Canady 257
- Family of Lucy Woodbridge and Daniel Epps 257
- Family of John Woodbridge and Abigail Leete 257
- Family of Benjamin Woodbridge and Mary Ward 257
- Family of Thomas Woodbridge and Mary Jones 258
- Family of Dorothy Woodbridge and Nathaniel Fryer 258
- Family of Timothy Woodbridge and Mehitabel Wyllis 258
- Family of Joseph Woodbridge and Martha Rogers 259
- Family of Martha Woodbridge and Samuel Ruggles 259
- Family of Mary Woodbridge and Samuel Appleton 259
- Family of Mehitable Marsh and Arthur Daggett 259
- Family of Noah Merrill and Abigail Cooper 260
- Family of Ichabod Merrill and Mary Merrill 260
- Family of Esther Merrill and Lot Norton 261
- Family of Joseph Merrill and Mary Merrill 261
- Family of Mehitable Merrill and William Seymour 261
- Family of Timothy Merrill and ? Plumb 262
- Family of Mary Merrill and John Thompson Jr. 262
- Family of Isaac Merrill and ??? Gillett 262
- Family of James Merrill and Jerusha Seymour 262
- Family of Rhoda Merrill and Reuben Gillett 263
- Family of Jonathan Merrill and Anna Gillett 263
- Family of Ashbel Merrill and Abigail Hart 264
- Family of Ruby Merrill and Darius Woodruff 264
- Family of Enos Merrill and Susan Noble Willard 265
- Family of Eliakim Merrill and Kegiah Loomis 266
- Family of Elias Merrill and Lydia Andrews 266
- Family of Bildad Merrill and Damaris Mix 267
- Family of Martin Merrill and Rhoda Case 268
- Family of Daniel Durland and Sarah Hawkesworth 268
- Family of Susanna Lane and Nathaniel Davis 269
- Family of Erastus Spalding and Jennet Mack 269

Index of Individuals 270

About the Author 293

Collins Publishing 294

  Books Published by Collins Publishing 294

North East Genealogical Research (NEGenRes) 296

Introduction

Many families in North America and Europe are descended from the William the Conqueror. Good record keeping of royal and noble families combined with modern genealogical databases now make it possible to trace many of today's families back for many centuries. This book does exactly that. It is not a history, it is a link-by-link genealogy connecting thousands of people alive today to this historic royal line. Here are the over 1550 families traced in this three volume set of books:

Acheson, Ackers, Ackworth, Acre, Adams, Adderley, Adelaide, Ahern, Ainsworth, Akin, Alabaster, Alan, Albany, Alber, Alcester, Alexander, Aleyn, Alfonso, Alice, Allen, Almy, Altimery, Alvarado, Ambrose, Ames, Amiot, Villeneuve, Anderson, Andrews, Angouleme, Angus, Anna, Tudor, Aplington, Appleton, Appleyard, Apsley, Ardene, Armistead, Arundel, Ashborne, Ashton, Aster, Astley, Aston, Atheling, Atkinson, Atwood, Aubrey, Auckland, Austin, Avison, Awbrey, Babcock, Bachelder, Badlesmere, Bagot, Bailey, Baker, Baldwin, Ball, Ballantyne, Ballard, Ballou, Bancroft, Bannister, Barclay, Bardolf, Barham, Barker, Barnaby, Barrett, Barringer, Bartlett, Barton, Bass, Basse, Bates, Batty, Baudrey, Beauchamp, Beauclerc, Beaufort, Beckwith, Beconsall, Belconger, Belden, Belknap, Bell, Benat, Benjamin, Bennett, Benway, Berenger, Berkeley, Berney, Berrigan, Bertin, Bessiles, Betts, Bidwell, Bigod, Birch, Bird, Birdsall, Birdseye, Birdsong, Biset, Biseth, Black, Blackburn, Blair, Blake, Blakeman, Blaylock, Bliss, Blithfield, Blount, Bohemia, Boleyn, Bolingbroke, Booth, Borthwick, Bostwick, Boteler, Boulter, Bournel, Bousquet, Bowen, Bowers, Bowles, Boyce, Boyd, Brabant, Brace, Braddock, Bradeen, Bradley, Bradshagh, Bradstreet, Braley, Bramshot, Brandt, Braose, Brashieur, Brasseur, Bray, Braye, Breed, Breland, Brereton, Bretagne, Brewse, Brigg, Brigham, Britany, Britian, Brittany, Brodes, Bronaaugh, Bronaugh, Bronson, Brooke, Brooks, Brown, Brownson, Bruce, Bruse, Bryan, Bulkeley, Bullard, Bunne, Burbank, Burdsell, Burges, Burgh, Burkett, Burleigh, Burley, Burling, Burnell, Burrows, Burte, Burton, Busby, Bush, Butler, Buxton, Byron, Calthorpe, Calvert, Cambell, Cameron, Campbell, Canady, Cane, Cansfield, Capell, Capet, Capps, Capron, Carey, Carl, Carleton, Carlson, Carmody, Carpenter, Carrick, Carter, Cartwright, Cary, Case, Casey, Castile, Castillo, Catford, Cauntelo, Cave, Chandler, Channing, Chapman, Chard, Charles, Charlesworth, Charlton, Chase, Chatellerault, Chatfield, Chauncey, Chaworth, Chedder, Chenail, Chenet, Cherleton, Chesley, Chester, Chetwood, Chisholm, Chisolm, Chowdhury, Christman, Clanranald, Clark, Clavell, Clawson, Cleveland, Clifford, Clinton, Clito, Close, Cobb, Coddington, Coe, Cogswell, Colburn, Cole, Coleman,

Colepepper, Collins, Comjaty, Compton, Comstock, Condron, Conger, Connolly, Conqueror, Conroy, Constable, Constance, Converse, Cook, Cooke, Coolidge, Cooper, Copeland, Copperdick, Corbet, Corcoran, Cordier, Corker, Cornell, Cornwall, Corrao, Costello, Cotes, Cottes, Cottingham, Cotton, Council, Courtenay, Couvent, Cowsart, Crafford, Crane, Crawford, Crist, Cromwell, Cronan, Cross, Crosse, Crowder, Cubbage, Culpepper, Cummings, Cunningham, Currie, Curson, Curtis, Custer, D'Arcy, Dacre, Daffydd, Daggett, Dahling, Dallas, Dalrymple, Dalton, Dammartin, Dane, Daniel, Daniels, d'Anjou, Darbe, Darcy, D'artois, Dashnaw, Davenport, David, Davis, Dawnes, de Anjou, de Arundel, de Astley, de Audley, de Auxy, de Banastre, de Bar, de Beauchamp, de Beaufort, de Beaumetz, de Beaumont, de Belmeis, de Bohun, de Bourbon, de Bourne, de Braose, de Bretagne, de Brewse, de Brienne, de Bruce, de Brus, de Burgh, de Carleton, de Carlton, de Carrick, de Charlton, de Chateaudun, de Chaworth, de Cherleton, de Clare, de Cobham, de Conde, de Conversano, de Dacre, de Dammartin, de Doncaster, de Driby, de Eaton, de Ferrers, de Fiennes, de France, de Freville, de Galloway, de Gaveston, de Geneville, de Geneville, de Gernet, de Goushill, de Gresley, de Grey, de Greystok, de Grosment, de Guines, de Hainault, de Hales, de Harcourt, de Hardentun, de Hardy, de Harrington, de Holland, de Hungria, de Joyeuse, de Kerswell, de Knightley, de La Grove, de La Guerche, de la Pole, de la Zouche, de LaBere, de Lacy, de L'Aigle, de Lancaster, de Latham, de Launde, de Leybourne, de Leybourne, de Lindsay, de Londres, de Longespee, de Longespic, de Longueval, de Lucy, de Lusignan, de Meschines, de Miraumont, de Montferrat, de Montfort, de Montmorency, de Morley, de Mortimer, de Motte, de Mountjoy, de Mowbray, de Multon, de Nesle, de Neville, de Normandie, de Northumberland, de Odyngsells, de Peverell, de Pilkington, de Ponthieu, de Quincy, de Radcliff, de Ridelisford, de Roches, de Roos, de Rumilly, de Saluzzo, de Saye, de Segrave, de Shardelowe, de Sherburne, de St Martin, de Stafford, de Stainton, de Stanley, de Talma, de Urswick, de Vendome, de Verdon, de Vere, de Villiers, de Wahull, de Warenne, de Warren, de Welles, de Wignacourt, de Willoughby, de Wynnington, Deane, Debeauchamp, DeBeaumont, DeBlackburn, Debois, DeBois, deBourbon, DeBourbon, deBourgogne, DeBourgogne, DeBraose, DeBrienne, DeBruce, DeBrus, deBurgh, DeCaen, deCantelou, DeCarlton, deCarrick, DeCarrick, DeClitheroe, deFerrers, deFrance*, DeGael, Deharrington, deHolland, deJoyeuse, Del Cid, DeLaPole, DeLeon, deLeybourne, DeLeyburn, DeLongueval, DeLusignan, DeMelun, Demeschines, DeMontfaucon, deNeville, DeNeville, Dennison, Denniston, DeNormandy, Denslow, DePadilla, DeProvence, DeQuincy, DeRus, Des Ancherins, DeSegrave, deSodington, Despencer, DeStainton, D'Estrees, DeTurnham, DeUfford, deValois, Devere, deVipount, DeWarenne, deWaterton, Dewey, Dewitt, Di Ceva, Dick, Dicken, Dickens, Dickson, Dion, Disney, dit Villeneuve, Dixon, Doak, Doane, Dobson, Dodd, Dodds, Dodge, Dolphin, Doney, Dorlandt, Dormer, Dorr, Doty, Douglas, Downey, Downton, Drake, Draviam, Drummond, du Bos, Dudek, Dudley, Dunbar, Dunolly, Durand, Durland, Dushame, Edmonds, Edmund, Edson, Edward, Edwards, Egsgard, Ehlers, Eleanor, Elliman, Ellingwood, Elliott, Ellmers, Ellsworth, Emerson, Emmons, Empringham, England, English, Ensworth, Entwysell, Epperson, Epps, Erskine, Esparza, Essick, Ettinger, Evans, Evarts, Eveleth, Evered, Everette, Ewens, Ewins, Eyre, Eytcheson, Fabbri, Fairclough, Farley, Farr, Farrar, Farwell, Fatmangle, Fausz, Fay, Fedorsak, Ferdinand, Fergan, Ferguson, Ferris, Fettiplace, Filmer, Finlayson, Fiske, Fitch, Fitton, Fitz Robert, Fitz Walter, FitzAlan, Fitzgeoffrey, Fitzgerald, FitzGerold, Fitzhammon, FitzHamon, Fitzjohn, FitzPayne, FitzRichard, Fitzrobert, FitzRobert, FitzWalter, Fitzwilliam, FitzWilliam, Flad, Flagg, Flanders, Fleming, Flete, Flynn, Folsom, Forbes, Forbis, Ford, Foroglou, Forrester, Forthe, Foule, Fowke, Fowler, Foz, France, Franceys, Francis, Franklin, Fraser, Freathy, Frederick, Freeman, Freethy, French, Frenchie, Frestel, Frieson, Frye, Fryer, Fuller, Furlong, Fychan, Galloway, Garcia, Gardiner, Gardner, Garey, Garland, Garlinghouse, Garrett, Gary, Gault, Gaunt, Gay, Geoffrey, George, Gerard, Gerrard, Gerrish, Gertrude, Giddings, Gifert, Gifford, Gilbert, Giles, Gill, Gilleain, Gillett, Girouard, Glendening, Gloucester, Goetschius, Goldblatt, Goldman, Goldstone, Goldthwaite, Goodale, Goodhue, Goodman, Goodrich, Gookin, Gordon, Gough, Goushill, Gradison, Graham, Granger, Grant, Grasty, Gray, Green, Greenham, Grey, Griffin, Griffith, Griggs, Griswold, Grosvenor, Guajardo, Guernsey, Gugle, Guilford, Guillaume, Guillaumine, Guille, Guy, Guyon, Gyllyiott, Hablett, Hagan, Hahn, Haight, Halbach, Hall, Hallock, Hamlin, Hamma, Haney, Hankeford, Hansen, Harcourt, Harden, Hardy, Harger, Hari, Harington, Harkness, Harper, Harrington, Harrison, Hart, Harvey, Harwood, Haskell, Haskin, Haskins, Hawker, Hawkesworth, Hawks, Hay, Hayward, Heath, Heaton, Hemingway, Henderson, Hendrix, Hendryx, Henry, Henry, Hepburn, Herbert, Hernandez, Hershey, Hester, Heyden, Hibbard, Higby, Higley, Hildreth, Hile, Hill, Hills, Hilton, Hinman, Hirthauran, Hirtle, Hobart, Hobbs, Hodgson, Hogan, Hohenstaufen, Hohler, Holand, Holcomb, Holden, Holdershaw, Holford, Holland, Holley, Hollister, Holmes, Hood, Hope, Hopetoun, Hopkins, Hopson, Hopton, Horne, Horner, Hough, Houghton, Houston, Howard, Howell, Howerton, Howland, Hubbard, Hubbell, Hudson, Hughes, Humphreville, Hungerford, Hunter, Hussey, Hutchinson, Hyde, Hymer, Ingram, Irby, Irvin, Irwin, Isabel, Isabel, Isabelle, Jackman, Jackson, Jacobson, Jankowia, Jannuzzi, Jarnagin, Jaume, Jeffrie, Jenkins, Jenney,

Jennings, Jewel, Joan, Joan, Joehlin, John, Johnson, Jones, Jordan, Jowet, Joyce, Karig, Keayne, Kehler, Keis, Keith, Kelleher, Kelley, Kellog, Kelly, Kemp, Kempe, Kendrick, Kennedy, Kent, Keppoch, Kerr, Kidd, King, Kirby, Kirkby, Kirkman, Klingler, Kliszawski, Kliszewski, Knight, Knollys, Knowles, Knowlton, Kortright, Krause, Kuster, Kynveton, Kyshe, La Zouche, LaBrum, Lafarr, Lafontaine, Lagoy, Lahr, Lake, Lakey, Lamb, Lambard, Lamont, Lamora, Lampley, Lancaster, Landon, Landry, Lane, Langille, Langton, Latham, Latimer, Lattimer, Lawrence, LaZouche, Le Blount, Le Despenser, Le Maistre, Le Strange, LeBlount, Ledespencer, Ledespenser, Lee, Leete, Legge, Leggett, Legh, Leigh, Leighton, LeMeschines, Lemoine, Lennox, Leonard, Leppard, LeStrange, Leverett, Leversedge, Levo, Lewis, Lightwood, Lilburn, Lindley, Lindsay, Lindsey, Linkroum, Linnell, Littleton, Llewellyn, Lochiel, Lockhart, Long, Longespee, Longford, Loomis, Lorwerth, Louis, Lovell, Low, Lowell, Lowestoft, Lowther, Lunsford, Lusignan, Luttrell, Lynch, Lyon, Lys, MacAdam, MacAlister, MacArthur, MacAulay, MacDonald, MacDougal, MacDougall, MacDuffie, MacEachan, MacFadyen, MacGhlasraich, MacGillivray, MacIain, MacIean, MacIntosh, Mack, Mackaskill, Mackay, Mackenzie, MacKenzie, Mackey, Mackinnon, MacKinnon, Mackintosh, Macklin, MacLachlan, MacLaine, MacLean, MacLeod, MacMartin, MacNachten, MacNeil, MacNiel, MacPherson, MacQuarrie, MacQueen, MacRory, MacVicar, Madigan, Madison, Mahon, Maine, Mainwaring, Maitland, Malcolm, Maldonado, Malina, Malkani, Mallory, Malone, Malory, Maltravers, Manby, Manett, Manicol, ManIntosh, ManKenzie, Manley, Mann, Manningham, Manrow, Mar, Marden, Markham, Marmion, Maroner, Marsh, Marshall, Marsham, Marstead, Martin, Martindale, Mathew, Matilda, Matteson, Matthews, Mauchline, Maud, Mauduit, Mauleverer, Mauleverer,, Mayhill, Mc Lean, McArthur, McCaslan, McCauley, McClelland, McClintic, McCrillis, McDonald, McDongal, McEachern, McFadyen, McGee, McGoldrick, McGoun, McGowin, McGregor, McHutcheon, McIntyre, Mckinnon, McLane, McLaughlin, McLean, McLeod, McMalvay, McMorris, McNeil, McNutt, McPhaul, McPherson, McQuarrie, Meador, Mean, Mehaffey, Meikle, Mennen, Menteith, Meriam, Meritt, Merriam, Merrill, Merriton, Messer, Messier, Milbury, Mills, Milne, Milstead, Mitchell, Mix, Moleyns, Molyneux, Molyns, Monfort, Moninges, Monroe, Montague, Montez, Montgomery, Moody, Mooney, Moor, Moores, Mordox, Moreau, Morgan, Morley, Morrell, Morrison, Morse, Mortimer, Moss, Motagu, Moton, Mottrom, Moulton, Mowbray, Mudge, Munoe, Munro, Munroe, Mure, Musselman, Muukari, Nash, Navarre, Naylor, Neale, Needham, Neiburg, Neidlinger, Nelson, Nerford, Neville, Newell, Newgate, Newhall, Nicholas, Nichols, Nicholson, Nickerson, Night, Nikeich, Noble, Nobles,

Normandy, Norrington, Norton, Norway, Notman, Nutt, O'Balbhan, Obeolan, O'Brien, O'Cahan, Ocington, O'Donnell, Oedel, Ogden, Oranch, Orisek, Orr, Orwell, Osgood, Otely, Otto, Overton, Owain, Paden, Pakenham, Palmer, Pantry, Papazoglou, Pardee, Parke, Parker, Parks, Parr, Parrin, Parsons, Patterson, Paull, Pawley, Pearce, Pearl, Peck, Peden, Peele, Pelesholle, Pemberton, Penman, Pennington, Penny, Pennyston, Perceval, Percy, Perez, Perrone, Persson, Peryente, Petersen, Phelps, Philbrook, Philip, Phillips, Pickett, Pierce, Pilkington, Pinkston, Piper, Pitkin, Pittman, Pittsley, Platt, Plumb, Pope, Poppy, Port, Porter, Potent, Powers, Pratt, Prendergast, Prescott, Prichard, Prisett, Proctor, Proulx, Provence, Provost, Purcell, Purefoy, Quaint, Radcliff, Radcliffe, Rand, Randes, Rankin, Ratcliffe, Raven, Raymond, Read, Reagan, Reed, Reene, Reeve, Reinke, Revels, Reynolds, Rhos, Rice, Richard, Richardson, Robert, Roberti, Robertson, Robinson, Rochfort, Rock, Rockefellier, Roet, Rogers, Rolls, Ros, Rose, Rosenburg, Ross, Rotch, Roughton, Royle, Rudkin, Ruggles, Rule, Runnels, Russell, Sage, Saint John, Salesbury, Salisbury, Saltman, Saltsman, Sanchez, Sancho, Sanderson, Sandys, Sanford, Sap, Sargent, Saunders, Saunford, Savage, Savoy, Sayers, Schilling, Schmidt, Schofield, Schoonmaker, Schoyer, Schrero, Schwabe, Schwartz, Scotland, Scott, Scroyne, Seghers, Seigel, Selleck, Sellors, Seton, Seymour, Shakespeare, Shareshull, Sharp, Sharpe, Shaw, Sheldon, Shelley, Shellman, Sherborne, Sherburne, Sherman, Shirley, Short, Sibley, Simon, Simon, Simonson, Sinclair, Skelton, Skinner, Smallwood, Smart, Smith, Smythe, Sneyd, Snow, Somerset, Soule, Southill, Spalding, Spencer, Spoelstra, Sponer, Sprung, St. Clair, St. John, Stafford, Standish, Stangwish, Stanley, Stapleton, Starkes, Starks, Steel, Stell, Stevens, Stewart, Stiles, Stocks, Stone, Stradling, Strange, Strathbogie, Strelly, Stringer, Strong, Stuart, Styles, Sullivan, Suprenant, Supski, Surrarrerr, Sutton, Swift, Sykes, Sylverson, Syngleton, Tabb, Taber, Taillefer, Talbot, Talcott, Talhelm, Talvaise, Taylor, Tempest, Tendring, Terkel, Tewfik, Thomas, Thompson, Thomsen, Thomson, Thorne, Tierney, Tillinghast, Tillson, Tilney, Tiptoft, Tirry, Tisdale, Todd, Tomlinson, Tommaso, Tomson, Toppen, Totteshurst, Tow, Towlson, Townsend, Trafford, Treat, Tredennick, Troutbeck, Trowbridge, Trumpour, Tryon, Tuck, Tucker, Tudor, Tull, Turnbull, Tuttle, Tweedie, Twigg, Tyler, Tyndall, Tyng, Tyrell, Ulrich, Una, Urraca, Usher, Ussher, Valois, Vannatten, Verts, Vetquosky, Viiala, Villiers, Violet, Visconti, Vollack, Von Hartleben, Waddington, Wagner, Wagstaffe, Wake, Walboldt, Walbolt, Waldo, Waldron, Wales, Walfield, Walkenden, Walker, Wall, Walp, Walter, Warburton, Ward, Warde, Wardle, Warenne, Warren, Warriner, Washington, Watson, Waymeyer, Weaver, Webb, Webber, Wedgwood, Weeden, Weeks, Wees, Welby, Wellborne, Weller, Welles, Wells, Wells Lady Willoughby, Wemhaner, Wemyss, Wenthlian,

Wentworth, Wertz, West, Westgate, Wetherbee, Wheeler, White, Whitehead, Whiting, Whitmore, Whitney, Whitten, Wicks, Wiesinger, WIittelsbach, Wilbore, Wilcox, Wilding, Wiley, Willard, Willcox, Willets, William, Williams, Willis, Willoughby, Wilsey, Wilson, Winans, Winchell, Winegar, Winn, Winter, Winthrop, Wittlesbach, Wolcott, Wood, Woodbridge, Woodcote, Woodruff, Woods, Woodstock, Worsley, Worthen, Wright, Wrighte, Wyatt, Wydeville, Wyllis, Wynne, Wyrrall, Yarde, Yerkey, York, Yorke, Young, Yuill, Ziegler, Ziska, Zouche.

William The Conqueror and Matilda of Flanders

1. William The^0 Conqueror was born on October 4, 1027, at Castle of Falaise in Chateau de Falaise, Falaise, Normandy, France. He was the son of Robert and Herleve "of Falaise".

   William was known by the title of Duke of Normandy, King of England. He died in the Convent of St. Gervais, Rouen, France, on September 9, 1087, at the age of 59.

   William married Matilda of Flanders in 1053 in Eu, Seine-Maritime, Haute-Normandie, France.

   Matilda of Flanders was born in Flanders, France, on November 24, 1031. She was the daughter of Baldwin and Adelaide.

   Matilda reached 51 years of age and died in Caen, Calvados, Basse-Normandy, France, on November 2, 1083.

   In Volume One of the set, we presented the first 18 generations of descendants of William and Matilda. In this volume we continue with generations 19 through 23.

Families of the Descendants of William the Conqueror and Matilda of Flanders.

19th Generation

Family of Jane Bulkeley and Maurice Wynne

653. Jane^{19} Bulkeley was born in 1531 in Beaumorris, Anglesy, Wales. She was the daughter of Richard Bulkeley and Catharine Griffith (586).

    Jane died in Gwynedd, Caernarvonshire, Wales, in 1553 at the age of 22.

    She married Maurice Wynne.

    Maurice Wynne was born in Caernary, Wales, in 1529. Maurice reached 51 years of age and died in Gwynedd, Caernarvonshire, Wales, on August 10, 1580.

    Son of Jane Bulkeley and Maurice Wynne:

    + 744   i.   George^{20} Wynne was born in London, England, in 1550.

Family of Robert Needham and Frances Ashton

654. Robert[19] Needham was born in 1535 in Shropshire, England. He was the son of Thomas Needham and Anne Talbot (587).

Robert died in Elizabeth City, Virginia, United States, in 1603 at the age of 68.

Robert married Frances Ashton on June 1, 1550, in England. They had eleven children.

Frances Ashton was born in Tixall, Staffordshire, England, in 1533. She was the daughter of Sir Edward Aston and Joan Bowles.

Frances reached 77 years of age and died in Staffordshire, England, on June 1, 1610.

Children of Robert Needham and Frances Ashton:

    i. Jane[20] Needham was born in London, England, in 1542. She died in England.

    ii. Maud Needham was born in Shavington, Shropshire, England, in 1550. She died in Cossington, Leicestershire, England, in 1635 at the age of 85.

    iii. Robert Needham was born in Shropshire, England, in 1555. He died in Elizabeth City, Virginia, United States, on November 26, 1631, at the age of 76.

    iv. Thomas Needham was born in Shavington, Shropshire, England, in 1566.

    v. Mary Margaret Needham was born in Hodnet, Shropshire, England, in 1568.

+ 745   vi. Dorothy Needham was born in Shavington, Shrops, England, in 1570.

    vii. Robert Needham was born in 1572. He died in 1627 at the age of 55.

    viii. Anne Needham was born in Shavington, Shropshire, England, in 1574.

    ix. Edmond Needham was born in Hampstead, Middlesex, England, in 1575. He died in Lynn, Essex, Massachusetts on May 16, 1677, at the age of 102.

       x.   Elizabeth Needham was born in Shavington, Shropshire, England, in 1578. She died in Hodnet, Shropshire, England, in 1617 at the age of 39.

       xi.   Alice Needham was born in Isle, Virginia on June 1, 1616. She died in Isle, Virginia on June 1, 1690, at the age of 74.

Family of Thomas Howard and Mary of Arundel

655. Thomas[19] Howard was born about 1536. He was the son of Sir Henry Howard (588) and Lady Frances Devere.

Thomas was known by the title of Knight of the Garter, 4th Duke of Norfolk'. He died in Executed-beheaded, Tower of London, London, Middlesex, England, on June 2, 1572, at the age of 36.

He married Mary of Arundel.

Mary of Arundel was born in 1540. Mary was known by the title of Duchess of Norfolk FitzAlan.

She reached 17 years of age and died in Arundel House, London, Middlesex, England, in August 1557.

Son of Thomas Howard and Mary of Arundel:

+   746   i.   Phillip[20] Howard was born in Arundel House, London, Norfolk, England, on June 28, 1557.

Family of John Allen and Elizabeth Alabaster

656. John[19] Allen was born in 1538 in Thaxted, Essex, England. He was the son of John Allen (589) and Margaret Leigh.

John died in Hatfield, Peverell, Essex, England, on June 22, 1558, at the age of 20.

John married Elizabeth Alabaster in 1553 in Thaxted, Essex, England.

Elizabeth Alabaster was born in Wix, Essex, England, in 1538. Elizabeth reached 100 years of age and died in Goldington, Bedfordshire, England, in 1638.

Children of John Allen and Elizabeth Alabaster:

       i.   Edmund[20] Allen was born in Thaxted, Essex, England, in 1558. He died in Hatfield, Essex, England, on September 12, 1616, at the age of 58.

+   747   ii.   Thomas Allen was born in Bedfordshire, England, in 1560.

iii. Richard Allyn was born in Braunton, Devon, England, in 1564. He died in Cambridge, Middlesex, Massachusetts, on May 10, 1652, at the age of 88.

iv. Elizabeth Allen was born in Thaxted, Essex, England, in 1565. She died in Bulmer, Essex, England, in 1665 at the age of 100.

v. George Allen was born in Weymouth, Dorset, England, in 1568. He died in Sandwich, Barnstable, Massachusetts, United States, on May 2, 1648, at the age of 80.

vi. Mary Allen was born in Thaxted, Essex, England, in 1568. She died in North Okenden, , England, in 1668 at the age of 100.

Family of George Allen and Katherine Starkes

657. George[19] Allen was born in 1568 in Weymouth, Dorset, England. He was the son of Ralph Allen (590) and Margaret Wyatt.

George died in Sandwich, Barnstable, Massachusetts, United States, on May 2, 1648, at the age of 80.

He married Katherine Starkes.

Katherine Starkes was born in Woking, Surrey, England, in 1605. Katherine reached 51 years of age and died in Sandwich, Barnstable, Massachusetts, United States, in 1656.

Son of George Allen and Katherine Starkes:

+ 748 i. Ralph[20] Allen was born in of Thureaston, Leicester, England, in 1621.

Family of Lady Mary Katherine Cary and Sir Francis Knollys

658. Lady Mary Katherine[19] Cary was born on May 19, 1524, in Chilton, Wiltshire, England. She was the daughter of Sir William Carey (523) and Mary Boleyn (592).

Lady died in Rotherford Grey, Oxfordshire, England, on January 15, 1568, at the age of 43.

She married Sir Francis Knollys.

Sir Francis Knollys was born in Rutherfield Greys Caversham, Oxfordshire, England, in 1514. He was the son of Robert Knollys and Lettice Pennyston.

Sir reached 82 years of age and died in Caversham, Oxfordshire, England, on January 15, 1596.

Son of Lady Mary Katherine Cary and Sir Francis Knollys:

+ 749 i. Sir William[20] Knowles was born in Rotherfield Grays, Oxfordshire, England, in 1544.

Family of Walter Hungerford and Ann Dormer

659. Sir Walter[19] Hungerford was born in 1532 in Hungerford, Somerset, England. He was the son of Walter Hungerford and Elizabeth, Baroness Hussey (593).

He was known by the title of Baron of Hungerford and Farle. He died in Farley Castle, Somerset, England, in 1596 at the age of 64.

He married Lady Ann Dormer.

Lady Ann Dormer was born in Eythorpe House, Waddesdon, Buckinghamshire, England, in 1525. Lady reached 115 years of age and died in Suffolk, England, in 1640.

Daughter of Sir Walter Hungerford and Lady Ann Dormer:

+ 750 i. Lady Lucy[20] Hungerford was born in Hungerford Castle, Somerset, England, in 1560.

Family of Thomas Yorke and Mary Sutton

660. Thomas[19] Yorke was born in 1520 in Ashby de la Launde, Lincolnshire, England. He was the son of Roger Yorke (594) and Eleanor Luttrell.

Thomas died in Ashby de la Launde, Lincolnshire, England, on September 7, 1574, at the age of 54.

He married Mary Sutton.

Mary Sutton was born in Washingborough, Lincolnshire, England, in 1509. She was the daughter of Simon Sutton and Emlyn Disney.

Mary reached 65 years of age and died on September 7, 1574.

Daughter of Thomas Yorke and Mary Sutton:

+ 751 i. Mary[20] Yorke was born in Lincoln, Lincolnshire, England, in 1540.

Family of Humphrey Styles and Elizabeth ?

661. Humphrey[19] Styles was born about 1487 in Suffolk, England. He was the son of John Styles and Margaret Elizabeth Tudor (595).

Humphrey died in Beckenham, Kent, England, on June 27, 1558, at the age of 71.

He married Elizabeth ?.

Elizabeth ? was born in England about 1490.

Son of Humphrey Styles and Elizabeth ?:

+ 752   i.   Humphrey[20] Stiles was born in London, Middlesex, England, in 1506.

Family of Elizabeth Yorke and Edmund Perceval

662.   Elizabeth[19] Yorke was born in 1515 in Walton, Somerset, England. She was the daughter of Sir Richard Yorke (596) and Eleanor Luttrell.

Elizabeth died in Carhampton, Somerset, England, United Kingdom, on September 8, 1601, at the age of 86.

She married Edmund Perceval.

Edmund Perceval was born in Walton, Somerset, England, in 1493. He was the son of James Perceval and Joan Chedder.

Edmund reached 58 years of age and died in Walton, Somerset, England, on September 21, 1551.

Daughter of Elizabeth Yorke and Edmund Perceval:

+ 753   i.   Christian[20] Perceval was born in Eastbury, Berkshire, England, in 1540.

Family of John Gray and Barbara Sanderson

663.   John[19] Gray was born in 1580 in Edinburgh, Midlothian, Scotland. He was the son of Gilbert Gray (597) and Christian Munro.

John was baptized in St Leonard, Shoreditch, Middlesex, England, on June 18, 1581. He died in Midlothian, Scotland.

He married Barbara Sanderson.

Barbara Sanderson was born in Edinburgh, Midlothian, Scotland, in 1584. Barbara died in Edinburgh, Midlothian, Scotland.

Son of John Gray and Barbara Sanderson:

+ 754   i.   James[20] Gray was born in Edinburgh, Midlothian, Scotland, on February 9, 1606.

Family of Sarah Winter and Robert Jordan

664. Sarah[19] Winter was born in 1564 in Ottery, St Mary, Devon, England. She was the daughter of Sir Knight William Winter (598) and Maria Langton.

Sarah was baptized in St John the Baptist, Hillingdon, Middlesex, England, on April 6, 1564. She died in England in 1664 at the age of 100.

Sarah married Robert Jordan in 1590 in Dorset, England.

Robert Jordan was born in Melcombe, Dorset, England, in 1562. He was the son of Thomas Jordan and Agnes Burte.

Robert reached 37 years of age and died in Jordans Journey, Henrico, Virginia, United States, on October 12, 1599.

Son of Sarah Winter and Robert Jordan:

+ 755 i. Capt Samuel Silas[20] Jordan was born in Dorset, England, in 1578.

Family of John Conger and Mary Kelly

665. John[19] Conger was born on September 8, 1633, in Yarmouth, Norfolk, England. He was the son of John Belconger (599) and Elizabeth Toppen.

John died in Woodbridge, Middlesex, New Jersey, United States, on August 27, 1712, at the age of 78.

At the age of 32, John married Mary Kelly on April 12, 1666, in Newbury, Essex, Massachusetts, United States, when she was 26 years old. They had nine children.

Mary Kelly was born in Newbury, Essex, Massachusetts, United States, on February 12, 1640. Mary reached 44 years of age and died in Woodbridge, Middlesex, New Jersey, United States, in 1685.

Children of John Conger and Mary Kelly:

    i. Mary[20] Conger was born in Newbury, Essex, Massachusetts, United States, on December 29, 1666. She died in Newbury, Essex, Massachusetts, United States, on December 29, 1666.

    ii. Enos Conger was born in Newbury, Essex, Massachusetts, United States, in 1667. He died in Woodbridge, Middlesex, New Jersey, United States, on November 21, 1689, at the age of 22.

    iii. Sarah Conger was born in Woodbridge, Middlesex, New Jersey, United States, in January 1668. She died in Woodbridge, Middlesex, New Jersey, United States, in 1702 at the age of 34.

iv. Joanna Conger was born in Woodbridge, Middlesex, New Jersey, United States, on August 1, 1670. She died in Piscataway, Middlesex, New Jersey, United States, on June 26, 1742, at the age of 71.

+ 756 v. John Conger was born in Woodbridge, Middlesex, New Jersey, United States, on May 24, 1674.

vi. Elizabeth Conger was born in Woodbridge, Middlesex, New Jersey on January 1, 1678. She died in Piscataway, Middlesex, New Jersey on May 10, 1731, at the age of 53.

vii. Lediah Conger was born in Woodbridge, Middlesex, New Jersey, United States, on January 1, 1679. She died in Woodbridge, Middlesex, New Jersey, United States, on December 28, 1692, at the age of 13.

viii. Jonathan Conger was born in Woodbridge, Middlesex, New Jersey, United States, on May 29, 1683. He died in Newark, Essex, New Jersey, on May 8, 1733, at the age of 49.

ix. Gershom Conger was born in Woodbridge, Middlesex, New Jersey, United States, in 1685. He died in Woodbridge, Middlesex, New Jersey, United States, in 1711 at the age of 26.

Family of John Thompson and Alice Freeman

666. John^{19} Thompson was born in 1589 in Little Preston, Northhamptonshire, England. He was the son of John Thompson (600) and Joane Evered.

John was baptized in Lancashire: Stalmine - Parish Register, 1583-1724. He died in Stratford, CT, Connecticut on January 29, 1679, at the age of 90.

At the age of 27, John married Alice Freeman on November 6, 1616, in Preston Capes, Northamptonshire, England, when she was 11 years old.

Alice Freeman was born in Preston Capes, Northamptonshire, England, on April 21, 1605. She was the daughter of Henry Freeman and Margaret Edwards.

Alice reached 58 years of age and died in New London, New London, Connecticut, on February 11, 1664.

Son of John Thompson and Alice Freeman:

+ 757 i. John^{20} Thompson was born in Preston Capes, Northamptonshire, England, on September 10, 1620.

Family of Ann Totteshurst and John Thomas

667. Ann[19] Totteshurst was born in 1540 in Chevening, Kent, England. She was the daughter of Thomas Totteshurst and Elizabeth Willoughby (601).

Ann died in Chevening, Kent, England, on April 15, 1633, at the age of 93.

She married John Thomas.

John Thomas was born in Chevening, Kent, England, in 1547. He was the son of Tristram Thomas and Elizabeth Madison.

He was buried in St Mary, Whitechapel, Middlesex, England, on August 16, 1603. John reached 56 years of age and died in Lenham, Kent, England, on August 17, 1603.

Son of Ann Totteshurst and John Thomas:

+ 758   i.   Benjamin[20] Thomas was born in Kent, England, in 1584.

Family of James Burges and Margaret Marsh

668. James[19] Burges was born in 1529 in Goudhurst, Kent, England. He was the son of Nicholas Burges (602) and Johana ?.

James died in Goudhurst, Kent, England, in 1590 at the age of 61.

He married Margaret Marsh.

Margaret Marsh was born in Goudhurst, Kent, England, in 1537. She was the daughter of Thomas Marsh and Margaret Ellen Cooke.

Margaret was baptized in Rotherfield, Sussex, England, on May 30, 1542. She was buried in East Langdon, Kent, on November 4, 1561. Margaret reached 26 years of age and died in Kent, England, in 1563.

Daughter of James Burges and Margaret Marsh:

+ 759   i.   Sarah[20] Burges was born in Goudhurst, Kent, England, in 1559.

Family of Richard Bennett and Elizabeth Tisdale

669. Richard[19] Bennett was born in 1528 in Wallingford, Berkshire, England. He was the son of Thomas Bennett (603) and Agnes Ann Molyns.

Richard died in Berkshire, England, in 1574 at the age of 46.

He married Elizabeth Tisdale.

Elizabeth Tisdale was born in Deanly, Berkshire, England, in 1530. Elizabeth reached 67 years of age and died in Somerset,

England/Wallingford, Berkshire, England/St. Bride's, Fleet St., London, England, on June 28, 1597.

Sons of Richard Bennett and Elizabeth Tisdale:

+ 760 i. William[20] Bennett was born in Mavesyn Ridware, Staffordshire, England, in 1556.

+ 761 ii. John Bennett was born in Clapcot, Wallingford, Berk, England, in 1560.

Family of Hezekiah Usher and Mary ?

670. Hezekiah[19] Usher was born in 1567 in Thorp Arch, Westriding, Yorkshire, England. He was the son of Matthew Usher (604) and Isabel Gyllyiott.

Hezekiah was known by the title of Captain. He died in at the Gambia River, Rhode Island, United States, on September 15, 1595, at the age of 28.

Hezekiah married Mary ? in 1591 in Middlesex, England.

Mary ? was born in London, Middlesex, England, in 1571.

Daughter of Hezekiah Usher and Mary ?:

+ 762 i. Dorothy Elizabeth[20] Usher was born in St Saviour, Surrey, England, in 1599.

Family of John Harrington and Isabella Markham

671. John[19] Harrington was born on April 21, 1525, in Stepney, Middlesex, England. He was the son of Alexander Harrington (605) and Elizabeth Moton.

John was baptized in England. He died in St Gregory by St Paul, London, England, on July 1, 1582, at the age of 57.

John married Isabella Markham in 1554 in Exton, England.

Isabella Markham was born in Of, Allerton, Nottinghamshire, England, on March 28, 1527. She was the daughter of Sir John Markham and Anne Strelly.

Isabella was baptized in England. Isabella reached 52 years of age and died in St Gregory by St Paul, London, England, on May 20, 1579. She was buried in London, Middlesex, England, England, on May 26, 1579.

Children of John Harrington and Isabella Markham:

      i.   Robert[20] Harrington was born in England about 1551. He died in Bourne, Lincoln Co., England, on December 6, 1601, at the age of 50.

      ii.   Elizabeth Harrington was born in Kelston, Somerset, Eng, in 1559.

+ 763   iii.   Sir John Harrington was born in Cannington, Somerset, England, on August 4, 1561.

      iv.   James Harrington was born in Exton, Rutlandshire, Eng, in 1565. He died in England in 1592 at the age of 27.

Family of Agnes Crosse and John Wolcott

672. Agnes[19] Crosse was born in Ash Prior Lydeard St Lawrence, Somerset, England. She was the daughter of John Cross (606) and Ursella Wentworth.

Agnes died in Tolland, Somerset, England, on November 2, 1623. She was buried in Tolland, Somerset, England, on April 5, 1637.

She married John Wolcott.

John Wolcott was born in Tolland, Somerset, England, on April 17, 1545. He was the son of John Wolcott and Agnes Butler.

Son of Agnes Crosse and John Wolcott:

+ 764   i.   Henry[20] Wolcott was born in Tolland, Somersetshire, England, on December 5, 1578.

Family of Alice Molyneux and James Prescott

673. Alice[19] Molyneux was born in 1531 in Sefton, Lancashire, England. She was the daughter of Richard Molyneux and Eleanore Radcliffe (607).

Alice died in Lancashire, England, on May 11, 1581, at the age of 50.

Alice married James Prescott in 1581 in Standish, Lancashire, England.

James Prescott was born in Standish Parish, Lancashire, England, in 1529. James reached 53 years of age and died in Drilby, Lincolnshire, England, on March 1, 1582.

Son of Alice Molyneux and James Prescott:

+ 765   i.   John[20] Prescott was born in Wigan, Lancashire, England, in 1576.

Family of Robert Hyde and Jane Davenport

674. Robert[19] Hyde was born in 1522 in Norbury, Cheshire, England. He was the son of Hamnet Hyde (608) and Margaret Warren.

Robert died in Norbury, Cheshire, England, in 1571 at the age of 49.

He married Jane Davenport.

Jane Davenport was born in Bramhall, Cheshire, England, in 1525. She was the daughter of William Davenport (389) and Blanch Warburton.

Jane reached 41 years of age and died in Cheshire, England, in 1566.

Son of Robert Hyde and Jane Davenport:

+ 766   i.   Robert[20] Hyde JR was born in Newbury, Chester, England, in 1543.

Family of George Gardiner and Margaret Neville

675. George[19] Gardiner was born in 1510 in Northumberland, England. He was the son of Stephen Gardiner (609) and Margaret De Grey.

George was known by the title of Reverend. He died in England in 1548 at the age of 38.

He married Margaret Neville.

Margaret Neville was born in Raby, Durham, England, in 1515. She was the daughter of Ralph Neville 4th Earl of Westmorland (509) and Countess Catherine Stafford Westmorland.

Margaret reached 44 years of age and died at Age: 41 in Shoreditch, London, England, on October 13, 1559. She was buried in Shoreditch, Greater London, England.

Son of George Gardiner and Margaret Neville:

+ 767   i.   George[20] Gardiner was born in Berwick-Upon-Tweed, Northumberland, England, in 1535.

Family of Hervey Bagot and Catherine Adderley

676. Sir Hervey[19] Bagot, 1st Baronet Bagot of Blithfield was born on February 8, 1591, in Checkley County, Stafford, England. He was the son of Sir Walter Bagot (610) and Lady Elizabeth Cave.

Hervey worked as a High Sheriff of Staffordshire in 1626.

He was known by the title of 1st Baronet Bagot in Blithfield Hall on May 31, 1627.

Hervey died in Trescott Grange, Staffordshire, England, on December 27, 1660, at the age of 69. He was buried in Blithfield, East Staffordshire Borough, Staffordshire, England.

He married Catherine Adderley.

Catherine Adderley was born in Wedington, Warwickshire, England, on January 10, 1594. She was the daughter of Humphrey Adderley and Elizabeth Capell.

Catherine reached 28 years of age and died in Blithfield, Staffordshire, England, on February 16, 1622.

Son of Sir Hervey Bagot 1st Baronet Bagot of Blithfield and Catherine Adderley:

+   768   i.   Sir Edward[20] Bagot, 2nd Baronet was born in Bagot Bromley, Staffordshire, England, on May 23, 1616.

Family of John Walker and Mary Jowet

677.   John[19] Walker was born in 1604 in Yorkshire, England. He was the son of Robert Walker (611) and Ann Heaton.

John was baptized in Yorkshire, England, on October 17, 1602. He died in Bolton, Yorkshire, England, in 1669 at the age of 65.

John married Mary Jowet in 1628.

Mary Jowet was born in Yorkshire, England, in 1608. Mary reached 50 years of age and died in Birstall, Yorkshire, England, in 1658.

Son of John Walker and Mary Jowet:

+   769   i.   William[20] Walker was born in Yorkshire, England, in 1630.

Family of Jean Baptiste Amiot and Genevieve Guyon

678.   Jean Baptiste[19] Amiot was born on June 25, 1658, in Ville De Quebec, Quebec, Pq. He was the son of Mathieu Amiot dit Villeneuve (612) and Marie Catherine Miville dit le Suisse.

Jean died in Quebec City, Pq, Canada, on September 19, 1685, at the age of 27.

At the age of 24, Jean married Genevieve Guyon on July 20, 1682, in Quebec, Quebec, Canada, when she was 16 years old.

Genevieve was baptized in Québec, Québec, between 1621 and 1671. Genevieve Guyon was born in Ville De Quebec, Quebec, Pq, Canada, on January 16, 1666.

She reached 20 years of age and died in Quebec, Quebec, Canada, on February 21, 1686.

Daughter of Jean Baptiste Amiot and Genevieve Guyon:

+ 770 i. Marie Anne[20] Amiot was born in Québec, Quebec, Canada, on September 29, 1685.

Family of John Townsend and Elizabeth Montgomery

679. John[19] Townsend was born in 1608 in Raynham Hall, Norfolk, England. He was the son of Thomas Townsend (613) and Mary Newgate.

John died in Oyster Bay, Long Island, New York on October 5, 1668, at the age of 60. He was buried in Oyster Bay, Nassau County, New York.

He married Elizabeth Montgomery.

Elizabeth Montgomery was born in Ballyleck, Monaghan, Ireland, in 1606. Elizabeth reached 78 years of age and died in Oyster Bay, Long Island, New York on February 24, 1684.

Son of John Townsend and Elizabeth Montgomery:

+ 771 i. John[20] Townsend was born in Oyster Bay, Nassau, New York, United States, in 1635.

Family of John Crubach McLean and Anne Campbell

680. John Crubach[19] McLean was born about 1603 in Ardgour, Scotland. He was the son of Allan MacLean (614) and Catherine Cameron.

John was known by the title of 8th MacLean of Ardgour. He died in Scotland in 1702 at the age of 99. John was buried in Isle of Coll, Argyll, Scotland.

John married Anne Campbell about 1630.

Anne Campbell was born in Isle os Skye, Scotland, about 1615. She was the daughter of Angus Campbell.

John Crubach McLean married Marion MacLean.

Marion MacLean was born about 1625. She was the daughter of Hector Maclean (799) and Jannet MacLean (701).

Marion reached 55 years of age and died about 1680.

Children of John Crubach McLean and Anne Campbell:

+ 772   i.   Ewen[20] MacLean was born about 1635.
+ 773   ii.   Lachlan McLean was born about 1636.
+ 774   iii.   Jannet McLean.
+ 775   iv.   Donald McLean.
            v.   Archibald McLean.
+ 776   vi.   Allan McLean.
            vii.   Beatrix McLean.
+ 777   viii.   Mary McLean.

Son of John Crubach McLean and Marion MacLean:

            i.   John McLean was born about 1655.

Family of Ewen the elder MacLean and Sarah MacLaine

681.   Ewen the elder[19] MacLean was born about 1605. He was the son of Allan MacLean (614) and Catherine Cameron.

Ewen died in 1691 at the age of 86.

He married Sarah MacLaine. She is the daughter of Hector Odhar MacLaine (570) and Beathag MacLean (688).

Family of Charles Maclean and Margaret Horner

682.   Charles[19] Maclean was born about 1610. He was the son of Allan MacLean (614) and Catherine Cameron.

Charles died on April 4, 1664, at the age of 54.

Charles married Margaret Horner on September 10, 1639.

Children of Charles Maclean and Margaret Horner:

            i.   John[20] Maclean.
            ii.   Janet Maclean.

Family of Mary MacLean and Charles MacLean

683.   Mary[19] MacLean. She is the daughter of Allan MacLean (614) and Catherine Cameron.

She married Charles MacLean. He is the son of Allan MacLean.

Mary MacLean married Charles Maclean.

Charles Maclean was born about 1598. He was the son of Allan Maclean (620) and Una MacDonald.

Charles was known by the title of 1st MacLean of Ardnacross.

"Charles, second son of Allan Mac Ian Duy, was tacksman of Ardnacross in Mull. He was invariably spoken of as Tearlach Mac Ailein, or Terlach Mac Allan. He purchased the lands of Drimnin from the Earl of Argyll, and gave them to his eldest son" Sinclair, pp. 436

Children of Mary MacLean and Charles Maclean:

+ 778 i. Lachlan[20] Maclean was born in Calgary, Isle of Mull, Argyll, Scotland, about 1635.
+ 779 ii. Allan the elder Maclean was born about 1641.
+ 780 iii. Allan the younger Maclean was born about 1643.
+ 781 iv. Donald MacLean was born about 1645.
+ 782 v. Hector Maclean was born about 1647.
+ 783 vi. Ewen Maclean was born about 1649.
       vii. Anne Maclean.
       viii. Florence Maclean.
       ix. Margaret Maclean.
       x. Mary Maclean.

Archibald Maclean

684. Archibald[19] Maclean was born about 1620. He was the son of Allan MacLean (614) and Catherine Cameron.

Archibald was known by the title of of Ardtun, of the family of Ardgour.

Children of Archibald Maclean:

+ 784 i. Marion[20] MacLean was born about 1650.
       ii. James Maclean.
       iii. Hector Maclean.

Family of Marion MacLean and John Roy MacLean

685. Marion[19] MacLean was born about 1622. She was the daughter of Allan MacLean (614) and Catherine Cameron.

She married John Roy MacLean.

John Roy MacLean was born about 1632. He was the son of John Garbh MacLean (807) and Florence Campbell.

John was known by the title of 1st MacLean of Totaranald.

"He was known as Iain Ruadh, or John Roy. He served under Sir Lachlan of Duart in Montrose's army. He was at Inverkeithing in 1651, and was severely wounded in the head. He was taken prisoner, and was kept in custody for a long time. He had a natural son named Ewen. He married Marion, daughter of Allan Maclean of Ardgour, and had by her Allan, Hector, Ann, Margaret, and Florence" Sinclair, pp.418

Children of Marion MacLean and John Roy MacLean:

+ 785   i.   Ann[20] MacLean was born about 1652.
+ 786   ii.   Allan MacLean was born about 1650.
+ 787   iii.   Hector MacLean.
           iv.   Margaret MacLean.
           v.   Florence MacLean.

Family of Lachalan Og MacLean and Flora MacLean

686. Lachalan Og[19] MacLean. He was the son of Allan MacLean (614) and Catherine Cameron.

Lachalan married Flora MacLean on July 5, 1659. She was the daughter of Hector MacLean.

Ewen MacLean

687. Ewen[19] MacLean was born about 1604. He was the son of Allan MacLean (615).

Ewen was known by the title of 3rd MacLean of Inverscadell.

Son of Ewen MacLean:

+ 788   i.   Allan[20] MacLean was born about 1631.

Family of Beathag MacLean and Hector Odhar MacLaine

688. Beathag[19] MacLean was born in 1579 in Isle of Mull, Argyll, Scotland. She was the daughter of Lachlan Mor MacLean (616) and Margaret Cunningham.

Beathag died in Lochbuie, Scotland.

She married Hector Odhar MacLaine.

Hector Odhar MacLaine was born in Lochbuie, Mull, Scotland, in 1575. He was the son of Hector MacLean (504) and Margaret Campbell.

Hector was known by the title of 9th MacLean of Lochbuie. Hector reached 53 years of age and died in Lochbuie, Scotland, in 1628.

Children of Beathag MacLean and Hector Odhar MacLaine:

- + 789   i.   Murdock Mor[20] MacLaine.
- + 790   ii.   Lachlan Mor MacLaine was born in Lochbuie, Mull, Scotland, in 1614.
- + 791   iii. Margaret MacLaine was born about 1612.
- + 792   iv.   Janet MacLaine.
-          v.   Allan MacLaine.
- + 793   vi.   Mary MacLaine.
- + 794   vii. Sarah MacLaine.

Family of Hector Og MacLean and Janet Mackenzie

689. Hector Og[19] MacLean was born in 1583 in Duart Castle, Isle of Mull, Scotland. He was the son of Lachlan Mor MacLean (616) and Margaret Cunningham.

Hector was known by the title of 14th Chief MacLean. He died in Tobermory, Isle of Mull, Scotland, in September 1623 at the age of 40.

He married Janet Mackenzie.

Janet Mackenzie was born in Cromarty, Ross & Cromarty, Scotland, in 1576.

Hector Og MacLean married Isabelle Acheson about 1595 in Scotland.

Isabelle Acheson was born in Aberlady, East Lothian, Scotland, in 1576. She was the daughter of Archibald Acheson.

Isabelle died in Scotland.

Children of Hector Og MacLean and Janet Mackenzie:

+ 795 i. Hector Mor[20] Maclean was born about 1603.

+ 796 ii. Lachlan MacLean was born in Scotland in 1606.

+ 797 iii. Finvola (Florence) MacLean was born about 1610.

Children of Hector Og MacLean and Isabelle Acheson:

+ 798 i. Donald MacLean was born in Duart, Argyll, Scotland, in 1600.

ii. John Dubh MacLean. John was known by the title of progenitor of the MacLeans of Sweden.

iii. Isabelle MacLean.

Family of Gillean Maclean and Mary the elder Maclean

690. Gillean[19] Maclean was born about 1583 in Isle of Mull, Argyll, Scotland. He was the son of Lachlan Mor MacLean (616) and Margaret Cunningham.

He married Mary the elder Maclean. Mary the elder Maclean was born about 1594. She was the daughter of Allan Maclean (620) and Una MacDonald.

Family of Lachlan Og MacLean and Marian Campbell

691. Lachlan Og[19] MacLean was born about 1584 in Scotland. He was the son of Lachlan Mor MacLean (616) and Margaret Cunningham.

Lachlan was known by the title of 1st MacLean of Torloisk. He died in Coll, Argyll, Scotland, in January 1642 at the age of 58.

He married Marian Campbell. She is the daughter of Duncan Campbell.

Lachlan Og MacLean married Margaret Stewart.

Lachlan Og MacLean married Marian MacDonald. They had twelve children.

Marian MacDonald was born in Scotland in 1594. Marian reached 12 years of age and died in Torloisk, Scotland, in 1606.

Son of Lachlan Og MacLean and Marian Campbell:

+ 799 i. Hector[20] Maclean was born in Coll, Argyll, Scotland, about 1610.

Children of Lachlan Og MacLean and Marian MacDonald:

+ 800 i. Jannet[20] MacLean was born in Scotland, United Kingdom, in 1600.

+ 801 ii. Mary MacLean was born in Scotland in 1603.

+	802	iii.	Lachlan Og Maclean was born about 1610.
		iv.	Allan Maclean was born in Ardnacross Mull Scotland about 1615. He died in Harris Scotland in 1651 at the age of 36.
+	803	v.	John Diuriach Maclean was born about 1625.
+	804	vi.	Julian MacLean was born in Torloisk, Mull, Scotland.
		vii.	Hector Maclean.
		viii.	Lachlan Catanach Maclean. Lachlan died on July 20, 1651. Killed in the Battle of Inverkeithing.
		ix.	Ewen Maclean. Ewen died on July 20, 1651. Killed in the Battle of Inverkeithing.
+	805	x.	Neil Maclean.
		xi.	Catherine Maclean.
		xii.	Isabella Maclean.

Family of Allan Maclean and Mary the younger Maclean

692. Allan^{19} Maclean was born about 1585. He was the son of Lachlan Mor MacLean (616) and Margaret Cunningham.

He married Mary the younger Maclean. She is the daughter of Allan Maclean (620) and Una MacDonald.

Family of Charles Maclean and Margaret MacLaine

693. Charles^{19} Maclean was born about 1592 in Isle of Mull, Argyll, Scotland. He was the son of Lachlan Mor MacLean (616) and Margaret Cunningham.

He married Margaret MacLaine. Margaret MacLaine was born about 1612.

Charles Maclean married Anna MacLean. Anna MacLean was born about 1595. She was the daughter of Hector MacLean (504) and Margaret Campbell.

Family of Janet MacLean and John Garbh MacLean

694. Janet^{19} MacLean was born about 1575. She was the daughter of Hector Roy MacLean (495) and Marion MacLean (617).

She married John Garbh MacLean.

John Garbh MacLean was born in Ardnamurchan, Argyll, Scotland, about 1590. He was the son of John Dubh MacLean (550) and Margaret Campbell.

John was known by the title of 1st MacLean of Drimnin. John reached 72 years of age and died in Midlothian, Scotland, on August 12, 1662. He was buried in Midlothian, Scotland, on August 12, 1662.

Daughter of Janet MacLean and John Garbh MacLean:

+ 806 i. Margaret[20] MacLean was born about 1620.

Family of Lachlan MacLean and Florence Macleod

695. Lachlan[19] MacLean was born about 1582 in Coll, Argyll, Scotland. He was the son of Hector Roy MacLean (495) and Marion MacLean (617).

Lachlan was known by the title of 6th MacLean of Coll. He died in Coll, Argyll, Scotland, in January 1642 at the age of 60.

He married Florence Macleod.

Florence Macleod was born in Isle of Harris, Hebrides, Inverness, Scotland, about 1580. She was the daughter of Tormod MacLeod.

Florence died in Scotland.

Children of Lachlan MacLean and Florence Macleod:

+ 807 i. John Garbh[20] MacLean was born in Isle of Coll, Argyllshire, Scotland, about 1600.
+ 808 ii. Hector MacLean was born about 1605.
+ 809 iii. Neil MacLean was born in Coll, Argyll, Scotland, about 1615.
  iv. Catherine MacLean.
+ 810 v. Jannet MacLean.

Family of John MacLean and Jannet Stuart

696. John[19] MacLean was born about 1580 in Isle of Coll, Argyllshire, Scotland. He was the son of Duncan MacLean.

He married Jannet Stuart.

Son of John MacLean and Jannet Stuart:

+ 811 i. Patrick[20] MacLean was born in Lochbuie, Argyll, Scotland, about 1610.

Family of Mary the elder Maclean and Gillean Maclean

697. Mary the elder[19] Maclean was born about 1594. She was the daughter of Allan Maclean (620) and Una MacDonald.

She married Gillean Maclean. Gillean Maclean was born in Isle of Mull, Argyll, Scotland, about 1583.

Family of Julian MacLean and Hector MacLean

698. Julian[19] MacLean was born about 1595. She was the daughter of Allan Maclean (620) and Una MacDonald.

She married Hector MacLean. They had three sons.

Hector MacLean was born about 1605. Hector is deceased. murdered by robbers.

Sons of Julian MacLean and Hector MacLean:

+ 935   i.   Lachlan[20] MacLean was born about 1635.
+ 936   ii.   Hector MacLean was born about 1645.
           iii.   Hugh MacLean.

Family of Charles Maclean and Mary MacLean

699. Charles[19] Maclean was born about 1598. He was the son of Allan Maclean (620) and Una MacDonald.

Charles was known by the title of 1st MacLean of Ardnacross.

He married Mary MacLean.

Children of Charles Maclean and Mary MacLean:

+ 778   i.   Lachlan[20] Maclean was born in Calgary, Isle of Mull, Argyll, Scotland, about 1635.
+ 779   ii.   Allan the elder Maclean was born about 1641.
+ 780   iii.   Allan the younger Maclean was born about 1643.
+ 781   iv.   Donald MacLean was born about 1645.
+ 782   v.   Hector Maclean was born about 1647.
+ 783   vi.   Ewen Maclean was born about 1649.
           vii.   Anne Maclean.
           viii.   Florence Maclean.
           ix.   Margaret Maclean.
           x.   Mary Maclean.

Family of Hector Maclean and Jannet MacLean

700. Hector[19] Maclean was born about 1601. He was the son of Allan Maclean (620) and Una MacDonald.

Hector was known by the title of 1st MacLean of Kinlochaline, 3rd MacLean of Morvern. He died in Scotland after 1641.

More facts and events for Hector Maclean:

He married Jannet MacLean.

Jannet MacLean was born in Scotland, United Kingdom, in 1600. Jannet reached 50 years of age and died in Torloisk Mull, Argyll, Scotland, in 1650.

Hector Maclean married Margaret Campbell.

Sons of Hector Maclean and Jannet MacLean:

+ 923   i.   John[20] Maclean was born in Duart Castle, Isle of Mull, Argyll, Scotland, about 1625.

           ii.   Lachlan Maclean.

Family of Jannet MacLean and Hector Maclean

701. Jannet[19] MacLean was born about 1620. She was the daughter of Allan Maclean (620) and Una MacDonald.

She married Hector Maclean. They had three daughters.

Hector Maclean was born in Coll, Argyll, Scotland, about 1610. Hector reached 73 years of age and died in Isle of Mull, Argyll, Scottland, in 1683.

Daughters of Jannet MacLean and Hector Maclean:

+ 917   i.   Marion[20] MacLean was born about 1625.

+ 918   ii.   Margaret MacLean was born in Torloisk, Mull, Scotland, about 1635.

           iii.   Mary Maclean.

Family of Mary the younger Maclean and Allan Maclean

702. Mary the younger[19] Maclean. She is the daughter of Allan Maclean (620) and Una MacDonald.

She married Allan Maclean. Allan Maclean was born about 1585.

Family of Lachlan Maclean and first wife unknown

703.   Lachlan[19] Maclean was born about 1600. He was the son of Allan Maclean (620) and ?.

   Lachlan was known by the title of of Calgary.

   He married first wife unknown.

   Lachlan Maclean married Anne ?.

Son of Lachlan Maclean and Anne ?:

+   812   i.   Allan[20] Maclean was born about 1630.

Family of John Diurach MacLean and Elizabeth MacLean

704.   John Diurach[19] MacLean was born about 1616. He was the son of Charles MacLean (622) and Julia MacGillivray.

   He married Elizabeth MacLean.

   Elizabeth MacLean was born about 1620. She was the daughter of Charles MacLean.

Son of John Diurach MacLean and Elizabeth MacLean:

+   813   i.   Hector[20] MacLean was born about 1656.

Family of Lachlan MacLean and Catherine Macdonald

705.   Lachlan[19] MacLean was born in 1618 in Grishermish, Scotland. He was the son of Charles MacLean (622) and Julia MacGillivray.

   Lachlan died in Grishermish, Scotland, on April 18, 1619, at the age of 1.

   He married Catherine Macdonald.

   Catherine Macdonald was born in Cromarty, Ross & Cromarty, Scotland, in 1600. Catherine reached 60 years of age and died in Cromarty, Ross & Cromarty, Scotland, in 1660.

Children of Lachlan MacLean and Catherine Macdonald:

+   814   i.   Donald[20] MacLean was born about 1618.
         ii.   Isabel MacLean was born in Duart, Mull, Scotland, in January 1620. She died in Scotland in 1657 at the age of 37.

Charles MacLean

706. Charles[19] MacLean was born about 1570. He was the son of Allan MacLean (623).

Daughter of Charles MacLean:

+ 815   i.   Margaret[20] MacLean was born about 1590.

Family of Charles MacLean and Flora MacNeil

707. Charles[19] MacLean. He is the son of Allan Og MacLean (624).

Charles was known by the title of 4th MacLean of Gigha.

He married Flora MacNeil.

Daughter of Charles MacLean and Flora MacNeil:

+ 815   i.   Margaret[20] MacLean was born about 1590.

Charles McLean

708. Charles[19] McLean was born about 1613. He was the son of Alister McLean (626) and Sally Campbell.

Son of Charles McLean:

     i.   John[20] McLean was born about 1633. He died in 1647 at the age of 14.

Family of Duncan McLean and Christian Nikeich

709. Duncan[19] McLean was born about 1617 in Scotland. He was the son of Alister McLean (626) and Sally Campbell.

Duncan married Christian Nikeich on January 28, 1655, in Kenmore, Scotland. They had three sons.

Christian Nikeich was born about 1630.

Sons of Duncan McLean and Christian Nikeich:

+ 816   i.   John Ban[20] McLean was born in Scotland about 1655.

+ 817   ii.   Duncan McLean was born in Argylleshire, Scotland, about 1656.

+ 1086   iii.   Angus MacLean was born in Argylleshire, Scotland, about 1657.

Donald Og MacLean

710. Donald Og[19] MacLean was born about 1645. He was the son of John MacLean (628).

Donald was known by the title of 4th MacLean of Hynish.

Sons of Donald Og MacLean:

+   818   i.   Lachlan[20] MacLean was born about 1680.

+   819   ii.   Allan MacLean.

Family of Hector MacLean and Marion MacQuarrie

711. Hector[19] MacLean was born about 1640. He was the son of Nial Ban MacLean (629) and Ann MacKenzie.

He married Marion MacQuarrie. She is the daughter of John MacQuarrie.

Sons of Hector MacLean and Marion MacQuarrie:

+   820   i.   Neil[20] MacLean was born about 1670.

+   821   ii.   Ewen MacLean was born about 1673.

Family of John MacLean and ? Campbell

712. John[19] MacLean was born about 1643. He was the son of Nial Ban MacLean (629) and Ann MacKenzie.

John was known by the title of 7th MacLean of Borreray. He died in 1723 at the age of 80.

He married ? Campbell.

Children of John MacLean and ? Campbell:

+   822   i.   Archibald[20] MacLean was born about 1668.

+   823   ii.   John MacLean.

+   824   iii. Neil MacLean.

                iv. Anne MacLean.

Family of Donald MacLean and Isabel Campbell

713. Donald[19] MacLean was born about 1645. He was the son of Nial Ban MacLean (629) and Ann MacKenzie.

He married Isabel Campbell.

Isabel Campbell was born about 1650. She was the daughter of John Campbell.

Children of Donald MacLean and Isabel Campbell:

+   825   i.   John[20] MacLean was born in Tiree, Argyll, Scotland, about 1670.

    ii. Charles MacLean.

    iii. Archibald MacLean.

    iv. Florence MacLean.

    v. Isabell MacLean.

    vi. Elizabeth MacLean.

Family of Charles MacLean and Florence MacLean

714.   Charles[19] MacLean was born about 1647. He was the son of Nial Ban MacLean (629) and Ann MacKenzie.

Charles died in Tiree, Argyll, Scotland.

He married Florence MacLean. They had nine children. She is the daughter of Niel MacLean.

Children of Charles MacLean and Florence MacLean:

+ 826   i. Donald[20] MacLean was born about 1675.
+ 827   ii. Ann MacLean was born about 1682.
+ 828   iii. Archibald MacLean was born about 1685.
+ 829   iv. Mary MacLean was born about 1700.
+ 830   v. Neil MacLean.
+ 831   vi. Lachlan MacLean.
        vii. John MacLean.
        viii. Catherine MacLean.
+ 832   ix. Isabel MacLean.

Ewen MacLean

715.   Ewen[19] MacLean. He is the son of Nial Ban MacLean (629) and Ann MacKenzie.

Son of Ewen MacLean:

        i. John[20] MacLean was born about 1620.

Allan MacLean

716.   Allan[19] MacLean. He is the son of Archibald MacLean (630) and a daughter of Mackaskill.

Allan was known by the title of 4th MacLean of Achnasaul.

Sons of Allan MacLean:

+ 833   i.   Donald[20] MacLean.

+ 834   ii.   Lachlan MacLean.

Rory MacLean

717.   Rory[19] MacLean. He is the son of Archibald MacLean (630) and a daughter of Mackaskill.

Son of Rory MacLean:

+ 835   i.   John[20] MacLean.

Family of Roderick MacLean and Marion MacLean

718.   Roderick[19] MacLean was born about 1623. He was the son of Lachlan MacLean (631) and Ann MacLean.

Roderick was known by the title of 4th MacLean of Grishipol.

He married an unknown woman.

Roderick MacLean married Marion MacDonald.

Roderick MacLean married Marion MacLean. She is the daughter of Donald MacLean.

Son of Roderick MacLean and an unknown woman:

+ 836   i.   Neil[20] MacLean.

Sons of Roderick MacLean and Marion MacLean:

     i.   Lachlan[20] MacLean was born about 1650. He was known by the title of 5th MacLean of Grishipol.

     ii.   John MacLean. John is deceased. died young without children.

Family of John MacLean and Margaret Mauchline

719.   John[19] MacLean was born about 1630 in Coll, Argyl, Scotland. He was the son of Lachlan MacLean (631) and Ann MacLean.

John was using a title in Grishpoll. He died in Coll, Argyll, Scotland.

He married Margaret Mauchline.

Margaret Mauchline was born in Duns, Berwick, Scotland, in 1645. Margaret died in Coll, Argyll, Island of Mull, Scotland.

Son of John MacLean and Margaret Mauchline:

+ 837   i.   John[20] McLean was born in Scotland about 1674.

Family of John MacLean and Elizabeth Matthews

720.   John[19] MacLean was born about 1678. He was the son of John MacLean (632) and a daughter of James Cubbage.

He married Elizabeth Matthews. They had three sons.

Sons of John MacLean and Elizabeth Matthews:

    i.   Lachlan[20] MacLean was born about 1705.
    ii.   James MacLean was born about 1707.
    iii.   Henry MacLean was born about 1709.

John MacLean

721.   John[19] MacLean was born about 1675. He was the son of Donald MacLean (633).

Son of John MacLean:

+ 838   i.   Lachlan[20] MacLean was born in Grimsary, Coll, Scotland, about 1715.

John MacLean

722.   John[19] MacLean was born about 1652. He was the son of Hector MacLean (634).

Son of John MacLean:

    i.   Donald[20] MacLean was born about 1679.

Donald MacLean

723.   Donald[19] MacLean. He is the son of Charles MacLean (635).

Son of Donald MacLean:

+ 839   i.   John[20] MacLean was born in 1724.

Family of John MacLean and Catherine MacLean

724.   John[19] MacLean was born about 1680. He was the son of Donald MacLean (636) and Mary MacLean.

John was known by the title of 2nd MacLean of Killean. He died about 1760 at the age of 80.

He married Catherine MacLean. They had five sons. She is the daughter of Hector MacLean.

Sons of John MacLean and Catherine MacLean:

+ 840   i.   Hector[20] MacLean was born about 1715.

         ii.   Donald MacLean.

         iii.   Neil MacLean.

         iv.   John MacLean.

         v.   Lachlan MacLean.

Family of Alexander MacLean and Agnes Chisholm

725.   Alexander[19] MacLean was born about 1625. He was the son of John MacLean (637) and Agnes Fraser.

Alexander died in September 1671 at the age of 46.

Alexander married Agnes Chisholm in November 1656.

Agnes Chisholm was born about 1636. She was the daughter of Alexander Chisholm.

Son of Alexander MacLean and Agnes Chisholm:

         i.   Allan[20] MacLean.

Family of John Og MacLean and Margaret Fowler

726.   John Og[19] MacLean was born about 1626. He was the son of John MacLean (637) and Agnes Fraser.

John was known by the title of 6th MacLean of Dochgarroch. He died about 1715 at the age of 89.

He married Margaret Fowler.

Margaret Fowler was born in of, Inverness, Inverness, Scotland, in 1651. She was the daughter of Ballie Fowler.

Children of John Og MacLean and Margaret Fowler:

+ 841   i.   John[20] MacLean was born in Dochgarroch, Inverness, Scotland, in 1673.

         ii.   Alexander MacLean.

		iii.	David MacLean.
		iv.	Donald MacLean.
		v.	Charles MacLean.
		vi.	Farquhar MacLean.
+	842	vii.	Janet MacLean.
+	843	viii.	Annie MacLean.

Donald MacLean

727.   Donald^{19} MacLean was born about 1630. He was the son of John MacLean (637) and Agnes Fraser.

Donald died about 1693 at the age of 63.

Son of Donald MacLean:

   i.   John^{20} MacLean.

Family of Bridget MacLean and Angus MacQueen

728.   Bridget^{19} MacLean. She is the daughter of John MacLean (637) and Agnes Fraser.

She married Angus MacQueen.

Family of Margaret MacLean and Donald Campbell

729.   Margaret^{19} MacLean. She is the daughter of John MacLean (637) and Agnes Fraser.

She married Donald Campbell.

Family of Jannet MacLean and Malcolm MacIntosh

730.   Jannet^{19} MacLean. She is the daughter of John MacLean (637) and Agnes Fraser.

She married Malcolm MacIntosh.

Family of Alexander MacLean and Agnes Chisolm

731.   Alexander^{19} MacLean was born in 1628 in Dochgarroch, Inverness, Scotland. He was the son of John MacLean (537) and Agnes Fraser.

Alexander died in September 1671 at the age of 43.

He married Agnes Chisolm.

Agnes Chisolm was born in Dochgarroch, Inverness, Scotland, in 1634. Agnes is deceased.

Son of Alexander MacLean and Agnes Chisolm:

+ 844 i. John Og[20] MacLean was born in Dochgarroch, Inverness, Scotland, in 1657.

Hector MacLean

732. Hector[19] MacLean was born about 1639. He was the son of David MacLean (639).

Son of Hector MacLean:

i. Lachlan[20] MacLean was born about 1669.

Hector MacLean

733. Hector[19] MacLean was born about 1610. He was the son of Donald MacLean (641).

Hector was known by the title of 6th MacLean of Kingerloch. He died about 1650 at the age of 40.

Son of Hector MacLean:

+ 845 i. Laclhlan[20] MacLean was born about 1635.

Family of James Borthwick and Margaret Hay

734. Lord James[19] Borthwick was born on June 24, 1570, in Borthwick, Midlothian, Scotland. He was the son of William Borthwick (642) and Grissel Scott.

James died in Scotland in December 1599 at the age of 29.

He married Margaret Hay.

Margaret Hay was born in Roxburghshire, Scotland, in 1570. Margaret reached 89 years of age and died on December 30, 1659.

Son of Lord James Borthwick and Margaret Hay:

+ 846 i. John[20] Borthwick was born in Borthwick, Midlothian, Scotland, in 1590.

Family of William Warren and Catherine Gookin

735. William[19] Warren was born on March 7, 1596, in Ripple, Kent, England. He was the son of John Warren (643) and Anne Crafford.

William died at Age: 39 in Ripple, Kent, England, on November 3, 1635, at the age of 39. He was buried in London, Greater London, England.

At the age of 23, William married Catherine Gookin on June 1, 1619, in Ripple, Kent, when she was 19 years old.

Catherine Gookin was born in Ripple, Kent, England, on October 7, 1599. Catherine reached 41 years of age and died in Canterbury, Kent, England, on February 9, 1641.

Son of William Warren and Catherine Gookin:

+ 847   i.   Thomas Warren[20] Warren was born in Kent, England, on January 30, 1624.

Family of Richard Hardy and Alice Wilson

736.   Richard[19] Hardy was born in 1567 in East Riding, Yorkshire, England. He was the son of Michael Hardy (644) and Alice Skelton.

Richard died in Isle of Wight, Virginia in 1645 at the age of 78.

Richard married Alice Wilson in 1603 in Yorkshire, England.

Alice Wilson was born in Shillington, Bedfordshire, England, on January 12, 1588. Alice reached 69 years of age and died in Bedfordshire, England, in 1658.

Son of Richard Hardy and Alice Wilson:

+ 848   i.   John[20] Hardy was born in Bedfordshire, England, about 1587.

Family of John Dudley and Elizabeth Leighton

737.   John[19] Dudley. He is the son of Simon Dudley (647) and Emma Saunders.

He married Elizabeth Leighton.

Son of John Dudley and Elizabeth Leighton:

+ 849   i.   Roger[20] Dudley was born about 1552.

Family of John Dudley and Elizabeth Leighton

738.   John[19] Dudley. He is the son of Simon Dudley (647) and Emma Saunders.

He married Elizabeth Leighton.

Son of John Dudley and Elizabeth Leighton:

+ 849   i.   Roger[20] Dudley was born about 1552.

Family of Judith Birdsall and Henry Cook

739. Judith[19] Birdsall was born in 1619 in England. She was the daughter of Henry Birdsall (648) and Judith Agnes Kempe.

She was buried in September 1689. Judith died in Salem, Essex, MA, on September 11, 1689, at the age of 70.

Judith married Henry Cook on June 29, 1639, in Salem, Essex, MA. They had fourteen children.

Henry Cook was born in England in 1615. He was the son of Edmund Cook and Elizabeth Nicholls.

Henry reached 46 years of age and died in Salem, Essex, MA, on December 25, 1661. He was buried in Salem, Essex, MA, on December 25, 1661.

Children of Judith Birdsall and Henry Cook:

+ 850   i.   Isaac[20] Cook was born in Salem, Essex, MA, on April 3, 1640.

       ii.   Samuel Cook was born in Salem, Essex, Massachusetts, on September 30, 1641. Samuel was buried between 1702 and 1703. He died in Wallingford, New Haven, Connecticut, on December 25, 1703, at the age of 62.

       iii.   Judith Cook was born in Salem, Essex, MA, on September 15, 1643. She died in September 1869 at the age of 225.

       iv.   Rachel Cook was born in Salem, Essex, MA, on September 25, 1645. Rachel was buried in 1740. She died in Enfield, Hartford, Connecticut, on December 10, 1740, at the age of 95.

       v.   John Cook was born in Salem, Essex, MA, on September 6, 1647. He died in Will Prob, 20 Mar 1716, in 1716 at the age of 68. John was buried in 1716.

       vi.   Henry Cook was born in Salem, Essex, Mass., in September 1648. He died in Y.

       vii.   Hannah Cook was born in Salem, Essex, Mass., in September 1648. She died in Y.

       viii.   Martha Cook was born in Salem, Essex, Massachusetts, on September 15, 1649. She died in Y.

       ix.   Mary Cook was born in Salem, Essex, MA, on September 15, 1649. She died in Y.

x.   Henry Cook was born in Salem, Essex, MA, on December 30, 1652. He died in 1705 at the age of 52. Henry was buried in 1705.

xi. Elizabeth Cook was born in Salem, Essex, Massachusetts, on September 9, 1654. She died in Salem, Essex, MA, in September 1654. Elizabeth was buried in Salem, Essex, MA, in September 1654.

xii. Hannah Cook was born in Salem, Essex, MA, on September 9, 1658. She died in Y.

xiii. John Cook was born in Salem, MA, on September 6, 1747. He died in Y.

xiv. Isaac Cook was born in Salem, MA, on April 3, 1840. He died in Y.

Family of Nathan Birdsall and Temperance Fowler Baldwin

740. Nathan[19] Birdsall was born on September 3, 1620, in Norwich, Norfolk, England. He was the son of Henry Birdsall (648) and Judith Agnes Kempe.

Nathan died in Longisland, Nassau, New York, United States, in 1696 at the age of 75.

Nathan married Temperance Fowler Baldwin in 1726 in Queens, New York.

Temperance Fowler Baldwin was born in Oyster Bay, Nassau, Long Island, Bahamas, in 1622. Temperance reached 94 years of age and died in Oyster Bay, Nassau, New York, United States, in 1716.

Son of Nathan Birdsall and Temperance Fowler Baldwin:

+ 851   i.   Henry[20] Birdsall was born in Oyster Bay, Nassau, New York, United States, in 1658.

Family of Elizabeth St. John and Samuel Whiting

741. Elizabeth[19] St. John was born on January 12, 1604, in Cayshoe, Bedfordshire, England. She was the daughter of Oliver St. John and Sarah Bulkeley (649).

Elizabeth was baptized in Cayshoe, Bdfds., England, on January 12, 1604. She died in Lynn, Essex, Massachusetts, United States, on March 3, 1677, at the age of 73.

She married Samuel Whiting.

Elizabeth St. John married Samuel Whiting.

Son of Elizabeth St. John and Samuel Whiting:

+ 852 i. Samuel[20] Whiting.

Son of Elizabeth St. John and Samuel Whiting:

+ 853 i. Samuel[20] Whiting.

Family of Olive Welby and Henry Farwell

742. Olive[19] Welby. She is the daughter of Richard Welby and Frances Bulkeley (651).

She married Henry Farwell. They have one daughter.

Daughter of Olive Welby and Henry Farwell:

+ 854 i. Olive[20] Farwell.

Family of Elizabeth Barker and William Freethy

743. Elizabeth[19] Barker was born in 1618 in Cornwall, England. She was the daughter of Robert Barker (652) and Catherine Ackworth.

Elizabeth died in York, York, Maine, United States, in 1688 at the age of 70. She was buried in St Sepulchre, Holborn, London, England, on April 29, 1690.

She married William Freethy.

William Freethy was born in Landrake, St Micheal, Cornwall, England, on August 22, 1612. He was the son of Alexander Freethy.

William reached 75 years of age and died in York, York, Maine on April 25, 1688.

Son of Elizabeth Barker and William Freethy:

+ 855 i. James[20] Freethy was born in York, York, Maine, United States, in 1651.

20th Generation

Family of George Wynne and Margaret Green

744. George[20] Wynne was born in 1550 in London, England. He was the son of Maurice Wynne and Jane Bulkeley (653).

George was baptized in Middlesex, England. He died in Lincolnshire, England, in 1610 at the age of 60. George was buried in St Mary Abchurch, London, England, in February 1610.

He married Margaret Green.

Margaret Green was born in Lincolnshire, England, in 1550. Margaret was baptized on April 13, 1551. Margaret was buried in St Mary Abchurch, London, England, in February 1610. She reached 60 years of age and died in Lincolnshire, England, in March 1610.

Son of George Wynne and Margaret Green:

+ 856 i. Edward[21] Wynne was born in Thornton Curtis, Lincolnshire, England, in 1570.

Family of Dorothy Needham and Richard Chetwood

745. Dorothy[20] Needham was born in 1570 in Shavington, Shrops, England. She was the daughter of Robert Needham (654) and Frances Ashton.

Dorothy died in England in 1629 at the age of 59.

She married Sir Richard Chetwood.

Sir Richard Chetwood was born about 1560. He was the son of Richard Chetwood and Alice De Wahull.

Sir died after 1631.

Daughter of Dorothy Needham and Sir Richard Chetwood:

+ 857 i. Grace[21] Chetwood was born about 1602.

Family of Phillip Howard and Anne Dacre

746. Phillip[20] Howard was born on June 28, 1557, in Arundel House, London, Norfolk, England. He was the son of Thomas Howard (655) and Mary of Arundel.

Phillip was known by the title of 20th Earl Arundal Saint Phillip. He died in Tower Hamlets, Greater London, England, on October 19, 1595, at the age of 38.

Phillip married Anne Dacre in 1571 in Finchingfield, Essex, England.

Anne Dacre was born in Gilsland, Carlisle, Cumberland, England, on April 12, 1557. Anne was known by the title of Countess of Arundel.

She reached 72 years of age and died in Shifnal, Shropshire, England, in 1630.

Son of Phillip Howard and Anne Dacre:

+ 858 i. Thomas[21] Howard was born in Finchingfield, Braintree District, Essex, England, on July 7, 1585.

Family of Thomas Allen and Mary Fairclough

747. Thomas[20] Allen was born in 1560 in Bedfordshire, England. He was the son of John Allen (656) and Elizabeth Alabaster.

Thomas died in Little Waltham, Essex, England, on April 14, 1635, at the age of 75.

Thomas married Mary Fairclough on July 30, 1582, in Goldington, Bedfordshire, England.

Mary Fairclough was born in Bedfordshire, England, in 1550. Mary reached 81 years of age and died in Bedfordshire, England, on April 30, 1631.

Daughter of Thomas Allen and Mary Fairclough:

+ 859 i. Jane[21] Allen was born in Odell, Bedfordshire, England, on January 17, 1587.

Family of Ralph Allen and Esther Susanna Swift

748. Ralph[20] Allen was born in 1621 in of Thureaston, Leicester, England. He was the son of George Allen (657) and Katherine Starkes.

Ralph worked as a Mason (not Ralph Allen the wheelwright of Sandwich) in Sandwich, Barnstable, Massachusetts. He died in Sandwich, Barnstable, Massachusetts, United States, on December 18, 1691, at the age of 70.

He married Esther Susanna Swift.

Esther Susanna Swift was born in Bocking, Essex, England, in 1622. Esther reached 69 years of age and died in Sandwich, Barnstable, Massachusetts, United States, in 1691.

Son of Ralph Allen and Esther Susanna Swift:

+ 860 i. Ebenezer[21] Allen was born on February 10, 1650.

Family of William Knowles and Dorothy Braye

749. Sir William[20] Knowles was born in 1544 in Rotherfield Grays, Oxfordshire, England. He was the son of Sir Francis Knollys and Lady Mary Katherine Cary (658).

William died in Banbury, Oxfordshire, England, on May 25, 1632, at the age of 88.

He married Dorothy Braye.

Dorothy Braye was born in England in 1540. Dorothy reached 65 years of age and died in Malmesbury, Wiltshire, England, on October 31, 1605.

Son of Sir William Knowles and Dorothy Braye:

+ 861 i. William[21] Knowles was born in Harwood, Bolton, Lancashire, England, in 1566.

Family of Lucy and John St John

750. Lady Lucy[20] Hungerford was born in 1560 in Hungerford Castle, Somerset, England. She was the daughter of Sir Walter Hungerford (659) and Lady Ann Dormer.

She was buried in St Dunstan in the West, London, England, on November 7, 1625. Lady died at Age: 67 in Lydiard Tregoze, Wiltshire, England, on June 27, 1627, at the age of 67.

She married Sir John St John.

Sir John St John was born in Lydiard Tregoze, Wiltshire, England, in 1560. Sir reached 34 years of age and died in Lydiard Tregoze, Wiltshire, England, on September 20, 1594.

Daughter of Lady Lucy Hungerford and Sir John St John:

+ 862 i. Lady Elizabeth Lucy[21] St. John was born in Lydiard Tregoze, Wiltshire, England, in 1580.

Family of Mary Yorke and Thomas Randes

751. Mary[20] Yorke was born in 1540 in Lincoln, Lincolnshire, England. She was the daughter of Thomas Yorke (660) and Mary Sutton.

Mary died in Lincoln, Lincolnshire, England, on February 27, 1596, at the age of 56. She was buried in Lincoln, Lincolnshire, England, after February 27, 1597. Buried in the Lincoln Cathedral. 1596/97 calendar issue.

She married Thomas Randes.

Thomas Randes was born in Nettleham, Lincolnshire, England, in 1546. He was the son of Henry Holbeach Randes and Joane Manett.

Thomas worked as a Preb (Prebendary?) of Lincoln Cathedral. Commissary of Lincoln and Stow. in Lincoln, Lincolnshire, England, between 1563 and

1608. Thomas reached 63 years of age and died in St Dunstan in the West, London, England, on February 17, 1609. He was buried at Lincoln Cathedral 1608/09 calendar issue in Lincoln, Lincolnshire, England, after February 17, 1609.

Daughter of Mary Yorke and Thomas Randes:

+ 863 i. Mary[21] Randes was born in Dustin, Northamptonshire, England, in 1571.

Family of Humphrey Stiles and Bridget Baudrey

752. Humphrey[20] Stiles was born in 1506 in London, Middlesex, England. He was the son of Humphrey Styles (661) and Elizabeth ?.

Humphrey died in Beckenham, Kent, England, on April 9, 1557, at the age of 51.

He married Bridget Baudrey.

Bridget Baudrey was born in London, England, in 1520. She was the daughter of Sir Thomas Baudrey.

Bridget reached 28 years of age and died in England in 1548.

Son of Humphrey Stiles and Bridget Baudrey:

+ 864 i. Edmond[21] Stiles was born in Sanborn, Warwickshire, England, in 1520.

Family of Christian Perceval and Richard Lowell

753. Christian[20] Perceval was born in 1540 in Eastbury, Berkshire, England. She was the daughter of Edmund Perceval and Elizabeth Yorke (662).

Christian died in Bedfordshire, England, in 1589 at the age of 49.

She married Richard Lowell.

Richard Lowell was born in Bristol City, Somerset, England, in 1547. He was the son of John Lowell and Apolyn Leversedge.

Richard reached 30 years of age and died in Somerset, England, on June 7, 1577.

Son of Christian Perceval and Richard Lowell:

+ 865 i. Percival[21] Lowell was born in Kingston Seymour, Somersetshire, England, in 1571.

Family of James Gray and Alison Gifert

754. James[20] Gray was born on February 9, 1606, in Edinburgh, Midlothian, Scotland. He was the son of John Gray (663) and Barbara Sanderson.

James died in Edinburgh, Midlothian, Scotland, after 1625.

He married Alison Gifert.

Alison Gifert was born in Edinburgh, Midlothian, Scotland, in 1608.

Son of James Gray and Alison Gifert:

+ 866 i. George[21] Gray was born in Edinburgh, Midlothian, Scotland, on April 14, 1625.

Family of Samuel Silas Jordan and Frances Baker

755. Captain Samuel Silas[20] Jordan was born in 1578 in Dorset, England. He was the son of Robert Jordan and Sarah Winter (664).

Sam died in Beggars Bush, Prince George, Virginia, United States, in April 1632 at the age of 54.

He married Frances Baker.

Frances Baker was born in London, England, in 1580. Frances reached 28 years of age and died in England in 1608.

Son of Capt Samuel Silas Jordan and Frances Baker:

+ 867 i. Thomas Fleming[21] Jordan was born in Wiltshire, England, on January 6, 1600.

Family of John Conger and Mary Tuttle

756. John[20] Conger was born on May 24, 1674, in Woodbridge, Middlesex, New Jersey. He was the son of John Conger (665) and Mary Kelly.

John died in Morris River, Salem, New Jersey, United States, on August 27, 1726, at the age of 52.

He married Mary Tuttle.

Mary Tuttle was born in Woodbridge, Province East Jersey, The Colonies, in 1678. She was the daughter of John Tuttle and Katherine Lane.

Mary reached 49 years of age and died in Woodbridge, Middlesex, New Jersey, United States, in 1727.

Son of John Conger and Mary Tuttle:

+ 868   i.   John^{21} Conger was born in Woodbridge, Middlesex, New Jersey, United States, in 1702.

Family of John Thompson and Ellen Harrison

757.   John^{20} Thompson was born on September 10, 1620, in Preston Capes, Northamptonshire, England. He was the son of John Thompson (666) and Alice Freeman.

John died in New Haven, New Haven, Connecticut, United States, on December 14, 1674, at the age of 54.

John married Ellen Harrison on February 25, 1650, in New Haven, New Haven, Connecticut.

Ellen Harrison was born in New Haven, New Haven, Connecticut in 1630. Ellen reached 36 years of age and died in New Haven, New Haven, Connecticut on March 29, 1666.

John Thompson married Dorothy Harrison.

Dorothy Harrison was born in England in 1620. Dorothy reached 46 years of age and died in New Haven, New Haven, Connecticut, United States, on March 29, 1666.

Son of John Thompson and Ellen Harrison:

+ 869   i.   Joseph^{21} Thompson was born in New Haven, New Haven, Connecticut, United States, on April 4, 1664.

Daughter of John Thompson and Dorothy Harrison:

+ 870   i.   Rebecca^{21} Thompson was born in New Haven, New Haven, Connecticut, United States, on January 26, 1651.

Family of Benjamin Thomas and Mirable Fitch

758.   Benjamin^{20} Thomas was born in 1584 in Kent, England. He was the son of John Thomas and Ann Totteshurst (667).

Benjamin died in Stratford, Fairfield, Connecticut, United States, in 1609 at the age of 25.

He married Mirable Fitch.

Mirable Fitch was born in Lenham, Kent, England, in 1591. Mirable reached 99 years of age and died in Stratford, Fairfield, Connecticut, United States, on April 13, 1690.

Son of Benjamin Thomas and Mirable Fitch:

+ 871 i. John[21] Thomas was born in Lemhan, Kent, England, in 1616.

Family of Sarah Burges and William Merriam

759. Sarah[20] Burges was born in 1559 in Goudhurst, Kent, England. She was the daughter of James Burges (668) and Margaret Marsh.

Sarah was baptized in England. She died in Hadlowe, Kent, England, on November 27, 1635, at the age of 76.

Sarah married William Merriam in 1580 in Kent, England.

William Merriam was born in Tudeley, Kent, England, on May 11, 1564. He was the son of William Meriam and Alice Hablett.

William was baptized in Goudhurst, Kent, on May 11, 1564. William reached 71 years of age and died in Hadlow, Kent, England, on November 27, 1635.

Son of Sarah Burges and William Merriam:

+ 872 i. Joseph[21] Merriam was born in Tudeley, Kent, England, in 1599.

Family of William Bennett and Joan Hodgson

760. William[20] Bennett was born in 1556 in Mavesyn Ridware, Staffordshire, England. He was the son of Richard Bennett (669) and Elizabeth Tisdale.

William was baptized in Mavesyn Ridware, Staffordshire, England, on February 18, 1551. He died in Sedgely, Staffordshire, England, on December 17, 1597, at the age of 41.

He married Joan Hodgson.

Joan Hodgson was born in Sedgely, Staffordshire, England, in 1560. Joan reached 65 years of age and died in Sedgely, Staffordshire, England, on August 2, 1625.

Son of William Bennett and Joan Hodgson:

+ 873 i. William[21] Bennett was born in Brindle, Lancashire, England, about 1579.

Family of John Bennett and Ann Weeks

761. John[20] Bennett was born in 1560 in Clapcot, Wallingford, Berk, England. He was the son of Richard Bennett (669) and Elizabeth Tisdale.

John died in England in 1625 at the age of 65.

He married Ann Weeks.

Ann Weeks was born in Salisbury, Wiltshire, England, in 1562. She was the daughter of Christopher Weeks.

Ann reached 39 years of age and died in England on February 9, 1601.

Son of John Bennett and Ann Weeks:

+ 874 i. Thomas[21] Bennett was born in Somerset, England, in 1580.

Family of Dorothy Elizabeth Usher and John Harwood

762. Dorothy Elizabeth[20] Usher was born in 1599 in St Saviour, Surrey, England. She was the daughter of Hezekiah Usher (670) and Mary ?.

Dorothy was baptized in St Christopher Le Stocks, London, England, on December 25, 1599. She died in London, Middlesex, England, in 1620 at the age of 21.

Dorothy married John Harwood in 1620 in London, Middlesex, England.

John Harwood was born in London, Middlesex, England, in 1600. He was the son of William Harwood and Elizabeth Greenham.

John was baptized in St Saviour, Surrey, England, on June 26, 1600. John reached 52 years of age and died in Middlesex, England, on February 16, 1652.

Children of Dorothy Elizabeth Usher and John Harwood:

i. John[21] Harwood was born in 1621. He died in London, Middlesex, England, on June 22, 1685, at the age of 64.

ii. Thomas Harwood was born in London, Middlesex, England, in 1623. He died in Boston, Suffolk, Massachusetts, United States, on January 5, 1706, at the age of 83.

iii. Hannah Harwood was born in London, Middlesex, England, in 1625. She died in Concord, Middlesex, Massachusetts, United States, on November 14, 1670, at the age of 45.

iv. Nathaniel Harwood was born in London, England, in 1626. He died in Concord, Middlesex, Massachusetts, United States, on February 7, 1716, at the age of 90.

v. Robert Harwood was born in London, Middlesex, England, in 1628. He died in Concord, Middlesex, Massachusetts, United States, in 1678 at the age of 50.

		vi.	Anne Harwood was born in London, Middlesex, England, in 1630.
+	875	vii.	Peter Harwood was born in Talbot, Maryland, United States, in 1633.

Family of John Harrington and Mary Rogers

763. Sir John[20] Harrington was born on August 4, 1561, in Cannington, Somerset, England. He was the son of John Harrington (671) and Isabella Markham.

He died in Bath, Somerset, England, on November 20, 1612, at the age of 51.

John married Mary Rogers on September 6, 1583, in Cannington, Somerset, England.

Mary Rogers was born in Somerset, Somerset, England, in 1565. She was the daughter of Thomas George Rogers and Joan Winter.

Mary reached 69 years of age and died in Wickham, Suffolk, England, in 1634.

Sons of Sir John Harrington and Mary Rogers:

		i.	Edward[21] Harrington was born in Bath, Northamptonshire, England, in 1584. He died in Northampton, Virginia, United States, in 1653 at the age of 69.
+	876	ii.	James Harrington was born in Bath, Somerset, England, in 1592.

Family of Henry Wolcott and Elizabeth Saunders

764. Henry[20] Wolcott was born on December 5, 1578, in Tolland, Somersetshire, England. He was the son of John Wolcott and Agnes Crosse (672).

Henry died in Windsor, Hartford, Connecticut, British Colonial America, on May 30, 1655, at the age of 76. He was buried in Windsor, Hartford, Connecticut, British Colonial America.

More facts and events for Henry Wolcott:

At the age of 27, Henry married Elizabeth Saunders on January 19, 1606, when she was 21 years old.

Elizabeth Saunders was born in Lydeard St Lawrence, Somerset, England, on December 20, 1584. She was the daughter of Thomas Saunders and Annie Blake.

Elizabeth was christened in Lydiard, Somerset, England, on December 20, 1584. She was buried in Windsor, Hartford, Connecticut, British Colonial America, in July 1655. Elizabeth reached 70 years of age and died in Windsor, Hartford, Connecticut, British Colonial America, on July 17, 1655.

Daughter of Henry Wolcott and Elizabeth Saunders:

+ 877 i. Anna[21] Wolcott was born in Gaulden Manor, Tolland, Somerset, England, in 1620.

Family of John Prescott and Elizabeth Manby

765. John[20] Prescott was born in 1576 in Wigan, Lancashire, England. He was the son of James Prescott and Alice Molyneux (673).

John died in Alford, Lincolnshire, England, on December 18, 1607, at the age of 31. He was buried on December 18, 1607.

John married Elizabeth Manby in 1603 in Driby, Lancashire, England.

Elizabeth Manby was born in Lincoln, Lincolnshire, England, in 1580. Elizabeth reached 32 years of age and died in Brigg, Lincolnshire, England, on May 15, 1612.

Son of John Prescott and Elizabeth Manby:

+ 878 i. James[21] Prescott was born in Driby, Lincs, England, on April 1, 1607.

Family of Robert Hydeand Annie Ardene

766. Robert[20] Hyde was born in 1543 in Newbury, Chester, England. He was the son of Robert Hyde (674) and Jane Davenport (447).

Robert died at Age: 71 in Stockport, Cheshire, Northamptonshire, England, on March 22, 1614, at the age of 71.

He married Annie Ardene.

Annie Ardene was born in Alvanley, Cheshire, England, in 1545. Annie reached 79 years of age and died in Stockport, Cheshire, England, on December 21, 1624.

Daughter of Robert Hyde JR and Annie Ardene:

+ 879 i. Maria[21] Hyde was born in Derby, Derbyshire, England, in 1579.

Family of George Gardiner and Dorothy Constable

767. George[20] Gardiner was born in 1535 in Berwick-Upon-Tweed, Northumberland, England. He was the son of George Gardiner (675) and Margaret Neville (577).

George died in Stepney, London, England, in June 1589 at the age of 54. He was buried in Beddington, Greater London, England.

He married Dorothy Constable.

Dorothy Constable was born in Wallington, Northumberland, England, in 1536. Dorothy reached 53 years of age and died in England in June 1589.

Son of George Gardiner and Dorothy Constable:

+ 880   i.   Thomas[21] Gardner was born in Dorchester, Dorset, England, in 1565.

Family of Edward Bagot and Mary Lambard

768. Sir Edward[20] Bagot, 2nd Baronet was born on May 23, 1616, in Bagot Bromley, Staffordshire, England. He was the son of Sir Hervey Bagot (676) and Catherine Adderley.

Edward was baptized in Penn, Staffordshire, England, on May 30, 1616. He died in Warwickshire, England, on May 30, 1673, at the age of 57.

He married Mary Lambard.

Mary Lambard was born in Buckinghamshire, England, in 1619. Mary reached 67 years of age and died in Warwickshire, England, on October 22, 1686.

Son of Sir Edward Bagot and Mary Lambard:

+ 881   i.   Sir Walter[21] Bagot 3rd Baronet was born in Staffordshire, England, on March 21, 1644.

Family of William Walker and Elizabeth Brigg

769. William[20] Walker was born in 1630 in Yorkshire, England. He was the son of John Walker (677) and Mary Jowet.

William died in Rothwell, Holy Trinity, Yorkshire, England, in 1672 at the age of 42.

William married Elizabeth Brigg in 1668.

Elizabeth Brigg was born in Kildwick, Yorkshire, England, on September 19, 1647. Elizabeth was baptized in Haworth, St Michael and All Angels,

Yorkshire, England, in April 1651. She reached 55 years of age and died in Yorkshire, England, in 1703.

Son of William Walker and Elizabeth Brigg:

+ 882 i. Thomas[21] Walker was born in Birstall, Yorkshire, England, in 1668.

Family of Marie Anne Amiot and Francois Michel Messier

770. Marie Anne[20] Amiot was born on September 29, 1685, in Québec, Quebec, Canada. She was the daughter of Jean Baptiste Amiot (678) and Genevieve Guyon.

Marie was baptized in Québec on 29, 1685. She died in Verchères, Quebec, Canada, on February 9, 1725, at the age of 39.

Marie married Francois Michel Messier on February 6, 1706, in Verchères, Quebec, Canada.

Francois Michel Messier was born in Montréal, Quebec, Canada, in 1679. He was the son of Michel Messier and Anne Lemoine.

Francois was baptized in 1679. Francois reached 70 years of age and died in Pointe-aux-Trembles, Quebec, Canada, on January 11, 1749.

Son of Marie Anne Amiot and Francois Michel Messier:

+ 883 i. Francois Michel[21] Messier was born in Verchères, Quebec, Canada, on April 18, 1707.

Family of John Townsend and Susanna Harcourt

771. John[20] Townsend was born in 1635 in Oyster Bay, Nassau, New York. He was the son of John Townsend (679) and Elizabeth Montgomery.

John died in Lusum, New York, United States, on January 5, 1721, at the age of 86.

He married Susanna Harcourt.

Susanna Harcourt was born in Hempstead, Nassau, New York, United States, in 1654. Susanna reached 28 years of age and died in Jerico, Nassau, New York, United States, on April 1, 1682.

Son of John Townsend and Susanna Harcourt:

+ 884 i. Solomon[21] Townsend was born in Queens, Lewis, New York, in 1667.

Family of Ewen MacLean and Mary MacLaine

772. Ewen[20] MacLean was born about 1635. He was the son of John Crubach McLean (680) and Anne Campbell.

Ewen was known by the title of 9th MacLean of Ardgour. He died in 1694 at the age of 59.

Ewen married Mary MacLaine on January 4, 1665.

Mary MacLaine was born in Scotland in 1651. She was the daughter of Lachlan Mor MacLaine (790) and Margaret MacLean (918).

Mary reached 78 years of age and died in December 1729.

Children of Ewen MacLean and Mary MacLaine:

+ 885   i.   Allan[21] MacLean was born in Argyll, Scotland, in 1668.
+ 886   ii.   Donald MacLean was born about 1670.
            iii.   Lachlan MacLean. Lachlan died at killed in a duel in Madrid, Spain.
            iv.   Charles MacLean was born about 1680.
            v.   John MacLean.
            vi.   Beatrix MacLean was born about 1672.
+ 887   vii.   Margaret MacLean.
            viii.   Marion MacLean.

Family of Lachlan McLean and Mary MacLean

773. Lachlan[20] McLean was born about 1636. He was the son of John Crubach McLean (680) and Anne Campbell.

Lachlan was known by the title of 3rd MacLean of Blaich.

Lachlan married Mary MacLean on October 4, 1668. She was the daughter of Hector MacLean.

Family of Jannet McLean and John Diuriach Maclean

774. Jannet[20] McLean. She is the daughter of John Crubach McLean (680) and Anne Campbell.

She married John Diuriach Maclean.

John Diuriach Maclean was born about 1625. He was the son of Lachlan Og MacLean (691) and Marian MacDonald.

Sons of Jannet McLean and John Diuriach Maclean:

+ 888   i.   Allan[21] MacLean was born about 1665.

+ 889   ii.   Hector Maclean was born about 1670.

Family of Donald McLean and Janet MacLean

775. Donald[20] McLean. He is the son of John Crubach McLean (680) and Anne Campbell.

He married Janet MacLean. She is the daughter of John MacLean.

Family of Allan McLean and Janet MacLean

776. Allan[20] McLean. He was the son of John Crubach McLean (680) and Anne Campbell.

Allan died in November 1709.

He married Janet MacLean.

Family of Mary McLean and John Maclean

777. Mary[20] McLean. She is the daughter of John Crubach McLean (680) and Anne Campbell.

She married John Maclean.

John Maclean was born in 1666. He was the son of Allan the elder Maclean (779) and Mary Cameron.

John was known by the title of 2nd MacLean of Drumnin. John reached 30 years of age and died in 1696.

Sons of Mary McLean and John Maclean:

     i.   Allan[21] Maclean was born about 1694. He was known by the title of 3rd MacLean of Drimnin.

          Allan died about 1723 at the age of 29. at age 29.

+ 890   ii.   Charles Maclean was born in Drimmin in Morven, Scotland, in 1695.

Family of Lachlan Maclean and Florence Fraser

778. Lachlan[20] Maclean was born about 1635 in Calgary, Isle of Mull, Argyll, Scotland. He was the son of Charles Maclean (699) and Mary MacLean (683).

Lachlan was known by the title of 1st MacLean of Calgary.

He married Florence Fraser.

Florence Fraser was born about 1635. She was the daughter of Farquhar Fraser and Jannet MacLean (810).

Lachlan Maclean married Ann MacLean.

Ann MacLean was born about 1652. She was the daughter of John Roy MacLean (933) and Marion MacLean (685).

Children of Lachlan Maclean and Florence Fraser:

+ 891   i.   Donald[21] Maclean was born in Calgary, Isle of Mull, Argyll, Scotland, about 1675.

+ 892   ii.   Florence MacLean.

Children of Lachlan Maclean and Ann MacLean:

       i.   Charles Maclean was born about 1660.

       ii.   Allan Maclean was born about 1662. He was known by the title of of Grulin.

       iii.   Peter Maclean.

+ 893   iv.   Marian Maclean.

Family of Allan the elder Maclean and Mary Cameron

779.   Allan the elder[20] Maclean was born about 1641. He was the son of Charles Maclean (699) and Mary MacLean (683).

Allan was known by the title of 1st MacLean of Drimnin. He died about 1670 at the age of 29. at age 29.

He married Mary Cameron. She is the daughter of John Cameron.

Children of Allan the elder Maclean and Mary Cameron:

+ 894   i.   Margaret[21] MacLean was born about 1665.

+ 895   ii.   John Maclean was born in 1666.

+ 896   iii.   Donald Maclean was born about 1668.

Family of Allan the younger Maclean and Una MacQuarrie

780.   Allan the younger[20] Maclean was born about 1643. He was the son of Charles Maclean (699) and Mary MacLean (683).

Allan was known by the title of 1st MacLean of Grulin. He died about 1720 at the age of 77.

He married Una MacQuarrie. She is the daughter of Donald MacQuarrie.

Children of Allan the younger Maclean and Una MacQuarrie:

+ 897   i.   Lachlan[21] Maclean was born about 1670.

+ 898   ii.   Charles Maclean was born about 1672.

+ 899   iii.   John MacLean was born about 1674.

+ 900   iv.   Margaret Maclean.

+ 901   v.   Jannet Maclean.

Family of Donald MacLean and Catherime MacQuarrie

781.   Donald[20] MacLean was born about 1645. He was the son of Charles Maclean (699) and Mary MacLean (683).

Donald was known by the title of od Aros.

He married Catherime MacQuarrie. They had three sons. She is the daughter of Donald MacQuarrie.

Sons of Donald MacLean and Catherime MacQuarrie:

+ 902   i.   Alexander[21] MacLean was born in 1690.

+ 903   ii.   Angus MacLean was born about 1691.

+ 904   iii.   Charles MacLean was born about 1692.

Family of Hector Maclean and Jannet MacLean

782.   Hector[20] Maclean was born about 1647. He was the son of Charles Maclean (699) and Mary MacLean (683).

He married Jannet MacLean. They had four sons.

Jannet MacLean was born about 1666. She was the daughter of Hector Roy MacLean (931) and Marion MacLean (917).

Sons of Hector Maclean and Jannet MacLean:

     i.   John[21] Maclean was born about 1675. He is deceased. unmarried.

     ii.   Donald Maclean was born about 1676. He is deceased. left no issue.

     iii.   Mary Maclean was born about 1678. He is deceased. unmarried.

iv. Lachlan Maclean. Lachlan is deceased. died young.

Family of Ewen Maclean and Marion MacLean

783. Ewen[20] Maclean was born about 1649. He was the son of Charles Maclean (699) and Mary MacLean (683).

He married Marion MacLean. Marion MacLean was born about 1650. She was the daughter of Archibald Maclean (684).

Family of Marion MacLean and Ewen Maclean

784. Marion[20] MacLean was born about 1650. She was the daughter of Archibald Maclean (684).

She married Ewen Maclean. Ewen Maclean was born about 1649.

Family of Ann MacLean and Lachlan Maclean

785. Ann[20] MacLean was born about 1652. She was the daughter of John Roy MacLean (933) and Marion MacLean (685).

She married Lachlan Maclean.

Lachlan Maclean was born in Calgary, Isle of Mull, Argyll, Scotland, about 1635.

Children of Ann MacLean and Lachlan Maclean:
- i. Charles[21] Maclean was born about 1660.
- ii. Allan Maclean was born about 1662. He was known by the title of of Grulin.
- iii. Peter Maclean.
- + 893 iv. Marian Maclean.

Family of Allan MacLean and Catherine MacLeod

786. Allan[20] MacLean was born about 1660. He was the son of John Roy MacLean (933) and Marion MacLean (685).

Allan was known by the title of 2nd MacLean of Totaranald.

He married Catherine MacLeod. She is the daughter of Roderick MacLeod.

Sons of Allan MacLean and Catherine MacLeod:
- + 905 i. Hector[21] MacLean was born about 1687.
- ii. Allan MacLean. Allan is deceased. died young by drowning.

Hector MacLean

787. Hector[20] MacLean. He is the son of John Roy MacLean (933) and Marion MacLean (685).

Son of Hector MacLean:

+ 906   i.   Allan[21] MacLean.

Allan MacLean

788. Allan[20] MacLean was born about 1631. He was the son of Ewen MacLean (687).

Allan was known by the title of 4th MacLean of Inverscadell.

Sons of Allan MacLean:

+ 907   i.   Charles[21] MacLean was born about 1665.
+ 908   ii.   Allan MacLean.

Family of Murdock Mor MacLaine and Julian Campbell

789. Murdock Mor[20] MacLaine. He was the son of Hector Odhar MacLaine (570) and Beathag MacLean (688).

Murdock was known by the title of 10th MacLean of Lochbuie. He died on January 8, 1663.

He married Julian Campbell. She is the daughter of Robert Campbell.

Family of Lachlan Mor MacLaine and Margaret MacLean

790. Lachlan Mor[20] MacLaine was born in 1614 in Lochbuie, Mull, Scotland. He was the son of Hector Odhar MacLaine (570) and Beathag MacLean (688).

Lachlan was known by the title of 11th MacLean of Lochbuie. He died in Lochaber, Scotland, in August 1687 at the age of 73.

He married Margaret MacLean.

Margaret MacLean was born in Torloisk, Mull, Scotland, about 1635. She was the daughter of Hector Maclean (799) and Jannet MacLean (701).

Lachlan Mor MacLaine married an unknown woman.

Children of Lachlan Mor MacLaine and Margaret MacLean:

+ 909   i.   Hector[21] MacLaine was born about 1640.
+ 910   ii.   Murdock Og MacLaine was born about 1635.

+ 911   iii.   John MacLaine.
+ 912   iv.   Mary MacLaine was born in Scotland in 1651.
         v.   Julia MacLaine.

Children of Lachlan Mor MacLaine and an unknown woman:

         i.   Charles MacLean. Charles died in Battle of Blenheim in 1704.
         ii.   Katherine MacLaine.

Family of Margaret MacLaine and Charles Maclean

791. Margaret[20] MacLaine was born about 1612. She was the daughter of Hector Odhar MacLaine (570) and Beathag MacLean (688).

She married Charles Maclean. Charles Maclean was born in Isle of Mull, Argyll, Scotland, about 1592. He was the son of Lachlan Mor MacLean (616) and Margaret Cunningham.

Family of Janet MacLaine and John Cambell

792. Janet[20] MacLaine. She is the daughter of Hector Odhar MacLaine (570) and Beathag MacLean (688).

She married John Cambell.

Family of Mary MacLaine and Neil Maclean

793. Mary[20] MacLaine. She is the daughter of Hector Odhar MacLaine (570) and Beathag MacLean (688).

She married Neil Maclean. He is the son of Lachlan Og MacLean (691) and Marian MacDonald.

Son of Mary MacLaine and Neil Maclean:

         i.   Lachlan[21] Maclean. Lachlan died in London, England.

Family of Sarah MacLaine and Hector McLean

794. Sarah[20] MacLaine. She is the daughter of Hector Odhar MacLaine (570) and Beathag MacLean (688).

She married Hector McLean. Hector died in 1654. murdered.

Sarah MacLaine married Ewen the elder MacLean. Ewen the elder MacLean was born about 1605.

Ewen reached 86 years of age and died in 1691.

Family of Hector Mor Maclean and Margaret MacLeod

795. Hector Mor[20] Maclean was born about 1603. He was the son of Hector Og MacLean (689) and Janet Mackenzie.

Hector was known by the title of 15th Chief MacLean. He died about 1630 at the age of 27.

He married Margaret MacLeod. She is the daughter of Roderick Ruairidh Macleod and Isabel MacDonald.

Family of Lachlan MacLean and Mary MacLeod

796. Lachlan[20] MacLean was born in 1606 in Scotland. He was the son of Hector Og MacLean (689) and Janet Mackenzie.

Lachlan was known by the title of 16th Chief MacLean, Knight Baronet. He died in Duart Castle, Isle of Mull, Argylishire, Scotland, on April 18, 1648, at the age of 42. Lachlan was buried in Isle od Iona.

He married Mary MacLeod.

Mary MacLeod was born in Dunvegan, Skye, Scotland, in 1605. She was the daughter of Roderick Ruairidh Macleod and Isabel MacDonald.

Children of Lachlan MacLean and Mary MacLeod:

      i.   Hector Ruadh[21] MacLean was born in 1626. He was known by the title of 17th Chief MacLean, 2nd Baronnet Morvern.

           Hector died in Battle of Innerkeithing, Fife, Scotland, on July 20, 1651, at the age of 25.

+ 913   ii.   Allan Maclean was born in Duart Castle, Mull, in 1641.

      iii.   Marian MacLean.

      iv.   Isabel MacLean.

      v.   Mary MacLean.

Family of Finvola (Florence) MacLean and John Garbh MacLean

797. Finvola (Florence)[20] MacLean was born about 1610. She was the daughter of Hector Og MacLean (689) and Janet Mackenzie.

She married John Garbh MacLean.

John Garbh MacLean was born in Isle of Coll, Argyllshire, Scotland, about 1600. He was the son of Lachlan MacLean (695) and Florence Macleod.

John was known by the title of 7th MacLean of Coll. John reached 78 years of age and died in Isle of Coll, Argyllshire, Scotland, in 1678.

Daughter of Finvola (Florence) MacLean and John Garbh MacLean:

+ 914 i. Catherine[21] MacLean was born about 1630.

Family of Donald MacLean and Finvole (Florence) MacLean

798. Donald[20] MacLean was born in 1600 in Duart, Argyll, Scotland. He was the son of Hector Og MacLean (689) and Isabelle Acheson.

Donald was known by the title of 1st MacLean of Brolass. He died after 1655.

Donald married Finvole (Florence) MacLean about 1648 in , Scotland. They had three sons.

Finvole (Florence) MacLean was born in Coll, Argyll, Scotland, about 1630. She was the daughter of John Garbh MacLean (807) and Florence Campbell.

Sons of Donald MacLean and Finvole (Florence) MacLean:

    i. Hector Mor[21] MacLean was born in Brolass, Mull, Scotland, about 1627. He is deceased. unmarried.

+ 915 ii. Hector Og MacLean was born in Brolass, Mull, Scotland, about 1631.

+ 916 iii. Lachlan MacLean was born in Brolass, Mull, Scotland, in 1650.

Family of Hector Maclean and Catherine Campbell

799. Hector[20] Maclean was born about 1610 in Coll, Argyll, Scotland. He was the son of Lachlan Og MacLean (691) and Marian Campbell.

Hector was known by the title of 2nd MacLean of Torloisk. He died in Isle of Mull, Argyll, Scottland, in 1683 at the age of 73.

He married Jannet MacLean. They had three daughters.

Jannet MacLean was born about 1620. She was the daughter of Allan Maclean (620) and Una MacDonald.

Hector Maclean married Catherine Campbell. She is the daughter of John Campbell.

Daughters of Hector Maclean and Jannet MacLean:

+ 917 i. Marion[21] MacLean was born about 1625.

| + | 918 | ii. | Margaret MacLean was born in Torloisk, Mull, Scotland, about 1635. |
| | | iii. | Mary Maclean. |

Children of Hector Maclean and Catherine Campbell:

+	919	i.	Lachlan MacLean was born about 1640.
+	920	ii.	John Maclean was born about 1642.
+	921	iii.	Isabella Maclean was born in Torloisk, Argyll, Scotland, about 1645.
+	922	iv.	Jannet MacLean was born about 1647.
		v.	Hector Maclean.

Family of Jannet MacLean and Hector Maclean

800. Jannet[20] MacLean was born in 1600 in Scotland, United Kingdom. She was the daughter of Lachlan Og MacLean (691) and Marian MacDonald.

Jannet died in Torloisk Mull, Argyll, Scotland, in 1650 at the age of 50.

She married Hector Maclean.

Hector Maclean was born about 1601. He was the son of Allan Maclean (620) and Una MacDonald.

Hector was known by the title of 1st MacLean of Kinlochaline, 3rd MacLean of Morvern. Hector died in Scotland after 1641.

Sons of Jannet MacLean and Hector Maclean:

| + | 923 | i. | John[21] Maclean was born in Duart Castle, Isle of Mull, Argyll, Scotland, about 1625. |
| | | ii. | Lachlan Maclean. |

Family of Mary MacLean and John Garbh MacLean

801. Mary[20] MacLean was born in 1603 in Scotland. She was the daughter of Lachlan Og MacLean (691) and Marian MacDonald.

Mary died in Ardnamurchan, Argyll, Scotland, in 1665 at the age of 62.

She married John Garbh MacLean.

John Garbh MacLean was born in Ardnamurchan, Argyll, Scotland, about 1590. He was the son of John Dubh MacLean (550) and Margaret Campbell.

John was known by the title of 1st MacLean of Drimnin. John reached 72 years of age and died in Midlothian, Scotland, on August 12, 1662. He was buried in Midlothian, Scotland, on August 12, 1662.

Children of Mary MacLean and John Garbh MacLean:

+ 924 i. Charles[21] MacLean was born about 1622.
+ 925 ii. Catherine McLean was born in Bunessan, Argyll, Scotland, in 1625.
    iii. Margaret McLean was born in Argyllshire, Scotland, about 1626. She died in Isle Mull, Argyll, Scotland, in 1660 at the age of 34.
    iv. Janet Kinlochlaine Maclean was born in Scotland about 1627. She died in Ardnamurchan, Argyll, Scotland, in 1700 at the age of 73.
    v. John Maclean was born about 1628.
    vi. Charles McLean was born in Scotland in 1630.
+ 926 vii. Hector MacLean was born about 1630.
+ 927 viii. Jannet MacLean.
+ 928 ix. Catherine MacLean.
    x. Donald MacLean.

Lachlan Og Maclean

802. Lachlan Og[20] Maclean was born about 1610. He was the son of Lachlan Og MacLean (691) and Marian MacDonald.

Son of Lachlan Og Maclean:

+ 929 i. Donald[21] Maclean was born about 1635.

Family of John Diuriach Maclean and Jannet McLean

803. John Diuriach[20] Maclean was born about 1625. He was the son of Lachlan Og MacLean (691) and Marian MacDonald.

He married Jannet McLean.

Sons of John Diuriach Maclean and Jannet McLean:

+ 888 i. Allan[21] MacLean was born about 1665.
+ 889 ii. Hector Maclean was born about 1670.

Family of Julian MacLean and Allan MacLaine

804. Julian[20] MacLean was born in Torloisk, Mull, Scotland. She is the daughter of Lachlan Og MacLean (691) and Marian MacDonald.

She married Allan MacLaine.

Allan MacLaine was born about 1675.

Children of Julian MacLean and Allan MacLaine:

+ 1197 i. John[21] MacLaine was born in 1724.

+ 1198 ii. Julian MacLaine was born about 1700.

+ 1199 iii. Finvola MacLaine.

Family of Neil Maclean and Mary MacLaine

805. Neil[20] Maclean. He is the son of Lachlan Og MacLean (691) and Marian MacDonald.

He married Mary MacLaine.

Son of Neil Maclean and Mary MacLaine:

i. Lachlan[21] Maclean. Lachlan died in London, England.

Family of Margaret MacLean and Hector McLean

806. Margaret[20] MacLean was born about 1620. She was the daughter of John Garbh MacLean (621) and Janet MacLean (694).

She married Hector McLean.

Hector McLean was born in Isle of Mull, Argyll, Scotland, about 1630. He was the son of Ewen McLean (948) and Catherine MacLean (563).

Hector was known by the title of 8th MacLean of Treshnish. Hector reached 63 years of age and died in Argylleshire, Scotland, in 1693.

Son of Margaret MacLean and Hector McLean:

+ 930 i. Ewen[21] McLean was born in Isle of Mull, Argyll, Scotland, about 1655.

Family of John Garbh MacLean and Florence Campbell

807. John Garbh[20] MacLean was born about 1600 in Isle of Coll, Argyllshire, Scotland. He was the son of Lachlan MacLean (695) and Florence Macleod.

John was known by the title of 7th MacLean of Coll. He died in Isle of Coll, Argyllshire, Scotland, in 1678 at the age of 78.

John married Florence Campbell about 1614 in Isle of Coll, Hebrides, Scotland.

Florence Campbell was born in Auchinbreck, Argyll-shire, Scotland, in 1595. She was the daughter of Sir Dugald Campbell and Mary Erskine.

Florence reached 41 years of age and died in Scotland in 1636.

John Garbh MacLean married Finvola (Florence) MacLean.

Finvola (Florence) MacLean was born about 1610.

Children of John Garbh MacLean and Florence Campbell:

+ 931   i.   Hector Roy[21] MacLean was born in Coll, Scotland, about 1625.
+ 932   ii.   Finvole (Florence) MacLean was born in Coll, Argyll, Scotland, about 1630.
+ 933   iii.   John Roy MacLean was born about 1632.
+ 934   iv.   Una MacLean was born about 1640.
           v.   Ewen or Hugh MacLean. Ewen died in 1651. killed at Inverkeithing.
           vi.   Jannet MacLean.

Daughter of John Garbh MacLean and Finvola (Florence) MacLean:

+ 914   i.   Catherine MacLean was born about 1630.

Daughter of John Garbh MacLean:

           i.   Finvola MacLean was born about 1630.

Family of Hector MacLean and Julian MacLean

808. Hector[20] MacLean was born about 1605. He was the son of Lachlan MacLean (695) and Florence Macleod.

Hector was known by the title of 1st MacLean of Muck. He is deceased. murdered by robbers.

He married Julian MacLean. They had three sons.

Julian MacLean was born about 1595. She was the daughter of Allan Maclean (620) and Una MacDonald.

Sons of Hector MacLean and Julian MacLean:

+ 935 i. Lachlan[21] MacLean was born about 1635.
+ 936 ii. Hector MacLean was born about 1645.
        iii. Hugh MacLean.

Family of Neil MacLean and Florence MacDonald

809. Neil[20] MacLean was born about 1615 in Coll, Argyll, Scotland. He was the son of Lachlan MacLean (695) and Florence Macleod.

Neil was known by the title of 1st MacLean of Drimnacross. He died in Drimnicross, Isle of Mull, Scotland, in 1651 at the age of 36.

He married Florence MacDonald.

Florence MacDonald was born in Morar, Inverness-shire, Scotland, in 1610.

Neil MacLean married Florence MacDonald.

Daughter of Neil MacLean and Florence MacDonald:

+ 937 i. Margaret[21] MacLean was born in Drimnicross, Isle of Mull, Scotland, about 1655.

Children of Neil MacLean and Florence MacDonald:

+ 938 i. Marian[21] MacLean was born about 1635.
+ 785 ii. Ann MacLean was born about 1652.
+ 939 iii. Allan MacLean was born about 1678.
+ 940 iv. Janet MacLean was born about 1685.
+ 941 v. Hector MacLean was born in Torrenstan.
        vi. Florence MacLean.
+ 942 vii. Margaret MacLean.

Family of Jannet MacLean and Farquhar Fraser

810. Jannet[20] MacLean. She is the daughter of Lachlan MacLean (695) and Florence Macleod.

She married Farquhar Fraser.

Daughter of Jannet MacLean and Farquhar Fraser:

+ 943 i. Florence[21] Fraser was born about 1635.

Patrick MacLean

811. Patrick[20] MacLean was born about 1610 in Lochbuie, Argyll, Scotland. He was the son of John MacLean (696) and Jannet Stuart.

Son of Patrick MacLean:

+ 944   i.   Duncan[21] MacLean.

Family of Allan Maclean and Una

812. Allan[20] Maclean was born about 1630. He was the son of Lachlan Maclean (703) and Anne ?.

Allan was known by the title of of Grulin.

He married Una.

Son of Allan Maclean and Una:

+ 945   i.   Charles[21] Maclean was born about 1650.

Family of Hector MacLean and Mary MacLean

813. Hector[20] MacLean was born about 1656. He was the son of John Diurach MacLean (704) and Elizabeth MacLean.

He married Mary MacLean. They had three sons.

Mary MacLean was born about 1660. She was the daughter of Ewen MacLean.

Sons of Hector MacLean and Mary MacLean:

       i.   Lachlan[21] MacLean was born about 1690.

+ 946   ii.   John MacLean was born in Balemartine Tyree Scotland about 1695.

+ 947   iii.   Donald MacLean was born about 1700.

Family of Donald MacLean and Isabella MacAdam

814. Donald[20] MacLean was born about 1618. He was the son of Lachlan MacLean (705) and Catherine Macdonald.

Donald was known by the title of merchant in Glasgow.

He married Isabella MacAdam.

Son of Donald MacLean and Isabella MacAdam:

       i.   Peter[21] MacLean was born about 1715. He died in London, England, in 1752 at the age of 37.

Family of Margaret MacLean and John McLean

815. Margaret[20] MacLean was born about 1590. She was the daughter of Charles MacLean (706).

She married John McLean. They had three sons.

John McLean was born about 1585.

Sons of Margaret MacLean and John McLean:

+ 948   i.   Ewen[21] McLean was born in Isle of Mull, Argyll, Scotland, about 1610.

       ii.   John Og McLean was born about 1616.

       iii.   Lachlan McLean.

John Ban McLean

816. John Ban[20] McLean was born about 1655 in Scotland. He was the son of Duncan McLean (709) and Christian Nikeich.

John died in Glasgow, Scotland, on April 21, 1723, at the age of 68.

Sons of John Ban McLean:

+ 949   i.   Farquhar[21] McLean was born in Scotland about 1676.

       ii.   John McLean.

Family of Duncan McLean and Janet McMalvay

817. Duncan[20] McLean was born about 1656 in Argylleshire, Scotland. He was the son of Duncan McLean (709) and Christian Nikeich.

Duncan married Janet McMalvay on April 24, 1695, in Lochgoilhead, Argyleshire, Scotland.

Janet McMalvay was born in Scotland about 1675.

Son of Duncan McLean and Janet McMalvay:

+ 950   i.   Donald[21] McLean was born in Lochgoilhead, Argyleshire, Scotland, on February 22, 1702.

Lachlan MacLean

818. Lachlan[20] MacLean was born about 1680. He was the son of Donald Og MacLean (710).

Lachlan was known by the title of 5th MacLean of Hynish.

Son of Lachlan MacLean:

+ 951   i.   Charles[21] MacLean was born about 1710.

Allan MacLean

819. Allan[20] MacLean. He is the son of Donald Og MacLean (710).

Son of Allan MacLean:

+ 952   i.   Charles[21] MacLean.

Neil MacLean

820. Neil[20] MacLean was born about 1670. He was the son of Hector MacLean (711) and Marion MacQuarrie.

Son of Neil MacLean:

+ 953   i.   John[21] MacLean was born in Tiree, Argyll, Scotland, in August 1707.

Ewen MacLean

821. Ewen[20] MacLean was born about 1673. He was the son of Hector MacLean (711) and Marion MacQuarrie.

Daughters of Ewen MacLean:

+ 954   i.   Catherine[21] MacLean was born about 1700.
+ 955   ii.   Mary MacLean was born about 1702.

Family of Archibald MacLean and a daughter of Samual MacDonald

822. Archibald[20] MacLean was born about 1668. He was the son of John MacLean (712) and ? Campbell.

Archibald was known by the title of 8th MacLean of Boreray. He died in 1739 at the age of 71.

He married a daughter of Samual MacDonald.

Archibald MacLean married a daughter of John MacDonald. They had three sons.

Sons of Archibald MacLean and a daughter of Samual MacDonald:

+ 956   i.   Neil Ban[21] MacLean was born about 1695.

           ii.   John MacLean was born about 1699.

Sons of Archibald MacLean and a daughter of John MacDonald:

+ 957   i.   Alexander MacLean was born about 1700.

           ii.   Hector MacLean was born about 1710.

           iii.   John MacLean was born about 1712.

John MacLean

823.   John[20] MacLean. He is the son of John MacLean (712) and ? Campbell.

Son of John MacLean:

           i.   John[21] MacLean.

Family of Neil MacLean and a daughter of Lachlan MacLean

824.   Neil[20] MacLean. He is the son of John MacLean (712) and ? Campbell.

He married a daughter of Lachlan MacLean.

Family of John MacLean and Florence MacLean

825.   John[20] MacLean was born about 1670 in Tiree, Argyll, Scotland. He was the son of Donald MacLean (713) and Isabel Campbell.

He married Florence MacLean.

Florence MacLean was born about 1675. She was the daughter of John MacLean.

Children of John MacLean and Florence MacLean:

           i.   Charles[21] MacLean was born about 1700.

           ii.   John MacLean.

           iii.   Donald MacLean.

           iv.   James MacLean.

           v.   Hugh MacLean.

           vi.   Isabel MacLean.

           vii.   Ann MacLean.

           viii.   Barbara MacLean.

Family of Donald MacLean and Isabella Campbell

826. Donald[20] MacLean was born about 1675. He was the son of Charles MacLean (714) and Florence MacLean.

He married Isabella Campbell.

Son of Donald MacLean and Isabella Campbell:

+ 958   i.   John[21] MacLean was born about 1700.

Family of Ann MacLean and Hector MacLean

827. Ann[20] MacLean was born about 1682. She was the daughter of Charles MacLean (714) and Florence MacLean.

She married Hector MacLean.

Hector MacLean was born about 1680. Hector was known by the title of 1st MacLean of Gallanach.

He reached 74 years of age and died on June 11, 1754.

"Hector, eldest son of Donald of Coll, was the progenitor of the Macleans of Gallanach. He lived in Mull. He was married and had two sons, Charles and Neil Ban. His descendants were known as Sliochd Eachainn Mhic Dhomhnaill, or the offspring of Hector the son of Donald," Sinclair, pp. 419

Son of Ann MacLean and Hector MacLean:

+ 959   i.   Neil Ban[21] MacLean was born about 1700.

Son of Ann MacLean:

+ 1239   i.   John[21] MacLean was born about 1740.

Family of Archibald MacLean and Susan Campbell

828. Archibald[20] MacLean was born about 1685. He was the son of Charles MacLean (714) and Florence MacLean.

Archibald was known by the title of Rev. in of Scour.

He married Susan Campbell.

Susan was known by the title of of Ardtun and Scamadale.

Children of Archibald MacLean and Susan Campbell:

+ 960   i.   Charles[21] MacLean was born about 1710.
+ 961   ii.   Barbara MacLean was born about 1732.

		iii.	John MacLean.
		iv.	Neil MacLean.
+	962	v.	Florence MacLean.
		vi.	Margaret MacLean.
+	963	vii.	Ann MacLean.

Family of Mary MacLean and John MacLean

829. Mary[20] MacLean was born about 1700. She was the daughter of Charles MacLean (714) and Florence MacLean.

She married John MacLean. John was known by the title of of Treshnish.

Family of Neil MacLean and Florence MacLean

830. Neil[20] MacLean. He is the son of Charles MacLean (714) and Florence MacLean.

He married Florence MacLean. They have two sons. She is the daughter of Donald MacLean.

Sons of Neil MacLean and Florence MacLean:

    i. Alexander[21] MacLean.

    ii. Lachlan MacLean.

Family of Lachlan MacLean and Maria Fatmangle

831. Lachlan[20] MacLean. He was the son of Charles MacLean (714) and Florence MacLean.

Lachlan died in the Brill in 1752.

He married Maria Fatmangle.

Daughter of Lachlan MacLean and Maria Fatmangle:

    i. Florentia[21] MacLean.

Family of Isabel MacLean and John MacLean

832. Isabel[20] MacLean. She is the daughter of Charles MacLean (714) and Florence MacLean.

She married John MacLean. John was known by the title of Rev.

Donald MacLean

833. Donald[20] MacLean. He is the son of Allan MacLean (716).

Donald was known by the title of 5th MacLean of Achnasaul.

Children of Donald MacLean:

- i. Allan[21] MacLean.
- ii. John MacLean. John was known by the title of 6th MacLean of Achnasaul.
- + 964 iii. Angus MacLean.
- iv. Neil MacLean.
- + 965 v. Margaret MacLean.

Lachlan MacLean

834. Lachlan[20] MacLean. He is the son of Allan MacLean (716).

Son of Lachlan MacLean:

- + 966 i. John[21] MacLean was born in of KILMORY about 1720.

John MacLean

835. John[20] MacLean. He is the son of Rory MacLean (717).

Sons of John MacLean:

- i. Murdock[21] MacLean.
- + 967 ii. Charles MacLean.

Neil MacLean

836. Neil[20] MacLean. He is the son of Roderick MacLean (718) and an unknown woman.

Son of Neil MacLean:

- i. John[21] MacLean.

Family of John McLean and Marritje DeWitt

837. John[20] McLean was born about 1674 in Scotland. He was the son of John MacLean (719) and Margaret Mauchline.

John died in Kingston, Ulster, New York on November 23, 1723, at the age of 49.

He married Marritje DeWitt.

Marritje DeWitt was born in Kingston, Ulster, New York in 1680. Marritje reached 53 years of age and died in Kingston, Ulster, New York in 1733.

Son of John McLean and Marritje DeWitt:

+ 968   i.   Cornelius[21] McLean was born in Shawangunk, Ulster, New York in 1701.

Family of Lachlan MacLean and Catherine Campbell

838. Lachlan[20] MacLean was born about 1715 in Grimsary, Coll, Scotland. He was the son of John MacLean (721).

He married Catherine Campbell. She is the daughter of John Campbell.

Son of Lachlan MacLean and Catherine Campbell:

+ 969   i.   John[21] MacLean was born about 1755.

Family of John MacLean and Christina MacLean

839. John[20] MacLean was born in 1724. He was the son of Donald MacLean (723).

John died in March 1808 at the age of 84.

He married Christina MacLean.

Christina MacLean was born in 1718. Christina reached 90 years of age and died in March 1808.

Children of John MacLean and Christina MacLean:

     i.   Allan[21] MacLean.

     ii.   Donald MacLean.

     iii.   Marion MacLean.

Hector MacLean

840. Hector[20] MacLean was born about 1715. He was the son of John MacLean (724) and Catherine MacLean.

Hector was known by the title of 3rd MacLean of Killean.

Sons of Hector MacLean:

+ 970   i.   Donald[21] MacLean.

     ii.   Dugald MacLean. Dugald died on June 25, 1818.

Family of John MacLean and Jannet Dallas

841. John[20] MacLean was born in 1673 in Dochgarroch, Inverness, Scotland. He was the son of John Og MacLean (726) and Margaret Fowler.

John was known by the title of 7th MacLean of Dochgarroch. He died in 1748 at the age of 75.

John married Jannet Dallas in 1700 in , Scotland.

Jannet Dallas was born in of, Cantray, Nairn, Scotland, in 1680. She was the daughter of William Dallas.

Children of John MacLean and Jannet Dallas:

      i.   John[21] MacLean was born about 1701. He died on April 16, 1746, at the age of 45. at the Battle of Culloden.

      ii.   Jannet MacLean was born in Dochgarroch, Inverness, Scotland, in 1704.

      iii.   William MacLean was born in Dochgarroch, Inverness, Scotland, in 1706. He died in storming of Gaudaloupe in 1753 at the age of 47.

      iv.   Mary MacLean was born in Dochgarroch, Inverness, Scotland, in 1707.

+ 971   v.   Charles MacLean was born in Dochgarroch, Inverness, Scotland, in March 1718.

Family of Janet MacLean and William MacIntosh

842. Janet[20] MacLean. She is the daughter of John Og MacLean (726) and Margaret Fowler.

She married William MacIntosh.

Family of Annie MacLean and James Ross

843. Annie[20] MacLean. She is the daughter of John Og MacLean (726) and Margaret Fowler.

She married James Ross.

Family of John Og MacLean and Margaret Fowler

844. John Og[20] MacLean was born in 1657 in Dochgarroch, Inverness, Scotland. He was the son of Alexander MacLean (731) and Agnes Chisolm.

John was known by the title of 8th MacLean of Dochgarroch. He died in 1707 at the age of 50.

He married Margaret Fowler.

Margaret Fowler was born in Dochgarroch, Inverness, Scotland, in 1661. Margaret reached 73 years of age and died on January 30, 1734.

Children of John Og MacLean and Margaret Fowler:

+ 972   i.   John[21] MacLean was born in Dochgarroch, Inverness, Scotland, on December 4, 1683.

+ 973   ii.   Alexander MacLean was born about 1685.

+ 974   iii.   David MacLean was born in Dochgarroch, Scotland, in 1692.

+ 975   iv.   Donald MacLean was born in Dochgarroch, Inverness, Scotland, about 1695.

         v.   Charles MacLean.

+ 976   vi.   Jannet MacLean.

+ 977   vii.   Annie MacLean.

Laclhlan MacLean

845.   Laclhlan[20] MacLean was born about 1635. He was the son of Hector MacLean (733).

Laclhlan was known by the title of 7th MacLean of Kingerloch.

Sons of Laclhlan MacLean:

+ 978   i.   Donald[21] MacLean was born about 1660.

         ii.   Hector MacLean.

         iii.   Alexander MacLean.

Family of John Borthwick and Lilias Ker

846.   John[20] Borthwick was born in 1590 in Borthwick, Midlothian, Scotland. He was the son of Lord James Borthwick (734) and Margaret Hay.

John died in Borthwick, Midlothian, Scotland, in November 1623 at the age of 33.

He married Lilias Ker.

Lilias Ker was born in West Lothian, Scotland, in 1587. Lilias reached 72 years of age and died on July 10, 1659.

Son of John Borthwick and Lilias Ker:

+ 979 i. Baron John[21] Borthwick was born in Prestongrange, East Lothian, Scotland, on February 9, 1615.

Family of Thomas Warren Warren and Jane Allen King

847. Thomas Warren[20] Warren was born on January 30, 1624, in Kent, England. He was the son of William Warren (735) and Catherine Gookin.

Thomas was baptized at Age: 0 in Ripple, Kent, on January 30, 1625. He died at Age: 46 in Smith S Fort, Surry, VA on April 21, 1670, at the age of 46. Thomas was buried in Surry County, Virginia.

Thomas married Jane Allen King in of VA.

Jane Allen King was born in Smiths Fort, Virginia, Surrey, England, on January 9, 1624. Jane reached 96 years of age and died in Surry, Surry, Virginia, United States, in 1721.

Son of Thomas Warren Warren and Jane Allen King:

+ 980 i. Robert[21] Warren was born in Smith Fort Creek, Surry, Virginia on March 13, 1667.

Family of John Hardy and Olive Council

848. John[20] Hardy was born about 1587 in Bedfordshire, England. He was the son of Richard Hardy (736) and Alice Wilson.

John died in Salem, Essex, Massachusetts, United States, on January 30, 1652, at the age of 65.

John married Olive Council in 1614 in Ashford, Kent, England.

Olive Council was born in Ashford, Kent, England, in 1595. Olive reached 60 years of age and died in Salem, Essex, Massachusetts, United States, on September 11, 1655.

Children of John Hardy and Olive Council:

+ 981 i. Joseph[21] Hardy was born in England in 1615.

+ 982 ii. Elizabeth Hardy was born in England about 1617.

      iii. Isabel hardy was born in England in 1620. She died in Isle of Wight, Isle of Wight, Virginia, United States, on August 7, 1693, at the age of 73.

iv. Martha Hardy was born in England in 1620. She died in Salem, Essex, Massachusetts, United States, in January 1688 at the age of 68.

Family of Roger Dudley and Susannah Thorne

849. Roger[20] Dudley was born about 1552. He was the son of John Dudley (737) and Elizabeth Leighton.

Roger died in 1585 at the age of 33.

He married Susannah Thorne.

Susannah Thorne was born in March 1560. She was the daughter of Thomas Thorne and Mary Purefoy (455).

Susannah died after October 29, 1588.

Son of Roger Dudley and Susannah Thorne:

+ 983 i. Thomas[21] Dudley was born in Northampton, England, in October 1576.

Family of Isaac Cook and Elizabeth Barton

850. Isaac[20] Cook was born on April 3, 1640, in Salem, Essex, MA. He was the son of Henry Cook and Judith Birdsall (739).

Isaac died in 1692 at the age of 51. He was buried in 1692.

Isaac married Elizabeth Barton on May 3, 1664.

Isaac Cook married Elizabeth Buxton on May 3, 1664, in Salem, Essex, Massachusetts. They had thirteen children.

Elizabeth Buxton was born in Salem, Essex, Massachusetts, about 1642. She was the daughter of Anthony Buxton and Elizabeth.

Elizabeth died in Y.

Children of Isaac Cook and Elizabeth Buxton:

i. Elizabeth[21] Cook was born in Salem, Essex, Massachusetts, on September 23, 1665. She died in Y.

ii. Isaac Cook was born in Salem, Essex, Massachusetts, on November 9, 1666. He died on April 6, 1671, at the age of 4.

iii. Mary Cook was born in Salem, Essex, MA, on September 12, 1668. She died in Y.

		iv.	Abigail Cook was born in Salem, Essex, Massachusetts, on April 12, 1670. She died in Y.
+	984	v.	Hannah Cook was born in Salem, Essex, Massachusetts, on October 15, 1671.
		vi.	John Cook was born in Salem, Essex, Massachusetts, on March 23, 1673. He died in Y.
		vii.	Isaac Cook was born in Salem, Essex, Massachusetts, on July 3, 1674. He died on October 8, 1679, at the age of 5.
		viii.	Rachel Cook was born in Salem, Essex, Massachusetts, on December 20, 1675. She died on October 15, 1679, at the age of 3.
		ix.	Ebenezer Cook was born in Salem, Essex, Massachusetts, on October 24, 1677. He died on October 20, 1679, at the age of 1.
		x.	Samuel Cook was born in Salem, Essex, Massachusetts, on October 1, 1679. He died in 1718 at the age of 38.
		xi.	Henry Cook was born in Salem, Essex, Massachusetts, about 1681. He died in Y.
+	985	xii.	Sarah Cook was born in 1682.
		xiii.	Lydia Cook was born in Salem, Essex, Massachusetts, about 1685. She died in Y.

Family of Henry Birdsall and Mary ?

851. Henry[20] Birdsall was born in 1658 in Oyster Bay, Nassau, New York. He was the son of Nathan Birdsall (740) and Temperance Fowler Baldwin.

Henry was known by the title of Captain. He died in Oyster Bay, Nassau, New York, United States, in 1699 at the age of 41.

He married Mary ?.

Mary ? was born in Matinecock, Livingston, New York, United States, in 1660. Mary died in USA.

Daughter of Henry Birdsall and Mary ?:

+ 986   i.   Mary[21] Birdsall was born in Jerusalem, Suffolk Long Island, New York in 1690.

Family of Samuel Whiting and Dorcas Chester

852. Samuel[20] Whiting. He is the son of Samuel Whiting and Elizabeth St. John (741).

He married Dorcas Chester. They have one son.

Son of Samuel Whiting and Dorcas Chester:

+ 987   i.   Samuel[21] Whiting.

Family of Samuel Whiting and Dorcas Chester

853. Samuel[20] Whiting. He is the son of Samuel Whiting and Elizabeth St. John (741).

He married Dorcas Chester. They have one son.

Son of Samuel Whiting and Dorcas Chester:

+ 988   i.   Samuel[21] Whiting.

Family of Olive Farwell and Benjamin Spalding

854. Olive[20] Farwell. She is the daughter of Henry Farwell and Olive Welby (742).

She married Benjamin Spalding. They have one son.

Son of Olive Farwell and Benjamin Spalding:

+ 989   i.   Edward[21] Spalding.

Family of James Freethy and Mary Milbury

855. James[20] Freethy was born in 1651 in York, York, Maine. He was the son of William Freethy and Elizabeth Barker (743).

James died in York, York, Maine, United States, on October 14, 1690, at the age of 39.

He married Mary Milbury.

Mary Milbury was born in York, York, Maine, United States, in 1651. She was the daughter of Henry Milbury and Daug Dixon.

Mary reached 84 years of age and died in York, York, Maine, United States, on May 22, 1735.

Daughter of James Freethy and Mary Milbury:

+ 990   i.   Elizabeth[21] Freethy was born in York, York County, Maine, in 1680.

21st Generation

Family of Edward Wynne and Mary Dorothy Berkeley

856.   Edward[21] Wynne was born in 1570 in Thornton Curtis, Lincolnshire, England. He was the son of George Wynne (744) and Margaret Green.

Edward died in Thornton Curtis, Lincolnshire, England, in 1645 at the age of 75.

He married Mary Dorothy Berkeley.

Mary Dorothy Berkeley was born in Worcestershire, England, in 1584. She was the daughter of Rowland Berkeley and Catherine Hayward.

Mary reached 24 years of age and died in Yorkshire, England, in 1608.

Son of Edward Wynne and Mary Dorothy Berkeley:

+ 991   i.   Edward[22] Winn was born in Ipswich, Suffolk, England, in 1599.

Family of Grace Chetwood and Peter Bulkeley

857.   Grace[21] Chetwood was born about 1602. She was the daughter of Sir Richard Chetwood and Dorothy Needham (745).

Grace died in April 1669 at the age of 67.

Grace married Peter Bulkeley in 1634 in Bedfordshire, England.

Peter Bulkeley was born in Odell, Bedfordshire, England, on January 31, 1583. He was the son of Edward Bulkeley (581) and Olive Irby.

Peter reached 76 years of age and died in Concord, MA, on March 9, 1659.

Peter and Grace had four children. All the children were born in America.

Children of Grace Chetwood and Peter Bulkeley:

+ 992   i.   Gershom[22] Bulkeley was born in Concord, MA, on December 26, 1635.

           ii.   Eleazer Bulkeley was born in 1638.

           iii.   Dorothy Bulkeley was born on August 2, 1640.

iv. Peter Bulkeley was born on August 12, 1643.

Family of Thomas Howard and Alethea Talbot

858. Thomas[21] Howard was born on July 7, 1585, in Finchingfield, Braintree District, Essex, England. He was the son of Phillip Howard (746) and Anne Dacre.

Thomas was known by the title of Earl of Arundle. He died in Padua, Provincia di Padova Veneto, Italy, on September 26, 1646, at the age of 61.

Thomas married Alethea Talbot in September 1606 in Whitehall, Middlesex, Connecticut.

Alethea Talbot was born in Metropolitan Borough of Sheffield, Yorkshire, England, in 1581. Alethea was known by the title of 13th Baroness of Furnivall.

She reached 73 years of age and died in Amsterdam, Noord-Holland, Netherlands, on June 3, 1654.

Daughter of Thomas Howard and Alethea Talbot:

+ 993 i. Mary Anne[22] Howard was born in Greenwich, Kent, England, in 1614.

Family of Jane Allen and Peter Bulkeley

859. Jane[21] Allen was born on January 17, 1587, in Odell, Bedfordshire, England. She was the daughter of Thomas Allen (747) and Mary Fairclough.

Jane died in Odell, Bedfordshire, England, on December 8, 1626, at the age of 39.

Jane married Peter Bulkeley in 1613.

Peter and Grace had four children. All the children were born in America.

Children of Jane Allen and Peter Bulkeley:

+ 994 i. Edward[22] Bulkeley was born in Odell, Bedfordshire, England, on June 17, 1614.

ii. Mary Bulkeley was born in Odell, Bedford, England, in August 1615. She died in Odell, Bedford, England, in January 1616.

iii. Thomas Bulkeley was born on April 11, 1617.

iv. Nathaniall Bulkeley was born in Odell, England, in November 1618. He died in Odell, England, in February 1629 at the age of 10.

v. John Bulkeley was born in February 1619.

vi. Marye Bulkeley was born in Odell, England, in November 1621. She died in Odell, England, in April 1624 at the age of 2.

vii. Joseph Bulkeley was born in May 1623.

viii. Benjamin Bulkeley was born in May 1624.

ix. Danill Bulkeley was born in August 1625.

x. Jabez Bulkeley was born in December 1626. She died in December 1629 at the age of 3.

Family of Ebenezer Allen and Abigail Hill

860. Ebenezer[21] Allen was born on February 10, 1650. He was the son of Ralph Allen (748) and Esther Susanna Swift.

Ebenezer died in , Bristol County, Massachusetts, British Colonial America, on May 18, 1725, at the age of 75. He was buried in Russells Mills, Dartmouth, Bristol, Massachusetts, British Colonial America.

He married Abigail Hill.

Abigail Hill was born in Salem, Essex, Massachusetts, British Colonial America, on November 16, 1651. Abigail reached 73 years of age and died on April 18, 1725.

Son of Ebenezer Allen and Abigail Hill:

+ 995 i. James B[22] Allen was born in Dartmouth, Bristol, Massachusetts, United States, on November 30, 1695.

Family of William Knowles and Grace Clavell

861. William[21] Knowles was born in 1566 in Harwood, Bolton, Lancashire, England. He was the son of Sir William Knowles (749) and Dorothy Braye.

William died in Bolton, Lancashire, England, on October 26, 1598, at the age of 32.

He married Grace Clavell.

Grace Clavell was born in Barston, Dorset, England, in 1570. She was the daughter of John Clavell and Millicent Gifford.

Grace was baptized in Church Knowle, Dorset, England, on 22, 1589. Grace reached 28 years of age and died in Bolton, Lancashire, England, on October 26, 1598.

Sons of William Knowles and Grace Clavell:

          i.   Andrew[22] Knowles was born in Bolton, Lancashire, England, on May 22, 1592. He died in Bolton, Lancashire, England, in 1660 at the age of 67.

+ 996   ii.   John Knowles was born in Waltham, Lincolnshire, England, on November 1, 1596.

Family of Elizabeth Lucy St. John and Allen Apsley

862. Lady Elizabeth Lucy[21] St. John was born in 1580 in Lydiard Tregoze, Wiltshire, England. She was the daughter of Sir John St John and Lady Lucy Hungerford (750).

Elizabeth died in Apsley, Sussex, England, on October 11, 1658, at the age of 78.

She married Sir Allen Apsley.

Sir Allen Apsley was born in London, England, in 1582. He was the son of John Apsley and Elizabeth Shelley.

He was baptized in London, Middlesex, England. He worked as a Lieutenant in the Tower of London in 1620.

Allen reached 48 years of age and died in Vinë, Elbasan, Albania, on May 24, 1630.

Daughter of Lady Elizabeth Lucy St. John and Sir Allen Apsley:

+ 997   i.   Lady Lucy[22] Apsley was born in Tower Hill, London, Middlesex, England, on January 29, 1620.

Family of Mary Randes and George Merriton

863. Mary[21] Randes was born in 1571 in Dustin, Northamptonshire, England. She was the daughter of Thomas Randes and Mary Yorke (751).

Mary died in Northampton, Northamptonshire, England, on October 22, 1632, at the age of 61.

She married George Merriton.

George Merriton was born in Yorkshire, England, in 1567. George reached 57 years of age and died in Charlemange, , England, on December 23, 1624.

Daughter of Mary Randes and George Merriton:

+ 998   i.   Anne[22] Merriton was born in Castle Leavington, Yorkshire, England, in 1605.

Family of Edmond Stiles and Mary Berney

864. Edmond[21] Stiles was born in 1520 in Sanborn, Warwickshire, England. He was the son of Humphrey Stiles (752) and Bridget Baudrey.

Edmond died in England before 1565.

He married Mary Berney.

Mary Berney was born in Reedham, Norfolk. England, in 1528. She was the daughter of John Berney and Margaret Read.

Mary reached 86 years of age and died in Fairsted, Essex, England, in 1614.

Son of Edmond Stiles and Mary Berney:

+ 999   i.   Thomas[22] Stiles was born in Millbrook, Bedfordshire, England, in December 1550.

Family of Percival Lowell and Rebecca Alice Goodale

865. Percival[21] Lowell was born in 1571 in Kingston Seymour, Somersetshire, England. He was the son of Richard Lowell and Christian Perceval (753).

Percival worked as a merchant lrg merchtile establishment in England, and America. He immigrated in 1639.

Percival died in Newbury, Essex, Massachusetts. He was buried in Newburyport, Essex, Massachusetts.

Percival married Rebecca Alice Goodale in 1594 in of Bristol, Norfolk, England.

Rebecca Alice Goodale was born in Kingston Seymour, Somerset, England, in 1575. Rebecca was christened in Kingston Seymour, Somerset, England, in 1575. Rebecca was buried in Newburyport, Essex, Massachusetts Bay Colony, British Colonial America, in December 1645. She reached 70 years of age and died in Newbury, Essex County, Massachusetts, United States of America, on December 28, 1645.

Daughter of Percival Lowell and Rebecca Alice Goodale:

+ 1000   i.   Joanna Percival[22] Lowell was born in Bristol, England, on August 20, 1619.

Family of George Gray and Sarah Cooper

866. George[21] Gray was born on April 14, 1625, in Edinburgh, Midlothian, Scotland. He was the son of James Gray (754) and Alison Gifert.

George died in Berwick, York, Maine, United States, in 1693 at the age of 67.

He married Sarah Cooper.

Sarah Cooper was born in Kittery, York, Maine, United States, in 1656. She was the daughter of Alexander Cooper.

Sarah reached 70 years of age and died in Kittery, York, Maine, United States, in July 1726.

Son of George Gray and Sarah Cooper:

+ 1001 i. Robert[22] Gray was born in Berwick, York County, Maine, in 1680.

Family of Thomas Fleming Jordan and Lucy Corker

867. Thomas Fleming[21] Jordan was born on January 6, 1600, in Wiltshire, England. He was the son of Capt Samuel Silas Jordan (755) and Frances Baker.

Thomas died at Age: 85 in Isle of Wight, Virginia, United States, on May 3, 1687, at the age of 87.

He married Lucy Corker.

Lucy Corker was born in Wiltshire, England, in 1604. She was the daughter of William Corker and Lucy White.

Lucy reached 96 years of age and died in Virginia, United States, in 1700.

Son of Thomas Fleming Jordan and Lucy Corker:

+ 1002 i. Thomas[22] Jordan was born in Chuckatuck, Nansemond, Virginia on July 7, 1634.

Family of John Conger and Zipporah Moores

868. John[21] Conger was born in 1702 in Woodbridge, Middlesex, New Jersey. He was the son of John Conger (756) and Mary Tuttle.

John died in Salisbury, Rowan, North Carolina, United States, on February 17, 1784, at the age of 82.

He married Zipporah Moores.

Zipporah Moores was born in Woodbridge, Middlesex, New Jersey, United States, on April 20, 1710. She was the daughter of Joshua Moores and Elizabeth Penman.

Zipporah reached 72 years of age and died in Woodbridge, Middlesex, New Jersey, United States, on March 14, 1783.

Daughters of John Conger and Zipporah Moores:

+ 1003   i.   Phoebe[22] Conger was born in Woodbridge, Middlesex, New Jersey in 1740.

           ii.   Elizabeth Conger was born in Woodbridge, Middlesex, New Jersey, United States, in 1742. She died in Rowan, North Carolina, United States, in 1796 at the age of 54.

Family of Joseph Thompson and Elizabeth Smith

869.   Joseph[21] Thompson was born on April 4, 1664, in New Haven, New Haven, Connecticut. He was the son of John Thompson (757) and Ellen Harrison.

Joseph died in Wallingford, New Haven, Connecticut, on December 14, 1711, at the age of 47.

He married Elizabeth Smith.

Elizabeth Smith was born in New Haven, New Haven, Connecticut, United States, on August 1, 1675. Elizabeth reached 68 years of age and died in West Haven, New Haven, Connecticut, United States, on November 14, 1743.

Son of Joseph Thompson and Elizabeth Smith:

+ 1004   i.   Ebenezer[22] Thompson was born in New Haven, New Haven, Connecticut, United States, on June 21, 1712.

Family of Rebecca Thompson and Daniel Thomas

870.   Rebecca[21] Thompson was born on January 26, 1651, in New Haven, New Haven, Connecticut. She was the daughter of John Thompson (757) and Dorothy Harrison.

Rebecca died in New Haven, New Haven, Connecticut, United States, in 1716 at the age of 64.

She married Daniel Thomas.

Daniel Thomas was born in New Haven, New Haven, Connecticut, United States, on February 13, 1644. He was the son of John Thomas (871) and Tabitha Charles.

Daniel reached 49 years of age and died in New Haven, New Haven, Connecticut, United States, in February 1694.

Sons of Rebecca Thompson and Daniel Thomas:

+ 1005 i. John[22] Thomas was born in Wallingford, CT in 1672.

+ 1006 ii. Israel Thomas was born in New Haven, New Haven, Connecticut, United States, in 1685.

Family of John Thomas and Tabitha Charles

871. John[21] Thomas was born in 1616 in Lemhan, Kent, England. He was the son of Benjamin Thomas (758) and Mirable Fitch.

John died at Age: 57 in New Haven, New Haven, Connecticut, United States, on December 15, 1671, at the age of 55. He was buried in New Haven, New Haven County, Connecticut, United States of America.

John married Tabitha Charles in 1639 in New Haven, New Haven, Connecticut.

Tabitha Charles was born in Basing, Hampshire, England, on June 15, 1618. Tabitha reached 71 years of age and died in New Haven, New Haven, Connecticut, United States, on April 1, 1690. She was buried in New Haven, New Haven County, Connecticut.

Son of John Thomas and Tabitha Charles:

+ 1007 i. Daniel[22] Thomas was born in New Haven, New Haven, Connecticut, United States, on February 13, 1644.

Family of Joseph Merriam and Sarah Goldstone

872. Joseph[21] Merriam was born in 1599 in Tudeley, Kent, England. He was the son of William Merriam and Sarah Burges (759).

Joseph died in Concord, Middlesex, Massachusetts, United States, on January 1, 1641, at the age of 42.

He married Sarah Goldstone.

Sarah Goldstone was born in of, Kent, England, in 1602. She was the daughter of John Goldstone and Frances Jeffrie.

Sarah reached 68 years of age and died in Concord, Middlesex, Massachusetts, United States, on March 12, 1670.

Son of Joseph Merriam and Sarah Goldstone:

+ 1008 i. William[22] Merriam was born in Kent, England, in 1628.

Family of William Bennett and Mary ?

873. William[21] Bennett was born about 1579 in Brindle, Lancashire, England. He was the son of William Bennett (760) and Joan Hodgson.

William died in Rehoboth, Bristol, Massachusetts, United States, in 1645 at the age of 66.

He married Mary ?.

Mary ? was born in Brindle, Lancashire, England, in 1581.

Son of William Bennett and Mary ?:

+ 1009 i. John[22] Bennett was born in Lancashire, England, in 1606.

Family of Thomas Bennett and Alice Pierce

874. Thomas[21] Bennett was born in 1580 in Somerset, England. He was the son of John Bennett (761) and Ann Weeks.

Thomas died in Isle of Wight, Virginia in 1642 at the age of 62.

He married Alice Pierce.

Alice Pierce was born in Heacham, Norfolk, England, in 1600. Alice reached 47 years of age and died in Isle, Virginia, United States, in 1647.

Children of Thomas Bennett and Alice Pierce:

+ 1010 i. Richard[22] Bennett was born in England on August 6, 1609.
- ii. Mary Bennett was born in Isle of Wight, Colonial Virginia, in 1627. She died in Colonial Virginia in 1700 at the age of 73.

Family of Peter Harwood and Elizabeth Garey

875. Peter[21] Harwood was born in 1633 in Talbot, Maryland. He was the son of John Harwood and Dorothy Elizabeth Usher (762).

Peter died in Maryland, United States, on July 1, 1675, at the age of 42.

Peter married Elizabeth Garey in 1657 in Talbot, Maryland.

Elizabeth Garey was born in England in 1633. Elizabeth reached 64 years of age and died in Talbot, Maryland, United States, on April 16, 1697.

Children of Peter Harwood and Elizabeth Garey:

- i. John[22] Harwood was born in 1664.
+ 1011 ii. Peter Harwood was born in Easton, Talbot, Maryland, United States, in 1668.

iii. Elizabeth Harwood was born in Talbot, Maryland, United States, in 1676. She died in Maryland, United States, in 1737 at the age of 61.

iv. William Harwood.

v. Nathaniel Harwood.

vi. Mary Harwood.

vii. James Harwood.

Family of James Harrington and Ann Clinton

876. James[21] Harrington was born in 1592 in Bath, Somerset, England. He was the son of Sir John Harrington (763) and Mary Rogers.

James died in Watertown, Middlesex, Massachusetts in 1630 at the age of 38.

James married Ann Clinton in 1615 in Bath, Somerset, England.

Ann Clinton was born in Bath, Somerset, England, in 1596. Ann reached 36 years of age and died in Charlestown, Middlesex, Massachusetts on December 25, 1632.

Children of James Harrington and Ann Clinton:

+ 1012 i. Robert[22] Harrington was born in England on October 1, 1616.

ii. Rebecca Harrington was born in England, Somerset, England, in 1622. She died in Cambridge, Middlesex, Massachusetts, in 1680 at the age of 58.

Family of Anna Wolcott and Matthew Griswold

877. Anna[21] Wolcott was born in 1620 in Gaulden Manor, Tolland, Somerset, England. She was the daughter of Henry Wolcott (764) and Elizabeth Saunders.

Anna died in New London, New London, Connecticut, British Colonial America, on November 29, 1704, at the age of 84. She was buried in New London, New London, Connecticut, British Colonial America, on December 1, 1704.

More facts and events for Anna Wolcott:

Anna married Matthew Griswold on October 16, 1646, in Windsor, Hartford, Connecticut.

Matthew Griswold was born in Kennilworth, Warwick, England, in 1620. He was the son of George Griswold and Honora Pawley.

Matthew worked as a Lawyer. He immigrated to With brother to Windsor in 1639.

He was buried in Old Lyme, New London, Connecticut, British Colonial America, in September 1698. Matthew reached 78 years of age and died in Lyme, New London, Connecticut, British Colonial America, on September 23, 1698.

Daughter of Anna Wolcott and Matthew Griswold:

+ 1013 i. Anna[22] Griswold was born in Saybrook, Middlesex, Connecticut on June 19, 1651.

Family of James Prescott and Mary Copeland

878. James[21] Prescott was born on April 1, 1607, in Driby, Lincs, England. He was the son of John Prescott (765) and Elizabeth Manby.

James died in Washingboro, England, in June 1639 at the age of 32.

He married Mary Copeland.

Mary reached -4 years of age and died in Kingston, Rockingham Co, NH, in 1639. Mary Copeland was born in Leigh, Lancashire, England, in 1643.

Son of James Prescott and Mary Copeland:

+ 1014 i. James[22] Prescott Sr was born in Derby, Lincolnshire, England, on November 25, 1643.

Family of Maria Hyde and George Tomlinson

879. Maria[21] Hyde was born in 1579 in Derby, Derbyshire, England. She was the daughter of Robert Hyde (766) and Annie Ardene.

Maria died in Derby, Derbyshire, England, on September 22, 1642, at the age of 63.

Maria married George Tomlinson on January 19, 1600, in St Peters, Derby, Derbyshire, England.

George Tomlinson was born in London, Middlesex, England, in 1575. He was the son of John Tomlinson and Barbara ?.

George was baptized on February 25, 1577. : Lancashire: Hawkshead - Parish Register, 1568-1704. George reached 53 years of age and died at

Age: 53 in Derby, Derbyshire, England, on May 14, 1628. He was buried in St Peter's Church, Derby, Derbyshire, England, on May 14, 1628.

Son of Maria Hyde and George Tomlinson:

+ 1015 i. Henry^{22} Tomlinson was born in Derby, Derbyshire, England, on November 22, 1606.

Family of Thomas Gardner and Elizabeth White

880. Thomas^{21} Gardner was born in 1565 in Dorchester, Dorset, England. He was the son of George Gardiner (767) and Dorothy Constable.

Thomas died in Salem, Essex, Massachusetts in 1635 at the age of 70.

He married Elizabeth White.

Elizabeth White was born in Stanton, St John, Oxfordshire, England, in 1564. Elizabeth reached 84 years of age and died in Little Bourton, Croperdy, Oxfordshire, England, on March 29, 1648.

Daughter of Thomas Gardner and Elizabeth White:

+ 1016 i. Rachel^{22} Gardner was born in Aldington, Kent, England, in 1608.

Family of Walter Bagot and Jane Salesbury

881. Sir Walter^{21} Bagot, 3rd Baronet Bagot was born on March 21, 1644, in Staffordshire, England. He was the son of Sir Edward Bagot (768) and Mary Lambard.

Walter died in Blithfield, Staffordshire, England, on February 15, 1704, at the age of 59.

He married Jane Salesbury.

Jane Salesbury was born in 1689425, Denbighshire, Wales, in 1650. Jane reached 45 years of age and died in Staffordshire, England, on July 20, 1695.

Son of Sir Walter Bagot and Jane Salesbury:

+ 1017 i. Sir Edward^{22} Bagot, 4th Baronet was born in Blithfield Hall, Staffordshire, on July 21, 1673.

Family of Thomas Walker and Anne Peele

882. Thomas^{21} Walker was born in 1668 in Birstall, Yorkshire, England. He was the son of William Walker (769) and Elizabeth Brigg.

Thomas died in Birstall, Yorkshire, England, in 1726 at the age of 58.

Thomas married Anne Peele in 1694. They had five sons.

Anne Peele was born in Birstall, Yorkshire, England, in 1674. Anne was baptized in Birstall, St Peter, Yorkshire, England, on July 28, 1675. She reached 80 years of age and died in Birstall, Yorkshire, England, in 1754.

Sons of Thomas Walker and Anne Peele:

    i.   Thomas[22] Walker was born in 1698. He died in 1760 at the age of 62.

    ii.   William Walker was born in 1699. He died in 1700 at the age of 1.

    iii.   John Walker was born in Yorkshire, England, in 1702. He died in Almondbury, Yorkshire, England, in 1766 at the age of 64.

    iv.   Robert Walker was born in 1706. He died in 1770 at the age of 64.

+ 1018   v.   George Walker was born in Brompton by, Yorkshire, England, in 1715.

Family of Francois Michel Messier and Marie Josephe Guyon

883. Francois Michel[21] Messier was born on April 18, 1707, in Verchères, Quebec, Canada. He was the son of Francois Michel Messier and Marie Anne Amiot (770).

Francois died in Varennes, Quebec, Canada, on November 4, 1749, at the age of 42.

At the age of 23, Francois married Marie Josephe Guyon on January 22, 1731, in Verchères, Quebec, Canada, when she was 20 years old.

Marie was baptized in Ile-d`Orléans, Québec, between 1705 and 1718. Marie Josephe Guyon was born in La Pérade, Quebec, Canada, on March 9, 1710.

She reached 52 years of age and died in Varennes, Quebec, Canada, on March 21, 1762.

Daughter of Francois Michel Messier and Marie Josephe Guyon:

+ 1019   i.   Marie Judith[22] Messier was born in Varennes, Quebec, Canada, on September 8, 1737.

Family of Solomon Townsend and Catherine Almy

884. Solomon[21] Townsend was born in 1667 in Queens, Lewis, New York. He was the son of John Townsend (771) and Susanna Harcourt.

Solomon died at died of snakebite while mowing in Newport, Newport, Rhode Island, United States, on January 13, 1717, at the age of 50.

He married Catherine Almy.

Catherine Almy was born in Portsmouth, Newport, Rhode Island, United States, on January 22, 1674.

Son of Solomon Townsend and Catherine Almy:

+ 1020 i. Solomon[22] Townsend was born in April 1701.

Family of Allan MacLean and Anne Cameron

885. Allan[21] MacLean was born in 1668 in Argyll, Scotland. He was the son of Ewen MacLean (772) and Mary MacLaine (912).

Allan was known by the title of 10th MacLean of Ardgour. He died in Scotland on November 10, 1756, at the age of 88.

He married Anne Cameron. They had nine children. She is the daughter of Ewen Cameron.

Children of Allan MacLean and Anne Cameron:

+ 1021 i. Isabella[22] MacLean was born about 1695.
- ii. Donald MacLean was born about 1696. He died in 1731 at the age of 35.
- iii. Ewen MacLean was born about 1698. He died in 1729 at the age of 31. died young on his way from Virginia.
+ 1022 iv. John MacLean was born about 1700.
- v. Archibald MacLean.
+ 1023 vi. Margaret MacLean was born about 1702.
- vii. Allan MacLean was born about 1705. He died in January 1753 at the age of 48. emigrated to Georgia and died there.
+ 1024 viii. Mary MacLean was born in Inverchaolain, Argyll, in 1715.
- ix. James MacLean. James died on June 1, 1767. killed in battle at sea.

Family of Donald MacLean and Janet MacLean

886. Donald[21] MacLean was born about 1670. He was the son of Ewen MacLean (772) and Mary MacLaine (912).

He married Janet MacLean. They had three sons. She is the daughter of Lachlan MacLean.

Sons of Donald MacLean and Janet MacLean:

      i.   Ewen[22] MacLean.

      ii.   John MacLean.

      iii.   Lachlan MacLean.

Family of Margaret MacLean and Allan MacLachlan

887. Margaret[21] MacLean. She is the daughter of Ewen MacLean (772) and Mary MacLaine (912).

She married Allan MacLachlan.

Daughter of Margaret MacLean and Allan MacLachlan:

+ 1025 i.   Margery[22] MacLachlan.

Allan MacLean

888. Allan[21] MacLean was born about 1665. He was the son of John Diuriach Maclean (803) and Jannet McLean (774).

Allan was known by the title of of Troloisk.

Daughters of Allan MacLean:

+ 1026 i.   Anna[22] MacLean.

+ 1027 ii.   Marjory MacLean.

Family of Hector Maclean and Mary MacLean

889. Hector[21] Maclean was born about 1670. He was the son of John Diuriach Maclean (803) and Jannet McLean (774).

He married Mary MacLean. Mary MacLean was born about 1702. She was the daughter of Ewen MacLean (821).

Family of Charles Maclean and Isabella Cameron

890. Charles[21] Maclean was born in 1695 in Drimmin in Morven, Scotland. He was the son of John Maclean (895) and Mary McLean (777).

Charles was known by the title of 4th MacLean of Drimnin. He died on April 16, 1746, at the age of 51. killed at the Battle of Culloden.

He married an unknown woman.

Charles Maclean married Isabella Cameron. They had four sons.

Son of Charles Maclean and an unknown woman:

+ 1028 i. Lachlan[22] Maclean was born about 1722.

Sons of Charles Maclean and Isabella Cameron:

+ 1029 i. Allan[22] MacLean was born in Scotland in 1724.

+ 1030 ii. John Maclean was born about 1726.

iii. Donald Maclean was born about 1727. He died in New York.

iv. Lachlan Maclean was born about 1728. He died in Jamaica in 1764 at the age of 36.

Family of Donald Maclean and Susanna Campbell

891. Donald[21] Maclean was born about 1675 in Calgary, Isle of Mull, Argyll, Scotland. He was the son of Lachlan Maclean (778) and Florence Fraser (943).

Donald was known by the title of 2nd MacLean of Calgary.

He married Susanna Campbell. They had three sons.

Susanna Campbell was born in Inverawe, Lorn, Argyll, Scotland, about 1684. Susanna reached 31 years of age and died in 1715.

Donald Maclean married Florence MacLean.

Sons of Donald Maclean and Susanna Campbell:

i. Charles[22] Maclean was born about 1700. He is deceased. died young.

+ 1031 ii. Alexander Maclean was born about 1705.

iii. Allan Maclean was born in Calgary, Isle of Mull, Argyll, Scotland, about 1710. He died on April 16, 1746, at the age of 36. killed at the Battle of Culloden.

Children of Donald Maclean and Florence MacLean:

i. Lachlan Maclean.

ii. Jean Maclean.

Family of Florence MacLean and Hector MacLean

892. Florence[21] MacLean. She is the daughter of Lachlan Maclean (778) and Florence Fraser (943).

She married Hector MacLean. Hector was known by the title of of 'Torrestan.

Florence MacLean married Donald Maclean.

Donald Maclean was born about 1668. He was the son of Allan the elder Maclean (779) and Mary Cameron.

Son of Florence MacLean and Donald Maclean:

    i.   Lachlan[22] Maclean.

Family of Marian Maclean and Hector MacLean

893. Marian[21] Maclean. She is the daughter of Lachlan Maclean (778) and Ann MacLean (785).

She married Hector MacLean. Hector was known by the title of of Muck.

Family of Margaret MacLean and Allan Maclean

894. Margaret[21] MacLean was born about 1665. She was the daughter of Allan the elder Maclean (779) and Mary Cameron.

She married Allan Maclean.

Allan Maclean was born about 1660. He was the son of Donald Maclean (929) and a daughter of MacGillvray.

"Allan, eldest son of Donald Maclean, was a captain under Sir John of Duart at the battle of Killiecrankie in 1689 and at Sheriffmuir in 1715." Sinclair, pp. 462

Children of Margaret MacLean and Allan Maclean:

+   1032 i.   Donald[22] Maclean was born about 1685.
          ii.   John Maclean. John is deceased. left no issue.
          iii. Florence Maclean.

Family of John Maclean and Mary McLean

895. John[21] Maclean was born in 1666. He was the son of Allan the elder Maclean (779) and Mary Cameron.

John was known by the title of 2nd MacLean of Drumnin. He died in 1696 at the age of 30.

He married Mary McLean.

Sons of John Maclean and Mary McLean:

        i.   Allan[22] Maclean was born about 1694. He was known by the title of 3rd MacLean of Drimnin.

            Allan died about 1723 at the age of 29. at age 29.

+ 890 ii.   Charles Maclean was born in Drimmin in Morven, Scotland, in 1695.

Family of Donald Maclean and Florence MacLean

896.   Donald[21] Maclean was born about 1668. He was the son of Allan the elder Maclean (779) and Mary Cameron.

He married Florence MacLean.

Son of Donald Maclean and Florence MacLean:

        i.   Lachlan[22] Maclean.

Family of Lachlan Maclean and Janet MacLeod

897.   Lachlan[21] Maclean was born about 1670. He was the son of Allan the younger Maclean (780) and Una MacQuarrie.

Lachlan was known by the title of 2nd MacLean of Grulin. He died about 1751 at the age of 81.

He married Janet MacLeod. She is the daughter of John MacLeod.

Lachlan Maclean married Ann Campbell.

Children of Lachlan Maclean and Janet MacLeod:

+ 1033 i.   Hector[22] Maclean was born about 1700.

+ 1034 ii.   Una Maclean.

Family of Charles Maclean and Marian MacLean

898.   Charles[21] Maclean was born about 1672. He was the son of Allan the younger Maclean (780) and Una MacQuarrie.

Charles was known by the title of 1st MacLean of Kilunaig. He died about 1741 at the age of 69.

He married Marian MacLean. She is the daughter of John MacLean.

Marian was using a title in of Tarbert.

Children of Charles Maclean and Marian MacLean:

+ 1035   i.   Allan the elder[22] Maclean was born about 1700.

+ 1036   ii.   Hector Maclean was born about 1702.

+ 1037   iii.   Donald Maclean was born about 1704.

           iv.   Allan the younger Maclean was born about 1706. He died about 1730 at the age of 24.

           v.   John Maclean was born about 1708.

+ 1038   vi.   Alexander Maclean was born about 1709.

           vii.   Lachlan Maclean was born about 1712. He died in 1762 at the age of 50.

           viii.   Archibald Maclean was born about 1714.

           ix.   Isabell Maclean.

           x.   Anne Maclean.

Family of John MacLean and Isabella Campbell

899.   John[21] MacLean was born about 1674. He was the son of Allan the younger Maclean (780) and Una MacQuarrie.

John was known by the title of 1st MacLean of Pennygoun.

He married Isabella Campbell.

Children of John MacLean and Isabella Campbell:

+ 1039   i.   Donald[22] MacLean was born in Isle of Mull, Argyll, Scotland, about 1700.

           ii.   Allan MacLean was born about 1705. He died in Caco Bay, Canada.

+ 1040   iii.   Una MacLean was born about 1714.

+ 1041   iv.   Janet MacLean was born about 1716.

+ 1042   v.   Catherine MacLean was born about 1718.

Family of Margaret Maclean and Hector MacLean

900.   Margaret[21] Maclean. She is the daughter of Allan the younger Maclean (780) and Una MacQuarrie.

She married Hector MacLean. Hector was known by the title of of Kilmory of the family of Lochbuie.

Family of Jannet Maclean and John Campbell

901. Jannet^{21} Maclean. She is the daughter of Allan the younger Maclean (780) and Una MacQuarrie.

She married John Campbell.

Alexander MacLean

902. Alexander^{21} MacLean was born in 1690. He was the son of Donald MacLean (781) and Catherime MacQuarrie.

Alexander died at was beheaded in Madrid, Spain, in 1739 at the age of 49.

Children of Alexander MacLean:

      i.   Don Andrew^{22} MacLean was born about 1720.

      ii.   Zeiretta MacLean.

Family of Angus MacLean and Anna MacLean

903. Angus^{21} MacLean was born about 1691. He was the son of Donald MacLean (781) and Catherime MacQuarrie.

He married Anna MacLean.

Family of Charles MacLean and Jean Campbell

904. Charles^{21} MacLean was born about 1692. He was the son of Donald MacLean (781) and Catherime MacQuarrie.

He married Jean Campbell.

Children of Charles MacLean and Jean Campbell:

+   1043 i.   Hector^{22} MacLean was born in Isle of Mull, Argyll, Scotland, about 1720.

      ii.   Margaret MacLean.

Family of Hector MacLean and Julian MacLachlan

905. Hector^{21} MacLean was born about 1687. He was the son of Allan MacLean (786) and Catherine MacLeod.

Hector was known by the title of 3rd MacLean of Totaranald.

He married Julian MacLachlan. She is the daughter of Alexamder MacLachlan.

Sons of Hector MacLean and Julian MacLachlan:

        i.   Allan[22] MacLean.

        ii.   Roderick MacLean.

Allan MacLean

906.   Allan[21] MacLean. He is the son of Hector MacLean (787).

Son of Allan MacLean:

+   1044   i.   Hector[22] MacLean.

Family of Charles MacLean and a daughter of Donald Cameron

907.   Charles[21] MacLean was born about 1665. He was the son of Allan MacLean (788).

Charles was known by the title of 5th MacLean of Inverscadell.

He married a daughter of Donald Cameron.

Charles MacLean married a daughter of Archibald MacLean.

a daughter of Archibald MacLean was born in Ardtur, Scotland.

Son of Charles MacLean and a daughter of Donald Cameron:

+   1045   i.   Allan[22] MacLean was born about 1700.

Son of Charles MacLean and a daughter of Archibald MacLean:

+   1046   i.   John[22] MacLean was born in Inverchaolain, Argyll, on May 20, 1716.

Allan MacLean

908.   Allan[21] MacLean. He is the son of Allan MacLean (788).

Son of Allan MacLean:

        i.   Allan[22] MacLean.

Family of Hector MacLaine and Margaret Campbell

909.   Hector[21] MacLaine was born about 1640. He was the son of Lachlan Mor MacLaine (790) and Margaret MacLean (918).

Hector was known by the title of 12th MacLean of Lochbuie. He died after 1707.

He married Margaret Campbell. She is the daughter of Colin Campbell.

Children of Hector MacLaine and Margaret Campbell:

+ 1047 i. Murdock^{22} MacLaine.
+ 1048 ii. John MacLaine was born about 1670.
+ 1049 iii. Allan MacLaine was born about 1675.
+ 1050 iv. Margaret MacLaine.
+ 1051 v. Mary MacLaine.
+ 1052 vi. Lachlan MacLaine.

Family of Murdock Og MacLaine and Anne Campbell

910. Murdock Og^{21} MacLaine was born about 1635. He was the son of Lachlan Mor MacLaine (790) and Margaret MacLean (918).

Murdock was known by the title of 10th MacLean of Lochbuie. He died about 1662 at the age of 27. before his father without issue.

He married Anne Campbell. She is the daughter of Hugh Campbell.

Family of John MacLaine and Isabel MacDougal

911. John^{21} MacLaine. He was the son of Lachlan Mor MacLaine (790) and Margaret MacLean (918).

John is deceased. before his father without issue.

He married Isabel MacDougal.

Family of Mary MacLaine and Ewen MacLean

912. Mary^{21} MacLaine was born in 1651 in Scotland. She was the daughter of Lachlan Mor MacLaine (790) and Margaret MacLean (918).

Mary died in December 1729 at the age of 78.

Mary married Ewen MacLean on January 4, 1665.

Ewen MacLean was born about 1635. Ewen reached 59 years of age and died in 1694.

Children of Mary MacLaine and Ewen MacLean:

+ 885 i. Allan^{22} MacLean was born in Argyll, Scotland, in 1668.

+	886	ii.	Donald MacLean was born about 1670.
		iii.	Lachlan MacLean. Lachlan died at killed in a duel in Madrid, Spain.
		iv.	Charles MacLean was born about 1680.
		v.	John MacLean.
		vi.	Beatrix MacLean was born about 1672.
+	887	vii.	Margaret MacLean.
		viii.	Marion MacLean.

Family of Allan Maclean and Julian Macleod

913. Allan[21] Maclean was born in 1641 in Duart Castle, Mull. He was the son of Lachlan MacLean (796) and Mary MacLeod.

Allan was baptized in Hilipoll Hough Kilkenneth Kilkenneth Mursta, Argyll, Scotland. He was known by the title of 18th Chief MacLean, 3rd Baronet Morvern.

Allan died in Scotland in 1674 at the age of 33.

He married Julian Macleod.

Julian Macleod was born in Glasgow, Lanarkshire, Scotland, in 1636. She was the daughter of John MacLeod.

Julian reached 14 years of age and died in 1650.

Sons of Allan Maclean and Julian Macleod:

		i.	Alexander[22] MacLean was born in Isle of Mull Scotland. Exiled to Ulster after losing Jacobite War in 1715 in 1670. He died in County, Tyrone, Ireland, in 1736 at the age of 66.
+	1053	ii.	John MacLean 4th. Baronet was born in Isle of Mull, Argyll, Scotland, about 1670.

Family of Catherine MacLean and Lachlan MacQuarrie

914. Catherine[21] MacLean was born about 1630. She was the daughter of John Garbh MacLean (807) and Finvola (Florence) MacLean (797).

She married Lachlan MacQuarrie.

Daughter of Catherine MacLean and Lachlan MacQuarrie:

+	1054	i.	Flora[22] MacQuarrie.

Family of Hector Og MacLean and Janet McNeil

915. Hector Og[21] MacLean was born about 1631 in Brolass, Mull, Scotland. He was the son of Donald MacLean (798) and Finvole (Florence) MacLean (932).

He married Janet McNeil.

Sons of Hector Og MacLean and Janet McNeil:

       i.   Donald[22] MacLean was born about 1657. He is deceased. died young.

+ 1055 ii.   John Hector Og MacLean was born about 1660.

Family of Lachlan MacLean and Isabella Maclean

916. Lachlan[21] MacLean was born in 1650 in Brolass, Mull, Scotland. He was the son of Donald MacLean (798) and Finvole (Florence) MacLean (932).

Lachlan was known by the title of 2nd MacLean of Brolass. He died in 1686 at the age of 36.

He married Isabella Maclean.

Isabella Maclean was born in Torloisk, Argyll, Scotland, about 1645. She was the daughter of Hector Maclean (799) and Catherine Campbell.

Isabella was known by the title of of Torloisk.

Sons of Lachlan MacLean and Isabella Maclean:

+ 1056 i.   Donald[22] MacLean was born in Brolass, Mull, Scotland, in 1671.

+ 1057 ii.   Allan MacLean was born about 1684.

Family of Marion MacLean and John Crubach McLean

917. Marion[21] MacLean was born about 1625. She was the daughter of Hector Maclean (799) and Jannet MacLean (701).

Marion died about 1680 at the age of 55.

Marion married Hector Roy MacLean on January 22, 1641, in Hogh on Tiree.

Hector Roy MacLean was born in Coll, Scotland, about 1625. He was the son of John Garbh MacLean (807) and Florence Campbell.

Hector was known by the title of 8th MacLean of Coll. Hector died in Isle of Coll, Argyll, Scotland, before 1676.

The eldest son, Hector Roy, married Marian, daughter of Hector MacLean of Torloisk. He died before his father, leaving issue two sons, Lachlan and Donald, and four daughters : Margaret, married first to Allan Stewart of Appin, and afterward to Donald MacLean of Kingerloch; Catherine, married to Hector MacLean of isle of Muck; Jannet, married to Hector, fifth son of Charles MacLean of Ardnacross; and Una, married to John MacLean of Achanasaul.

"Hector Roy received, in 1642, a charter of Coll, Rum, Muck, and two-thirds of Ouinish. He was of a warlike nature He fought at the battle of Inverlochy, in 1645, and probably at the battle of Inverkeithing, in 1651," Sinclair, pp. 374

Marion MacLean married John Crubach McLean.

John Crubach McLean was born in Ardgour, Scotland, about 1603. John reached 99 years of age and died in Scotland in 1702.

Children of Marion MacLean and Hector Roy MacLean:

+ 1058 i. Lachlan[22] MacLean was born in Coll, Argyll, Scotland, about 1652.

+ 1059 ii. Donald MacLean was born in Coll, Argyll, Scotland, in 1656.

+ 1060 iii. Catherine MacLean was born about 1665.

+ 1061 iv. Jannet MacLean was born about 1666.

+ 1062 v. Margaret MacLean.

+ 1063 vi. Una MacLean.

Son of Marion MacLean and John Crubach McLean:

i. John McLean was born about 1655.

Family of Margaret MacLean and Lachlan Mor MacLaine

918. Margaret[21] MacLean was born about 1635 in Torloisk, Mull, Scotland. She was the daughter of Hector Maclean (799) and Jannet MacLean (701).

She married Lachlan Mor MacLaine.

Lachlan Mor MacLaine was born in Lochbuie, Mull, Scotland, in 1614. Lachlan reached 73 years of age and died in Lochaber, Scotland, in August 1687.

Children of Margaret MacLean and Lachlan Mor MacLaine:

+ 909   i.   Hector[22] MacLaine was born about 1640.

+ 910   ii.   Murdock Og MacLaine was born about 1635.

+ 911   iii.   John MacLaine.

+ 912   iv.   Mary MacLaine was born in Scotland in 1651.

        v.   Julia MacLaine.

Family of Lachlan MacLean and Barbara MacDonald

919.   Lachlan[21] MacLean was born about 1640. He was the son of Hector Maclean (799) and Catherine Campbell.

Lachlan was known by the title of 3rd MacLean of Torloisk. He died in 1687 at the age of 47.

He married Barbara MacDonald.

Barbara MacDonald was born in of Paiblisgeary, North Uist, Outer Hebrides, Scotland, in 1640. She was the daughter of Alexander MacDonald.

Children of Lachlan MacLean and Barbara MacDonald:

        i.   Alexander[22] MacLean was born in 1686. He was known by the title of 4th MacLean of Torloisk.

            Alexander died in Battle Of Brihuega, Spain, in 1715 at the age of 29.

        ii.   Hector MacLean was born about 1687. He is deceased. at age 18.

        iii.   Jannet MacLean.

Family of John Maclean and Catherine Campbell

920.   John[21] Maclean was born about 1642. He was the son of Hector Maclean (799) and Catherine Campbell.

John was known by the title of 1st MacLean of Tarbert.

He married Catherine Campbell. She is the daughter of Donald Campbell.

Children of John Maclean and Catherine Campbell:

+ 1064   i.   Donald[22] Maclean was born in Torloisk, Mull, Scotland, about 1672.

        ii.   John Maclean was born about 1673.

\+ 1065 iii. Marion Maclean was born about 1678.

Family of Isabella Maclean and Lachlan MacLean

921. Isabella[21] Maclean was born about 1645 in Torloisk, Argyll, Scotland. She was the daughter of Hector Maclean (799) and Catherine Campbell.

Isabella was known by the title of of Torloisk.

She married Lachlan MacLean.

Lachlan MacLean was born in Brolass, Mull, Scotland, in 1650. Lachlan reached 36 years of age and died in 1686.

Sons of Isabella Maclean and Lachlan MacLean:

\+ 1056 i. Donald[22] MacLean was born in Brolass, Mull, Scotland, in 1671.

\+ 1057 ii. Allan MacLean was born about 1684.

Family of Jannet MacLean and Hector Maclean

922. Jannet[21] MacLean was born about 1647. She was the daughter of Hector Maclean (799) and Catherine Campbell.

She married Hector Maclean.

Hector Maclean was born about 1660. He was the son of John Maclean (923) and Mary Campbell.

Hector was known by the title of 3rd MacLean of Kinlochaline.

Son of Jannet MacLean and Hector Maclean:

\+ 1066 i. Angus[22] Maclean was born about 1690.

Family of John Maclean and Mary Campbell

923. John[21] Maclean was born about 1625 in Duart Castle, Isle of Mull, Argyll, Scotland. He was the son of Hector Maclean (700) and Jannet MacLean (800).

John was known by the title of 2nd MacLean of Kinlochaline. He was known by the title of 2nd Laird of Kinlochaline.

John died in Isle of Mull, Argyll, Scotland, in 1681 at the age of 56.

More facts and events for John Maclean:

He married Mary Campbell.

Mary Campbell was born in Scotland, United Kingdom, in 1625. She was the daughter of John Campbell.

John Maclean married Una MacLean. Una MacLean was born about 1640. She was the daughter of John Garbh MacLean (807) and Florence Campbell.

Children of John Maclean and Mary Campbell:

+   i.   Allan[22] Maclean was born about 1657.
+ 1067   ii.   Hector Maclean was born about 1660.
+ 1068   iii.   William McLean was born in Scotland in 1670.
          iv.   Jannet Maclean.

Family of Charles MacLean and Marian MacLean

924.   Charles[21] MacLean was born about 1622. He was the son of John Garbh MacLean (621) and Mary MacLean (801).

Charles was known by the title of 2nd MacLean of Drimnin.

He married Marian MacLean.

Marian MacLean was born about 1635. She was the daughter of Neil MacLean (809) and Florence MacDonald.

Children of Charles MacLean and Marian MacLean:

+ 1069   i.   Allan[22] MacLean was born about 1655.
          ii.   Hector MacLean. Hector is deceased. killed in the Spanish Service.
          iii.   John MacLean. John died at killed in Queen Anne's War in Flanders, Belgium.
          iv.   Mary MacLean.

Family of Catherine McLean and Hector McLean

925.   Catherine[21] McLean was born in 1625 in Bunessan, Argyll, Scotland. She was the daughter of John Garbh MacLean (621) and Mary MacLean (801).

Catherine died in Isle of Mull, Argyll, Scotland, in 1660 at the age of 35.

Catherine married Hector McLean in 1650 in Argylleshire, Scotland.

Hector McLean was born in Isle of Mull, Argyll, Scotland, about 1630. He was the son of Ewen McLean (948) and Catherine MacLean (563).

Hector was known by the title of 8th MacLean of Treshnish. Hector reached 63 years of age and died in Argyllshire, Scotland, in 1693.

Children of Catherine McLean and Hector McLean:

      i.   Lachlan[22] McLean was born in Scotland in 1652.

      ii.   Donald McLean was born in Scotland in 1654. He died in Scotland.

      iii.   Archibald McLean was born in Scotland in 1658. He is deceased. died young.

      iv.   Janet McLean was born in Scotland in 1658.

      v.   Flora MacLean was born in Isle of Mull, Argyll, Scotland, in 1660. She died in Minginish, Inverness-shire, Scotland, in 1702 at the age of 42.

Family of Hector MacLean and Florence McLean

926. Hector[21] MacLean was born about 1630. He was the son of John Garbh MacLean (621) and Mary MacLean (801).

He married Florence McLean.

Florence McLean was born about 1635. She was the daughter of Ewen McLean (948) and Catherine MacLean (563).

Children of Hector MacLean and Florence McLean:

+ 1070   i.   Charles[22] MacLean was born about 1655.

+ 1071   ii.   Janet MacLean was born about 1670.

+ 1072   iii. John MacLean.

           iv.   Hugh MacLean.

           v.   Florence MacLean.

Family of Jannet MacLean and Malcolm MacDuffie

927. Jannet[21] MacLean. She is the daughter of John Garbh MacLean (621) and Mary MacLean (801).

She married Malcolm MacDuffie.

Family of Catherine MacLean and Ewen MacLean

928. Catherine[21] MacLean. She is the daughter of John Garbh MacLean (621) and Mary MacLean (801).

She married Ewen MacLean.

Family of Donald Maclean and a daughter of MacGillvray

929. Donald[21] Maclean was born about 1635. He was the son of Lachlan Og Maclean (802).

He married a daughter of MacGillvray. They had three sons. She is the daughter of Martin MacGillvray.

Sons of Donald Maclean and a daughter of MacGillvray:

+ 1073 i. Allan[22] Maclean was born about 1660.
+ 1074 ii. Lachlan Maclean was born about 1665.
      iii. John Maclean was born about 1670. He died at left no issue in Flanders.

Family of Ewen McLean and Margaret MacLean

930. Ewen[21] McLean was born about 1655 in Isle of Mull, Argyll, Scotland. He was the son of Hector McLean (1091) and Margaret MacLean (806).

Ewen was known by the title of 9th MacLean of Treshnish. He died in Killfinon, Mull, Scotland, in 1702 at the age of 47. Ewen was buried in Killfinon, Mull, Scotland, in 1702.

He married an unknown woman.

Ewen McLean married Margaret MacLean in 1690.

Margaret MacLean was born in Drimnicross, Isle of Mull, Scotland, about 1655. She was the daughter of Neil MacLean (809) and Florence MacDonald.

Sons of Ewen McLean and an unknown woman:

+ 1075 i. John[22] Mclean was born in Treshnish, Isle of Mull, Argyll, Scotland, in 1680.
+ 1076 ii. Lachlan McLean was born in Coll, Argyll, Scotland, about 1685.

Sons of Ewen McLean and Margaret MacLean:

+ 1077 i. Hector McLean was born in Isle of Mull, Argyll, Scotland, in 1696.

| + | 1078 | ii. | John McLean was born about 1699. |

Family of Hector Roy MacLean and Marion MacLean

931. Hector Roy[21] MacLean was born about 1625 in Coll, Scotland. He was the son of John Garbh MacLean (807) and Florence Campbell.

Hector was known by the title of 8th MacLean of Coll. He died in Isle of Coll, Argyll, Scotland, before 1676.

Hector married Marion MacLean on January 22, 1641, in Hogh on Tiree.

Marion MacLean was born about 1625. Marion reached 55 years of age and died about 1680.

Children of Hector Roy MacLean and Marion MacLean:

+	1058	i.	Lachlan[22] MacLean was born in Coll, Argyll, Scotland, about 1652.
+	1059	ii.	Donald MacLean was born in Coll, Argyll, Scotland, in 1656.
+	1060	iii.	Catherine MacLean was born about 1665.
+	1061	iv.	Jannet MacLean was born about 1666.
+	1062	v.	Margaret MacLean.
+	1063	vi.	Una MacLean.

Family of Finvole (Florence) MacLean and Donald MacLean

932. Finvole (Florence)[21] MacLean was born about 1630 in Coll, Argyll, Scotland. She was the daughter of John Garbh MacLean (807) and Florence Campbell.

Finvole married Donald MacLean about 1648 in , Scotland. They had three sons.

Donald MacLean was born in Duart, Argyll, Scotland, in 1600. Donald died after 1655.

Sons of Finvole (Florence) MacLean and Donald MacLean:

		i.	Hector Mor[22] MacLean was born in Brolass, Mull, Scotland, about 1627. He is deceased. unmarried.
+	915	ii.	Hector Og MacLean was born in Brolass, Mull, Scotland, about 1631.
+	916	iii.	Lachlan MacLean was born in Brolass, Mull, Scotland, in 1650.

Family of John Roy MacLean and an unknown woman

933. John Roy^{21} MacLean was born about 1632. He was the son of John Garbh MacLean (807) and Florence Campbell.

John was known by the title of 1st MacLean of Totaranald.

He married an unknown woman.

John Roy MacLean married Marion MacLean.

Marion MacLean was born about 1622.

John Roy MacLean married an unknown woman.

Son of John Roy MacLean and an unknown woman:

        i.   Ewen^{22} MacLean.

Children of John Roy MacLean and Marion MacLean:

+   785 i.   Ann^{22} MacLean was born about 1652.

+   786 ii.   Allan MacLean was born about 1660.

+   787 iii. Hector MacLean.

           iv. Margaret MacLean.

           v.   Florence MacLean.

Son of John Roy MacLean and an unknown woman:

        i.   Lachlan MacLean.

Family of Una MacLean and John Maclean

934. Una^{21} MacLean was born about 1640. She was the daughter of John Garbh MacLean (807) and Florence Campbell.

She married John Maclean. John Maclean was born in Duart Castle, Isle of Mull, Argyll, Scotland, about 1625.

John reached 56 years of age and died in Isle of Mull, Argyll, Scotland, in 1681.

Lachlan MacLean

935. Lachlan^{21} MacLean was born about 1635. He was the son of Hector MacLean (808) and Julian MacLean (698).

Son of Lachlan MacLean:

+   1079 i.   John^{22} MacLean was born about 1660.

Family of Hector MacLean and Catherine MacLean

936. Hector[21] MacLean was born about 1645. He was the son of Hector MacLean (808) and Julian MacLean (698).

Hector was known by the title of 2nd MacLean of Muck.

He married Catherine MacLean.

Catherine MacLean was born about 1665.

Children of Hector MacLean and Catherine MacLean:

+ 1211   i.   Lachlan[22] MacLean was born in Isle of Muck, Argyll, Scotland, about 1670.
+ 1212   ii.   Hector MacLean was born about 1672.
         iii.   Julian MacLean.

Family of Margaret MacLean and Ewen McLean

937. Margaret[21] MacLean was born about 1655 in Drimnicross, Isle of Mull, Scotland. She was the daughter of Neil MacLean (809) and Florence MacDonald.

Margaret married Ewen McLean in 1690.

Ewen McLean was born in Isle of Mull, Argyll, Scotland, about 1655. Ewen reached 47 years of age and died in Killfinon, Mull, Scotland, in 1702.

Sons of Margaret MacLean and Ewen McLean:

+ 1077   i.   Hector[22] McLean was born in Isle of Mull, Argyll, Scotland, in 1696.
+ 1078   ii.   John McLean was born about 1699.

Family of Marian MacLean and Charles MacLean

938. Marian[21] MacLean was born about 1635. She was the daughter of Neil MacLean (809) and Florence MacDonald.

She married Charles MacLean.

Charles MacLean was born about 1622.

Children of Marian MacLean and Charles MacLean:

+ 1069   i.   Allan[22] MacLean was born about 1655.
         ii.   Hector MacLean. Hector is deceased. killed in the Spanish Service.

iii. John MacLean. John died at killed in Queen Anne's War in Flanders, Belgium.

iv. Mary MacLean.

Family of Allan MacLean and Catherine MacLean

939. Allan[21] MacLean was born about 1678. He was the son of Neil MacLean (809) and Florence MacDonald.

Allan worked as a Professor in Edinburgh, Midlothian, Scotland. He was known by the title of 1st MacLean of Grishipol.

Allan died in Grishipoll, Coll, Argyll, Scotland.

He married Catherine MacLean.

Catherine MacLean was born in Balliphetrish, Tiree, Argyll, Scotland. She is the daughter of Hugh MacLean.

Children of Allan MacLean and Catherine MacLean:

+ 1080 i. Allan[22] MacLean was born in Grishispol, Argyll, Scotland, on August 1, 1715.

ii. Lachlan MacLean.

+ 1081 iii. John MacLean.

iv. Neil MacLean.

+ 1082 v. Florence MacLean.

+ 1083 vi. Mary MacLean.

Family of Janet MacLean and Charles MacLean

940. Janet[21] MacLean was born about 1685. She was the daughter of Neil MacLean (809) and Florence MacDonald.

She married Charles MacLean.

Charles MacLean was born about 1705. He was the son of Hector MacLean.

Charles was known by the title of 2nd MacLean of Gallanach.

"Charles, son of Hector, son of Donald of Coll, married Janet, youngest daughter of Neil Maclean of DrimnacrOSS, and haul by her a son named Lachlan. Charles fought at the battle of Culloden in 1746." Sinclair, pp. 420

Son of Janet MacLean and Charles MacLean:

+ 1084 i. Lachlan[22] MacLean was born in 1730.

Family of Hector MacLean and Florence MacLean

941. Hector[21] MacLean was born in Torrenstan. He was the son of Neil MacLean (809) and Florence MacDonald.

Hector was known by the title of 2nd MacLean of Drimnacross. He died on August 21, 1689. in the battle of Dunkeld.

He married Florence MacLean. She is the daughter of Lachlan MacLean.

Son of Hector MacLean and Florence MacLean:

+ 1085 i. Lachlan[22] MacLean.

Family of Margaret MacLean and Donald MacLean

942. Margaret[21] MacLean. She is the daughter of Neil MacLean (809) and Florence MacDonald.

She married Donald MacLean. Donald was using a title in of Arighoulan.

Margaret MacLean married Ewen MacLean. Ewen was using a title in of Trishnish.

Family of Florence Fraser and Lachlan Maclean

943. Florence[21] Fraser was born about 1635. She was the daughter of Farquhar Fraser and Jannet MacLean (810).

She married Lachlan Maclean.

Lachlan Maclean was born in Calgary, Isle of Mull, Argyll, Scotland, about 1635.

Children of Florence Fraser and Lachlan Maclean:

+ 891 i. Donald[22] Maclean was born in Calgary, Isle of Mull, Argyll, Scotland, about 1675.

+ 892 ii. Florence MacLean.

Duncan MacLean

944. Duncan[21] MacLean. He is the son of Patrick MacLean (811).

Son of Duncan MacLean:

+ 1086 i. Angus[22] MacLean was born in Argylleshire, Scotland, about 1657.

Family of Charles Maclean and Marianna ?

945. Charles[21] Maclean was born about 1650. He was the son of Allan Maclean (812) and Una.

Charles was known by the title of of Kilunaig.

He married Marianna ?.

Son of Charles Maclean and Marianna ?:

+ 1087 i. Alexander[22] MacLean.

Family of John MacLean and Marion MacQueen

946. John[21] MacLean was born about 1695 in Balemartine Tyree Scotland. He was the son of Hector MacLean (813) and Mary MacLean.

John worked as a Captain (Army). He died on April 18, 1746, at the age of 51. killed a day after the Battle of Culloden.

He married Marion MacQueen.

Son of John MacLean and Marion MacQueen:

+ 1088 i. Hugh[22] MacLean was born in Guirdil, Isle of Rum, Scotland, in 1738.

Family of Donald MacLean and Anne MacLean

947. Donald[21] MacLean was born about 1700. He was the son of Hector MacLean (813) and Mary MacLean.

He married Anne MacLean. She is the daughter of Charles MacLean.

Donald MacLean married Mary MacLean. She is the daughter of John MacLean.

Daughter of Donald MacLean and Anne MacLean:

+ 1089 i. Mary[22] MacLean.

Children of Donald MacLean and Mary MacLean:

    i. Lachlan[22] MacLean.

+ 1090 ii. Mary MacLean.

Family of Ewen McLean and Catherine MacLean

948. Ewen[21] McLean was born about 1610 in Isle of Mull, Argyll, Scotland. He was the son of John McLean (625) and Margaret MacLean (815).

Ewen was known by the title of 7th MacLean of Treshnish. He died at Killed in the Battle of Inverkeithing in Inverkeithing, Fife, Scotland, on July 20, 1651, at the age of 41.

Ewen married Catherine MacLean in 1624.

Catherine MacLean was born about 1590. She was the daughter of Allan MacLean (497).

Catherine reached 61 years of age and died in Isle Mull, Argyll, Scotland, on July 20, 1651.

Children of Ewen McLean and Catherine MacLean:

+ 1091 i. Hector[22] McLean was born in Isle of Mull, Argyll, Scotland, about 1630.

+ 1092 ii. Florence McLean was born about 1635.

Farquhar McLean

949. Farquhar[21] McLean was born about 1676 in Scotland. He was the son of John Ban McLean (816).

Farquhar died in probably in Cameron, near Lochuie, Mull, Scotland.

Sons of Farquhar McLean:

+ 1093 i. Farquhar[22] McLean was born about 1701.

+ 1094 ii. Hector McLean was born in Cameron, Mull, Scotland, about 1706.

Family of Donald McLean and Catherine Stewart

950. Donald[21] McLean was born on February 22, 1702, in Lochgoilhead, Argyleshire, Scotland. He was the son of Duncan McLean (817) and Janet McMalvay.

Donald died in 1795 at the age of 92.

Donald married Catherine Stewart on April 25, 1734, in Inveraray and Glenaray, Argyll, Scotland. They had three sons.

Catherine Stewart was born in Scotland about 1717.

Sons of Donald McLean and Catherine Stewart:

+ 1095 i. Lachlan[22] McLean was born in Inveraray, Argyll, Scotland, on February 19, 1735.

ii. John McLean was born in Inveraray, Argyll, Scotland, on August 23, 1737.

+ 1096 iii. Duncan McLean was born about 1739.

Charles MacLean

951. Charles[21] MacLean was born about 1710. He was the son of Lachlan MacLean (818).

Charles was known by the title of 6th MacLean of Hynish.

Children of Charles MacLean:

+ 1097 i. John[22] MacLean was born about 1735.
+ 1098 ii. Lachlan MacLean.
       iii. Mary MacLean.

Charles MacLean

952. Charles[21] MacLean. He is the son of Allan MacLean (819).

Son of Charles MacLean:

  i. Donald Roy[22] MacLean.

Family of John MacLean and Deborah Adams

953. John[21] MacLean was born in August 1707 in Tiree, Argyll, Scotland. He was the son of Neil MacLean (820).

John died in Danbury, CT, on April 7, 1805, at the age of 97.

He married Deborah Adams. She is the daughter of Samuel Adams.

Family of Catherine MacLean and Allan MacLean

954. Catherine[21] MacLean was born about 1700. She was the daughter of Ewen MacLean (821).

She married Allan MacLean. Allan MacLean was born about 1695.

Allan was using a title in of Grishipol.

Family of Mary MacLean and Hector Maclean

955. Mary[21] MacLean was born about 1702. She was the daughter of Ewen MacLean (821).

She married Hector Maclean. Hector Maclean was born about 1670.

Family of Neil Ban MacLean and a daughter of William MacDonald

956. Neil Ban[21] MacLean was born about 1695. He was the son of Archibald MacLean (822) and a daughter of Samual MacDonald.

Neil was known by the title of 9th MacLean of Boreray. He died after 1760.

He married a daughter of William MacDonald.

Children of Neil Ban MacLean and a daughter of William MacDonald:

    i.   Donald[22] MacLean was born about 1725. He was known by the title of 10th MacLean of Boeray.

    ii.   John MacLean was born about 1726.

    iii.   Archibald MacLean.

    iv.   William MacLean.

    v.   Allan MacLean.

    vi.   Marion MacLean.

    vii.   Margaret MacLean.

Alexander MacLean

957. Alexander[21] MacLean was born about 1700. He was the son of Archibald MacLean (822) and a daughter of John MacDonald.

Son of Alexander MacLean:

    i.   Archibald[22] MacLean. Archibald was known by the title of of North Uist.

Family of John MacLean and Florence MacLean

958. John[21] MacLean was born about 1700. He was the son of Donald MacLean (826) and Isabella Campbell.

He married Florence MacLean. They had three sons. She is the daughter of John MacLean.

Sons of John MacLean and Florence MacLean:

    i.   Donald[22] MacLean was born in Inverchaolain, Argyll, Scotland, about 1721.

    ii.   Charles MacLean.

    iii.   Archibald MacLean.

Neil Ban MacLean

959. Neil Ban²¹ MacLean was born about 1700. He was the son of Hector MacLean and Ann MacLean (827).

Son of Neil Ban MacLean:

+ 1099   i.   Charles²² MacLean was born about 1720.

Family of Charles MacLean and Catherine MacLean

960. Charles²¹ MacLean was born about 1710. He was the son of Archibald MacLean (828) and Susan Campbell.

He married Catherine MacLean.

Catherine MacLean was born in Isle of Muck, Argyll, Scotland, about 1705.

Children of Charles MacLean and Catherine MacLean:

     i.   Archibald²² MacLean was born about 1735. He died in 1817 at the age of 82.

     ii.   Mary MacLean.

     iii.   Isabel MacLean.

Family of Barbara MacLean and Hugh McLean

961. Barbara²¹ MacLean was born about 1732. She was the daughter of Archibald MacLean (828) and Susan Campbell.

She married Hugh McLean. Hugh McLean was born about 1730.

Family of Florence MacLean and Donald MacLean

962. Florence²¹ MacLean. She is the daughter of Archibald MacLean (828) and Susan Campbell.

She married Donald MacLean. Donald was known by the title of of Muck.

Family of Ann MacLean and Hugh MacLean

963. Ann²¹ MacLean. She is the daughter of Archibald MacLean (828) and Susan Campbell.

She married Hugh MacLean. Hugh was using a title in of Langamull.

Angus MacLean

964. Angus²¹ MacLean. He is the son of Donald MacLean (833).

Son of Angus MacLean:

+ 1100 i. Rory Mor[22] MacLean.

Family of Margaret MacLean and John MacLean

965. Margaret[21] MacLean. She is the daughter of Donald MacLean (833).

She married John MacLean.

John MacLean was born in of KILMORY about 1720. He was the son of Lachlan MacLean (834).

Son of Margaret MacLean and John MacLean:

+ 1101 i. John Mor[22] MacLean was born in Kilmory Isle of Rum about 1743.

Family of John MacLean and Margaret MacLean

966. John[21] MacLean was born about 1720 in of KILMORY. He was the son of Lachlan MacLean (834).

He married Margaret MacLean.

Son of John MacLean and Margaret MacLean:

+ 1101 i. John Mor[22] MacLean was born in Kilmory Isle of Rum about 1743.

Charles MacLean

967. Charles[21] MacLean. He is the son of John MacLean (835).

Sons of Charles MacLean:

      i. Neil[22] MacLean.

+ 1102 ii. Donald MacLean.

Family of Cornelius McLean and Sarah Schoonmaker

968. Cornelius[21] McLean was born in 1701 in Shawangunk, Ulster, New York. He was the son of John McLean (837) and Marritje DeWitt.

Cornelius died in Kingston, Ulster, New York, United States, in 1762 at the age of 61.

He married Sarah Schoonmaker.

Sarah Schoonmaker was born in Kingston, Ulster, New York, United States, on March 2, 1707. Sarah reached 57 years of age and died in Rochester, Ulster, New York, United States, on June 27, 1764.

Son of Cornelius McLean and Sarah Schoonmaker:

+ 1103 i. John[22] McLean was born in Kingston, Ulster, New York, United States, on May 28, 1727.

Family of John MacLean and Finvola MacLean

969. John[21] MacLean was born about 1755. He was the son of Lachlan MacLean (838) and Catherine Campbell.

He married Finvola MacLean.

Finvola MacLean was born about 1780. She was the daughter of Hector MacLean.

Children of John MacLean and Finvola MacLean:

- i. Lachlan[22] MacLean.
- ii. John Og MacLean.
- iii. Donald MacLean.
- iv. Mary MacLean.
- v. Margaret MacLean.
- vi. Catherine MacLean.

+ 1104 vii. Murdoch MacLean.

Family of Donald MacLean and Susan Haney

970. Donald[21] MacLean. He is the son of Hector MacLean (840).

He married Susan Haney.

Family of Charles MacLean and Marjory MacIntosh

971. Charles[21] MacLean was born in March 1718 in Dochgarroch, Inverness, Scotland. He was the son of John MacLean (841) and Jannet Dallas.

Charles was known by the title of 8th MacLean of Dochgarroch. He died in 1778 at the age of 59.

Charles married Marjory MacIntosh on Thursday, November 22, 1753.

Marjory MacIntosh was born about 1715. She was the daughter of Angus MacIntosh.

Marjory was buried on November 14, 1763.

Children of Charles MacLean and Marjory MacIntosh:

    i. John[22] MacLean was born in September 1754. He was known by the title of 9th MacLean of Dochgarroch.

    John died on October 7, 1826, at the age of 72.

    ii. Angus MacLean was born in March 1758. He died on January 11, 1794, at the age of 35.

    iii. Phineas MacLean was born in March 1759. He is deceased. died young.

+ 1105   iv. William MacLean was born on July 20, 1762.

+ 1106   v. Jannet MacLean was born in January 1756.

    vi. Barbara MacLean was born in July 1761. She died on June 13, 1849, at the age of 87.

+ 1107   vii. Marjory MacLean was born in November 1763.

Family of John MacLean and Christina Dallas

972. John[21] MacLean was born on December 4, 1683, in Dochgarroch, Inverness, Scotland. He was the son of John Og MacLean (844) and Margaret Fowler.

John was known by the title of 9th MacLean of Dochgarroch. He died on January 7, 1748, at the age of 64.

He married Christina Dallas. She is the daughter of Alexander Dallas.

Children of John MacLean and Christina Dallas:

    i. John[22] MacLean was born about 1710. He died on April 16, 1746, at the age of 36. Battle of Culloden.

+ 1108   ii. Charles MacLean was born about 1712.

    iii. William MacLean was born about 1714. He died in Gaudeloupe in 1753 at the age of 39.

    iv. Jannet MacLean.

    v. Mary MacLean.

Family of Alexander MacLean and Mary Campbell

973. Alexander^{21} MacLean was born about 1685. He was the son of John Og MacLean (844) and Margaret Fowler.

Alexander died about 1736 at the age of 51.

He married Mary Campbell. They had three sons.

Mary Campbell was born about 1687.

Sons of Alexander MacLean and Mary Campbell:

+ 1109 i. William^{22} Mclean was born in Isle of Mull, Argyll, Scotland, in 1702.
+ 1110 ii. Robert MacLean was born about 1710.
+ 1111 iii. William MacLean was born about 1712.

Family of David MacLean and Anna Gordon

974. David^{21} MacLean was born in 1692 in Dochgarroch, Scotland. He was the son of John Og MacLean (844) and Margaret Fowler.

David was baptized in Scotland on November 1, 1692. He died in 1719 at the age of 27.

David married Anna Gordon in 1720 in of Inverness, Scotland.

Sons of David MacLean and Anna Gordon:

+ 1112 i. Alexander^{22} MacLean was born in Dochgarroch, Inverness, Scotland, in 1720.
+ 1113 ii. John MacLean was born in Dochgarroch, Inverness, Scotland, about 1722.

Family of Donald MacLean and ? Campbell

975. Donald^{21} MacLean was born about 1695 in Dochgarroch, Inverness, Scotland. He was the son of John Og MacLean (844) and Margaret Fowler.

Donald is deceased. Argyllshire, Scotland.

He married ? Campbell.

Son of Donald MacLean and ? Campbell:

+ 1114 i. Lachlan^{22} MacLean was born about 1720.

Family of Jannet MacLean and William MacIntosh

976. Jannet[21] MacLean. She is the daughter of John Og MacLean (844) and Margaret Fowler.

She married William MacIntosh.

Family of Annie MacLean and James Ross

977. Annie[21] MacLean. She is the daughter of John Og MacLean (844) and Margaret Fowler.

She married James Ross.

Donald MacLean

978. Donald[21] MacLean was born about 1660. He was the son of Laclhlan MacLean (845).

Donald was known by the title of 8th MacLean of Kingerloch. He died in May 1726 at the age of 66.

Sons of Donald MacLean:

+ 1115   i.   Lachlan[22] MacLean was born about 1690.
           ii.   Allan MacLean.

Family of Baron John Borthwick and Lady Mary Elizabeth Kerr

979. Baron John[21] Borthwick was born on February 9, 1615, in Prestongrange, East Lothian, Scotland. He was the son of John Borthwick (846) and Lilias Ker.

Baron died in Borthwick, Midlothian, Scotland, on November 27, 1675, at the age of 60.

He married Lady Mary Elizabeth Kerr.

Lady Mary Elizabeth Kerr was born in Prestongrange, East Lothian, Scotland, on September 6, 1633. Lady reached 72 years of age and died in Canongate, Midlothian, Scotland, on July 23, 1706. She was buried in Midlothia, Scotland.

Son of Baron John Borthwick and Lady Mary Elizabeth Kerr:

+ 1116   i.   Thomas[22] Borthwick was born in , Midlothian, Scotland, in 1645.

Family of Robert Warren and Anne ?

980. Robert[21] Warren was born on March 13, 1667, in Smith Fort Creek, Surry, Virginia. He was the son of Thomas Warren Warren (847) and Jane Allen King.

Robert died at Age: 54 in Surry, Surry, Virginia, United States, on May 15, 1721, at the age of 54. He was buried in Surry County, Virginia.

Robert married Anne ? in 1685 in Surry, Surry, Virginia.

Anne ? was born in Virginia, United States, in 1674. Anne reached 43 years of age and died in Surry, Surry, Virginia, United States, on June 21, 1717.

Son of Robert Warren and Anne ?:

+ 1117 i. Robert[22] Warren was born in Surry, Surry, Virginia, United States, on January 11, 1700.

Joseph Hardy

981. Joseph[21] Hardy was born in 1615 in England. He was the son of John Hardy (848) and Olive Council.

Joseph died in 1638 at the age of 23.

Sons of Joseph Hardy:

+ 1118 i. John[22] Hardy was born in Ipswich, Essex, Massachusetts Bay, British Colonial America, in 1646.

    ii. William Hardy.

Family of Elizabeth Hardy and Roger Haskell

982. Elizabeth[21] Hardy was born about 1617 in England. She was the daughter of John Hardy (848) and Olive Council.

Elizabeth died in Marblehead, Essex, Massachusetts on May 11, 1676, at the age of 59.

Elizabeth married Roger Haskell in 1639 in Beverly, Essex, Massachusetts.

Roger Haskell was born in Wincanton, Somerset, England, on March 6, 1613/14. He was the son of William Haskell and Elinor Foule.

Roger reached 53 years of age and died in Beverly, Essex, Massachusetts on June 16, 1667.

Son of Elizabeth Hardy and Roger Haskell:

+ 1119 i. John[22] Haskell was born in Salem, Essex, Massachusetts in 1648.

Family of Thomas Dudley and Dorothy Yorke

983. Thomas[21] Dudley was born in October 1576 in Northampton, England. He was the son of Roger Dudley (849) and Susannah Thorne (513).

Thomas died in Roxbury, MA, on July 31, 1653, at the age of 76.

Thomas married Dorothy Yorke on April 25, 1603, in Hardingstone near Northampton.

Dorothy Yorke was born in Roxbury, MA. She was the daughter of Edmund York.

Dorothy died in December 1643.

Thomas Dudley married Dorothy ?.

Children of Thomas Dudley and Dorothy Yorke:

+	1120	i.	Patience[22] Dudley was born in February 1618.
+	1121	ii.	Mercy Dudley was born in Northampton, England, in 1621.
+	1122	iii.	Samuel Dudley.
		iv.	Thomas Dudley.
+	1123	v.	Anne Dudley.
+	1124	vi.	Sarah Dudley.
		vii.	Deborah Dudley.
		viii.	Dorothy Dudley.
+	1125	ix.	Joseph Dudley.
+	1126	x.	Paul Dudley.

Family of Hannah Cook and William King

984. Hannah[21] Cook was born on October 15, 1671, in Salem, Essex, Massachusetts. She was the daughter of Isaac Cook (850) and Elizabeth Buxton.

Hannah married William King on June 4, 1695, in Salem, Essex, Massachusetts.

William King was born in Salem, Essex, MA, in June 1669. He was the son of John King and Elizabeth Goldthwaite.

William reached 79 years of age and died in November 1748.

Hannah Cook married William Cook on June 4, 1695.

Children of Hannah Cook and William King:

      i.   Hannah[22] King was born in Salem, Essex, MA, on January 21, 1696. She died in Y.

      ii.   William King was born in Salem, Essex, MA, on January 1, 1699. He died in Y.

      iii.   Abigail King was born in Salem, Essex, MA, on February 16, 1701. She died in Y.

      iv.   Lydia King was born in Salem, Essex, MA, on December 16, 1702. She died in Y.

+ 1127 v.   Mehitable King was born in Salem, Essex, MA, on October 15, 1705.

      vi.   Henry King was born in Salem, Essex, MA, on June 22, 1707. He died in Y.

      vii.   Isaac King was born in Salem, Essex, MA, in 1709. He died in Y.

Family of Sarah Cook and Isaac Merrill

985.   Sarah[21] Cook was born in 1682. Sarah died in Y.

At the age of 24, Sarah married Isaac Merrill on May 2, 1706, in Northampton, Mass., when he was 24 years old.

Isaac Merrill was born in Hartford, CT, on March 11, 1682. He was the son of John Merrill and Sarah Margaret Watson.

Isaac reached 59 years of age and died in West Hartford, CT, in 1742.

[Copy of Hebron.FTW]

[Merrill full 2.FTW]

      Moved from Hartford to West Hartford after 1719.

Children of Sarah Cook and Isaac Merrill:

+ 1128 i.   Noah[22] Merrill was born in Hartford, CT, on May 8, 1707.

+ 1129 ii.   Timothy Merrill was born in Hartford, CT, on March 22, 1709.

          iii.   Isaac Merrill was born in Hartford, CT, on March 9, 1712. He died before 1715.

+ 1130 iv.   Eliakim Merrill was born in Hartford, CT, before August 8, 1714.

+ 1131 v. Joseph Merrill was born in Hartford, CT, before December 2, 1716.

+ 1132 vi. Sarah Merrill was born before May 24, 1719.

+ 1133 vii. Esther Merrill was born in West Hartford, CT, before November 19, 1721.

viii. Isaac Merrill was born in West Hartford, CT, before January 21, 1728. He died before 1749.

Family of Mary Birdsall and John Gerret Dorlandt

986. Mary[21] Birdsall was born in 1690 in Jerusalem, Suffolk Long Island, New York. She was the daughter of Henry Birdsall (851) and Mary ?.

Mary was baptized in Kirkby Overblow, Yorkshire, England, on August 30, 1695. She died in Hempstead, Livingston, New York on September 9, 1749, at the age of 59.

She married John Gerret Dorlandt.

John Gerret Dorlandt was born in Brooklyn, Kings, New York, United States, on March 29, 1688. John reached 55 years of age and died in Norwich, Livingston, New York, United States, in 1744.

Son of Mary Birdsall and John Gerret Dorlandt:

+ 1134 i. Daniel[22] Durland was born in Long Island City, Queens, New York, about 1737.

Family of Samuel Whiting and Elizabeth Read

987. Samuel[21] Whiting. He is the son of Samuel Whiting (852) and Dorcas Chester.

He married Elizabeth Read. They have one daughter.

Daughter of Samuel Whiting and Elizabeth Read:

+ 1135 i. Katherine[22] Whiting.

Family of Samuel Whiting and Elizabeth Read

988. Samuel[21] Whiting. He is the son of Samuel Whiting (853) and Dorcas Chester.

He married Elizabeth Read. They have one daughter.

Daughter of Samuel Whiting and Elizabeth Read:

+ 1135   i.   Katherine²² Whiting.

Family of Edward Spalding and Mary Adams

989.   Edward²¹ Spalding. He is the son of Benjamin Spalding and Olive Farwell (854).

He married Mary Adams. They have one son.

Edward Spalding married Mary Adams. They have one son.

Son of Edward Spalding and Mary Adams:

+ 1136   i.   Ephraim²² Spalding.

Son of Edward Spalding and Mary Adams:

+ 1136   i.   Ephraim²² Spalding.

Family of Elizabeth Freethy and Robert Gray

990.   Elizabeth²¹ Freethy was born in 1680 in York, York County, Maine. She was the daughter of James Freethy (855) and Mary Milbury.

Elizabeth died in York, York County, Maine, on May 4, 1754, at the age of 74.

She married Robert Gray.

Robert Gray was born in Berwick, York County, Maine, in 1680. Robert reached 91 years of age and died in York, York County, Maine, in 1771.

Son of Elizabeth Freethy and Robert Gray:

+ 1153   i.   Joshua²² Gray was born in York, York, Maine, on November 17, 1714.

22nd Generation

Family of Edward Winn and Joanna Sargent

991.   Edward²² Winn was born in 1599 in Ipswich, Suffolk, England. He was the son of Edward Wynne (856) and Mary Dorothy Berkeley.

Edward died in Woburn, Middlesex, Massachusetts, on September 5, 1682, at the age of 83.

He married Joanna Sargent.

Joanna Sargent was born in Eng, Massachusetts, in 1607. Joanna reached 42 years of age and died in Woburn, Middlesex, Massachusetts, on March 8, 1649.

Daughter of Edward Winn and Joanna Sargent:

+ 1137 i. Ann[23] Winn was born in Woburn, Middlesex, Massachusetts, on September 26, 1626.

Family of Gershom Bulkeley and Sarah Chauncey

992. Gershom[22] Bulkeley was born on December 26, 1635, in Concord, MA. He was the son of Peter Bulkeley (650) and Grace Chetwood (857).

Gershom died in Glastonbury, CT, on December 2, 1713, at the age of 77.

He married Sarah Chauncey.

Sarah Chauncey was born in Ware, Hertfordshire, England, on June 13, 1631. She was the daughter of Charles Chauncey and Catherine Eyre.

Sarah reached 67 years of age and died in Wethersfield, Hartford, Connecticut, United States, on June 3, 1699.

Children of Gershom Bulkeley and Sarah Chauncey:

+ 1138 i. Catherine[23] Bulkeley was born in Wethersfield, Hartford, Connecticut, United States, in 1660.
+ 1139 ii. Dorothy Bulkeley was born in 1662.
+ 1140 iii. Peter Bukeley was born in 1664.
+ 1141 iv. Charles Bulkeley.
+   v. Edward Bukeley. Edward died on August 27, 1748.
+   vi. John Bukeley. John died in June 1731.

Family of Mary Anne Howard and Jeffery Ferris

993. Mary Anne[22] Howard was born in 1614 in Greenwich, Kent, England. She was the daughter of Thomas Howard (858) and Alethea Talbot.

Mary was known by the title of Lady. She died in Stamford, Fairfield, Connecticut, United States, on July 31, 1658, at the age of 44.

Mary married Jeffery Ferris in 1635 in Greenwich, Fairfield County, Connecticut.

Jeffery Ferris was born in Leicestershire, England, in 1610. Jeffery reached 56 years of age and died in Greenwich, Fairfield, CT on May 31, 1666.

Son of Mary Anne Howard and Jeffery Ferris:

+ 1142 i. John[23] Ferris was born in Leicester, England, in 1634.

Family of Edward Bulkeley and Lucien ?

994. Edward[22] Bulkeley was born on June 17, 1614, in Odell, Bedfordshire, England. He was the son of Peter Bulkeley (650) and Jane Allen (859).

Edward was baptized in Odell, Beds, England, on June 12, 1614. He died in Chelmsford, Middlesex, Massachusetts, United States, on January 2, 1696, at the age of 81.

He married Lucien ?.

Lucien ? was born in Chelmsford, Middlesex, Massachusetts, United States, in 1616. Lucien reached 63 years of age and died in Chelmsford, Middlesex, Massachusetts, United States, on April 10, 1679.

Children of Edward Bulkeley and Lucien ?:

+ 1143 i. Peter[23] Bulkeley was born in Concord, Middlesex, Massachusetts, United States, on January 3, 1641.

+ 1144 ii. Peter Bulkeley.

+ 1145 iii. Elizabeth Bulkeley was born in Concord, MA.

Family of James B Allen and Mary Akin

995. James B[22] Allen was born on November 30, 1695, in Dartmouth, Bristol, Massachusetts. He was the son of Ebenezer Allen (860) and Abigail Hill.

James died in Dartmouth, Bristol, Massachusetts, United States, on April 29, 1771, at the age of 75.

He married Mary Akin.

Mary Akin was born in Dartmouth, Bristol, Massachusetts. Mary died in 1787.

Sons of James B Allen and Mary Akin:

+ 1146 i. Prince[23] Allen was born in Dartmouth, Bristol, Massachusetts, United States, about 1720.

 ii. Ebenezer Allen was born in Dartmouth, Bristol, Massachusetts, United States, on December 16, 1727. He died in Alive when his father died. on December 16, 1807, at the age of 80.

Family of John Knowles and Jemima Aster

996. John[22] Knowles was born on November 1, 1596, in Waltham, Lincolnshire, England. He was the son of William Knowles (861) and Grace Clavell.

John was baptized in St Bartholomew the Great, London, England, on December 23, 1621. He died in Eastham, Barnstable, Massachusetts, United States, on April 10, 1685, at the age of 88.

He married Jemima Aster.

John Knowles married Elizabeth Willis.

Elizabeth Willis was born in Isleworth, London, England, in 1621. Elizabeth reached 63 years of age and died in Ely, Norfolk, England, in 1684.

Son of John Knowles and Jemima Aster:

+ 1147 i. John[23] Knowles was born in Hampton, Rockingham, New Hampshire, United States, in 1625.

Son of John Knowles and Elizabeth Willis:

+ 1148 i. Richard[23] Knowles was born in Bolton, Lancashire, England, on September 17, 1614.

Family of Lucy Apsley and John Hutchinson

997. Lady Lucy[22] Apsley was born on January 29, 1620, in Tower Hill, London, Middlesex, England. She was the daughter of Sir Allen Apsley and Lady Elizabeth Lucy St. John (862).

Lucy was baptized in England. She died in Below, Mecklenburg-Strelitz, Mecklenburg-Vorpommern, Germany, in 1680 at the age of 59. She was buried in Owthorpe, Nottinghamshire, England, in 1681.

At the age of 18, she married John Hutchinson on July 3, 1638, in St Andrew Holborn, London, England, when he was 22 years old.

John Hutchinson was born in Nottingham, Nottinghamshire, England, on September 15, 1615. He was the son of Thomas Hutchinson and Lady Margaret Byron.

John was baptized in England. He worked as a Governor of Nottingham Castle between 1643 and 1647.

John was known by the title of Lord of Radcliffe. He was buried in St Margaret's Church, Owthorpe, England, in September 1644. John reached 48 years of age and died in Sandown Castle, Kent, England, on September 11, 1664.

Son of Lucy Apsley and John Hutchinson:

+ 1149 i. John[23] Hutchinson was born in Nottingham, Nottinghamshire, England, on September 6, 1641.

Family of Anne Merriton and Francis Wright

998. Anne[22] Merriton was born in 1605 in Castle Leavington, Yorkshire, England. She was the daughter of George Merriton and Mary Randes (863).

Anne died in Bolton Upon Swale, Yorkshire, England, on March 19, 1670, at the age of 65.

She married Francis Wright.

Francis Wright was born in Bolton Upon Swale, Yorkshire, England, about 1601. He was the son of Francis Wright and Grace Beckwith.

Francis was known by the title of Rev. Francis reached 54 years of age and died in Bolton On Swale, Yorkshire, England, on November 29, 1655.

Son of Anne Merriton and Francis Wright:

+ 1150 i. Richard Whittington[23] Wright was born in London, Middlesex, England, in 1633.

Family of Thomas Stiles and Maria ?

999. Thomas[22] Stiles was born in December 1550 in Millbrook, Bedfordshire, England. He was the son of Edmond Stiles (864) and Mary Berney.

Thomas died at Age: 64 in Millbrook, Bedfordshire, England, on March 7, 1614, at the age of 63.

He married Maria ?.

Maria ? was born in Bedfordshire, England, in 1563. Maria reached 51 years of age and died in Bedfordshire, England, on March 20, 1614.

Son of Thomas Stiles and Maria ?:

+ 1151 i. Francis[23] Stiles was born in Milbrook, Bedfordshire, England, on August 1, 1602.

Family of Joanna Percival Lowell and William Gerrish

1000. Joanna Percival[22] Lowell was born on August 20, 1619, in Bristol, England. She was the daughter of Percival Lowell (865) and Rebecca Alice Goodale.

Joanna died in Newbury, Essex, Massachusetts, United States, on June 18, 1677, at the age of 57.

She married William Gerrish.

William Gerrish was born in Bristol, Somerset, England, on August 20, 1617. He was the son of Capt. William Gerrish and Elizabeth (Ann) Parker.

William was christened in Bath Abbey, Somerset, England, in December 1617. He worked as an associated with father in business, merchant. William worked as a Merchant & Selectman. He worked as an associated with father in business, merchant.

William was known by the title of Captain. William reached 69 years of age and died in Lebanon, York, Maine, on August 9, 1687. He was buried in Massachusetts Baptist Temple, Tyngsborough, Middlesex, Massachusetts Bay, British Colonial America, on August 11, 1687.

Son of Joanna Percival Lowell and William Gerrish:

+   1152   i.   John^{23} Gerrish was born in Newbury, Essex, Massachusetts, United States, on February 12, 1646.

Family of Robert Gray and Elizabeth Freethy

1001. Robert^{22} Gray was born in 1680 in Berwick, York County, Maine. He was the son of George Gray (866) and Sarah Cooper.

Robert died in York, York County, Maine, in 1771 at the age of 91.

He married Elizabeth Freethy.

Elizabeth Freethy was born in York, York County, Maine, in 1680. She was the daughter of James Freethy (855) and Mary Milbury.

Elizabeth reached 74 years of age and died in York, York County, Maine, on May 4, 1754.

Son of Robert Gray and Elizabeth Freethy:

+   1153   i.   Joshua^{23} Gray was born in York, York, Maine, on November 17, 1714.

Family of Thomas Jordan and Margaret Brasseur

1002. Thomas^{22} Jordan was born on July 7, 1634, in Chuckatuck, Nansemond, Virginia. He was the son of Thomas Fleming Jordan (867) and Lucy Corker.

Thomas died in Chuckatuck, Nansemond, Virginia on October 8, 1699, at the age of 65. He was buried in Suffolk City, Virginia.

Thomas married Margaret Brasseur in 1659 in Isle of Wight, Isle of Wight, Virginia.

Margaret Brasseur was born in Chuckatuck, Nansemond, Virginia on July 17, 1642. She was the daughter of Robert Brashieur and Elizabeth Florence Fowke.

Margaret reached 66 years of age and died in Chuckatuck, Nansemond, Virginia on October 7, 1708.

Son of Thomas Jordan and Margaret Brasseur:

+ 1154   i.   James[23] Jordan was born in Nansemond, Virginia on November 23, 1665.

Family of Phoebe Conger and Benjamin Coddington

1003. Phoebe[22] Conger was born in 1740 in Woodbridge, Middlesex, New Jersey. She was the daughter of John Conger (868) and Zipporah Moores.

Phoebe died in Greenwich, Cumberland, New Jersey in September 1813 at the age of 73.

Phoebe married Benjamin Coddington in 1761.

Benjamin Coddington was born in Woodbridge, Middlesex, New Jersey in 1730. He was the son of Benjamin Coddington and Katherine Martin.

Benjamin reached 62 years of age and died in Greenwich, Cumberland, New Jersey on January 25, 1792. He was buried in Warren, Somerset County, New Jersey.

Children of Phoebe Conger and Benjamin Coddington:

    i.   Benjamin[23] Coddington was born in Woodbridge, Middlesex, New Jersey, United States, in 1762. He died in Waterford, Washington, Ohio, United States, in 1823 at the age of 61.

    ii.   Joseph Coddington was born in Pennsylvania, United States, on May 1, 1763. He died in Mason, Warren, Ohio, United States, on August 5, 1833, at the age of 70.

    iii.   Phoebe Coddington was born in Woodbridge, Middlesex, New Jersey, United States, in 1766.

    iv.   Moses Coddington was born in Woodbridge, Middlesex, New Jersey, United States, on January 16, 1768. He died in Parke, Indiana, United States, in 1853 at the age of 84.

    v.   Rhoda Coddington was born in Woodbridge, Middlesex, New Jersey, United States, in 1775.

		vi.	Jonathan Coddington was born in Montgomery, Orange, New York, United States, in 1776. He died in Bloomingburgh, Sullivan, New York, United States, on September 11, 1855, at the age of 79.
+	1155	vii.	John Coddington was born in Hector, Schuyler, New York, United States, on April 14, 1778.

Family of Ebenezer Thompson and Esther Stevens

1004. Ebenezer[22] Thompson was born on June 21, 1712, in New Haven, New Haven, Connecticut. He was the son of Joseph Thompson (869) and Elizabeth Smith.

Ebenezer died in Plymouth, Plymouth, Massachusetts, United States, on November 28, 1775, at the age of 63.

At the age of 20, Ebenezer married Esther Stevens on March 20, 1733, when she was 17 years old.

Esther Stevens was born in New Haven, New Haven, Connecticut, United States, on May 17, 1715. Esther reached 98 years of age and died in Scituate, Plymouth, Massachusetts, United States, on July 27, 1813. She was buried in Norwell, Plymouth County, Massachusetts.

Son of Ebenezer Thompson and Esther Stevens:

+	1156	i.	John[23] Thompson was born in New York in 1736.

Family of John Thomas and Mary Ford

1005. John[22] Thomas was born in 1672 in Wallingford, CT. He was the son of Daniel Thomas (1007) and Rebecca Thompson (870).

John died in New Haven, New Haven, CT, on January 25, 1711, at the age of 39. He was buried in Connecticut.

He married Mary Ford.

Mary Ford was born in New Haven, New Haven, Connecticut, United States, on September 11, 1676. She was the daughter of Samuel Ford and Elizabeth Hopkins.

Mary reached 35 years of age and died in Chestnut Hill New Haven, New Haven, Connecticut, United States, on June 30, 1712.

Son of John Thomas and Mary Ford:

+ 1157   i.   Recompense[23] Thomas was born in New Haven, New Haven, Connecticut, United States, on November 2, 1709.

Family of Israel Thomas and Sarah Humphreville

1006.   Israel[22] Thomas was born in 1685 in New Haven, New Haven, Connecticut. He was the son of Daniel Thomas (1007) and Rebecca Thompson (870).

Israel died in New Haven, New Haven, Connecticut, United States, in 1767 at the age of 82.

He married Sarah Humphreville.

Sarah Humphreville was born in New Haven, New Haven, Connecticut, United States, on April 2, 1695. She was the daughter of Samuel Humphrevile and Sarah Gray.

Sarah reached 32 years of age and died in New Haven, New Haven, Connecticut, United States, on June 27, 1727.

At the age of 42, Israel Thomas married Mehitabel Wolcott on June 27, 1727, in New Haven, New Haven, Connecticut, United States, when she was 37 years old. Mehitabel Wolcott was born in New Haven, New Haven, Connecticut, United States, on November 30, 1689.

Mehitabel reached 19 years of age and died in 1709.

Children of Israel Thomas and Sarah Humphreville:

     i.   Sarah[23] Thomas was born in Litchfield, Litchfield, Connecticut, United States, on March 28, 1716. She died in Woodbury, Litchfield, Connecticut, United States, on September 5, 1796, at the age of 80.

     ii.   Israel Thomas was born in New Haven, New Haven, Connecticut, United States, on June 5, 1720. He died in New Haven, New Haven, Connecticut, United States, in 1784 at the age of 63.

     iii.   Moses Thomas was born in New Haven, New Haven, Connecticut, United States, on February 5, 1721. He died in Milanville, Wayne, Pennsylvania, United States, in November 1762 at the age of 41.

     iv.   Gershom Thomas was born in New Haven, New Haven, Connecticut, United States, on March 17, 1725. He died in Bethany, New Haven, Connecticut, United States, on April 13, 1792, at the age of 67.

+ 1158 v. Lois Thomas was born in New Haven, CT, on June 27, 1727.

Family of Daniel Thomas and Rebecca Thompson

1007. Daniel[22] Thomas was born on February 13, 1644, in New Haven, New Haven, Connecticut. He was the son of John Thomas (871) and Tabitha Charles.

Daniel died in New Haven, New Haven, Connecticut, United States, in February 1694 at the age of 49.

He married Rebecca Thompson.

Rebecca Thompson was born in New Haven, New Haven, Connecticut, United States, on January 26, 1651. Rebecca reached 64 years of age and died in New Haven, New Haven, Connecticut, United States, in 1716.

Sons of Daniel Thomas and Rebecca Thompson:

+ 1005 i. John[23] Thomas was born in Wallingford, CT in 1672.

+ 1006 ii. Israel Thomas was born in New Haven, New Haven, Connecticut, United States, in 1685.

Family of William Merriam and Elizabeth Breed

1008. William[22] Merriam was born in 1628 in Kent, England. He was the son of Joseph Merriam (872) and Sarah Goldstone.

William died in Lynn, Essex, Massachusetts, United States, on May 22, 1689, at the age of 61.

He married Elizabeth Breed.

Elizabeth Breed was born in Lynn, Essex, Massachusetts, United States, on December 26, 1634. She was the daughter of Allen Breed and Elizabeth Wheeler.

Elizabeth reached 41 years of age and died in Lynn, Essex, Massachusetts, United States, on October 11, 1676.

Son of William Merriam and Elizabeth Breed:

+ 1159 i. John[23] Merriam was born in Lynn, Essex, Massachusetts on April 25, 1671.

Family of John Bennett and Anne Quaint

1009. John[22] Bennett was born in 1606 in Lancashire, England. He was the son of William Bennett (873) and Mary ?.

John died in Wavendon, Buckinghamshire, England, on February 5, 1671, at the age of 65.

He married Anne Quaint.

Anne Quaint was born in Wavendon, Buckinghamshire, England, on November 12, 1610. Anne reached 60 years of age and died in Wavendon, Buckinghamshire, England, on May 18, 1671. She was buried in St Katherine Cree, London, England, on August 25, 1671.

Daughter of John Bennett and Anne Quaint:

+ 1160 i. Elizabeth[23] Benat was born in Hambledon, Buckinghamshire, England, on June 4, 1653.

Family of Richard Bennett and Anne Barham

1010. Richard[22] Bennett was born on August 6, 1609, in England. He was the son of Thomas Bennett (874) and Alice Pierce.

Richard was known by the title of Governor. He died in Isle of Wight, Isle of Wight, Virginia, United States, on April 12, 1675, at the age of 65.

He married Anne Barham.

Anne Barham was born in James River, Buckingham, Virginia, United States, on June 1, 1624. She was the daughter of Robert Barham and Katherine Filmer.

Anne reached 57 years of age and died in Isle Wight, Virginia, United States, in 1682.

Son of Richard Bennett and Anne Barham:

+ 1161 i. Richard[23] Bennett was born in Upper Parish, Isle of Wight, Virginia, United States, in 1645.

Family of Peter Harwood and Elizabeth Taylor

1011. Peter[22] Harwood was born in 1668 in Easton, Talbot, Maryland. He was the son of Peter Harwood (875) and Elizabeth Garey.

Peter died in Easton, Talbot, Maryland, United States, on September 25, 1756, at the age of 88.

Peter married Elizabeth Taylor on September 20, 1690, in Third Haven Quaker Meeting, Talbot County, Maryland.

Elizabeth Taylor was born in Kent Island, Kent, Maryland, United States, in 1669. Elizabeth reached 87 years of age and died in Talbot, Maryland, United States, on September 25, 1756.

Children of Peter Harwood and Elizabeth Taylor:

      i.   Samuel[23] Harwood was born in Tuckahoe, Talbot, Maryland, United States, in 1692. He died in Talbot, Maryland, United States, on February 9, 1781, at the age of 89.

+ 1162   ii.   Elizabeth Harwood was born in Tuckahoe, Talbot, Maryland, United States, in 1694.

      iii.   Peter Harwood was born in Tuckahoe, Talbot, Maryland, United States, in 1697. He died in 1734 at the age of 37.

      iv.   Sarah Harwood was born in MH, Talbot, Maryland, United States, in 1700. She died on October 15, 1755, at the age of 55.

      v.   Mary Harwood was born in Tuckahoe, Talbot, Maryland, United States, in 1703. She died in Talbot, Maryland, United States, in 1748 at the age of 45.

      vi.   Robert Harwood was born in Tuckahoe, Talbot, Maryland, United States, on June 20, 1709. He died in September 1781 at the age of 72.

      vii.   Peter Harwood was born in Tuckahoe, Talbot, Maryland, United States, on April 3, 1721. He died in Talbot, Maryland, United States, on November 5, 1748, at the age of 27.

Family of Robert Harrington and Susanna George

1012.   Robert[22] Harrington was born on October 1, 1616, in England. He was the son of James Harrington (876) and Ann Clinton.

Robert died in Watertown, Middlesex, Massachusetts on May 17, 1707, at the age of 90.

Robert married Susanna George on October 10, 1648, in Watertown, Middlesex, Massachusetts.

Susanna George was born in Watertown, Middlesex, Massachusetts in 1632. Susanna reached 62 years of age and died in Watertown, Middlesex, Massachusetts on July 6, 1694.

Children of Robert Harrington and Susanna George:

    i. Susanna[23] Harrington was born in Watertown, Middlesex, Massachusetts on August 18, 1649. She died in Framingham, Middlesex, Massachusetts on July 6, 1694, at the age of 44.

    ii. John Harrington was born in Watertown, Middlesex, Massachusetts, on August 24, 1651. He died in Watertown, Middlesex, Massachusetts, on August 24, 1741, at the age of 90.

    iii. Mary Harrington was born in Watertown, Middlesex, Massachusetts on January 12, 1663. She died in Watertown, Middlesex, Massachusetts on September 8, 1716, at the age of 53.

    iv. Thomas Harrington was born in Watertown, Middlesex, Massachusetts on April 20, 1665. He died in Watertown, Middlesex, Massachusetts on March 29, 1712, at the age of 46.

+ 1163   v. Edward Harrington was born in Watertown, MA, on March 2, 1668.

    vi. Sarah Harrington was born in Watertown, Middlesex, Massachusetts on March 10, 1670. She died in Menot, Middlesex, Massachusetts on November 28, 1710, at the age of 40.

Family of Anna Griswold and Abraham Bronson

1013. Anna[22] Griswold was born on June 19, 1651, in Saybrook, Middlesex, Connecticut. She was the daughter of Matthew Griswold and Anna Wolcott (877).

Anna died in Old Lyme, Connecticut, on April 13, 1721, at the age of 69. She was buried in Meeting House, Hill Cemetery, Lyme, New London, Connecticut.

More facts and events for Anna Griswold:

At the age of 23, Anna married Abraham Bronson on September 2, 1674, in Lyme, Connecticut when he was 26 years old.

Abraham Bronson was born in Hartford, Hartford, Connecticut on November 28, 1647. He was the son of John Brownson and Frances Hills.

Abraham was christened in Hartford, Hartford, Connecticut, United States, on November 28, 1647. Abraham reached 71 years of age and died in Old Lyme, Connecticut, on June 27, 1719. He was buried in Meeting House Hill Cemetery, Lyme, New London, Connecticut.

Daughter of Anna Griswold and Abraham Bronson:

+ 1164 i. Elizabeth[23] Bronson was born in Lyme, New London, Connecticut on August 12, 1682.

Family of James Prescott Sr and Mary Boulter

1014. James[22] Prescott Sr was born on November 25, 1643, in Derby, Lincolnshire, England. He was the son of James Prescott (878) and Mary Copeland.

James died in Kingston, Rockingham, New Hampshire, United States, on November 23, 1728, at the age of 84.

He married Mary Boulter.

Mary Boulter was born in Exeter, Rockingham, New Hampshire, United States, on May 15, 1648. Mary was baptized in Exeter, Rockingham, New Hampshire. She reached 87 years of age and died in Kingston, Rockingham, New Hampshire, United States, on October 4, 1735.

Children of James Prescott Sr and Mary Boulter:

+ 1165 i. Joshua[23] Prescott was born in Hampton, Norfolk, NH, on March 1, 1669.

ii. James Prescott was born in Hampton, Rockingham, New Hampshire, United States, on September 1, 1671. He died in Hampton Falls, Rockingham, New Hampshire, United States, in 1746 at the age of 74.

iii. Rebecca Prescott was born in Hampton, Rockingham, New Hampshire, United States, on April 15, 1673. She died in Hampton Falls, Rockingham, New Hampshire, United States, on August 17, 1704, at the age of 31.

iv. Mary Prescott was born in Hampton, Rockingham, New Hampshire, United States, on June 11, 1677. She died in Kingston, Rockingham, New Hampshire, United States, on January 3, 1740, at the age of 62.

v. Abigail Prescott was born in Hampton, Rockingham, New Hampshire, United States, on November 19, 1679. She died in Portsmouth, Rockingham, New Hampshire, United States, in 1779 at the age of 99.

vi. Nathaniel Prescott was born in Hampton, Rockingham, New Hampshire, United States, on November 19, 1683. He died in

Kensington, Rockingham, New Hampshire, United States, on February 26, 1771, at the age of 87.

vii. Samuel Prescott was born in Hampton Falls, Rockingham, New Hampshire, United States, on March 14, 1697. He died in Hampton Falls, Rockingham, New Hampshire, United States, on June 12, 1759, at the age of 62.

Family of Henry Tomlinson and Alice Johnson

1015. Henry[22] Tomlinson was born on November 22, 1606, in Derby, Derbyshire, England. He was the son of George Tomlinson and Maria Hyde (879).

Henry died in Stratford, Fairfield, Connecticut on March 16, 1681, at the age of 74. He was buried in Stratford, Fairfield County, Connecticut.

He married Alice Johnson.

Alice Johnson was born in Derby, Derbyshire, England, in 1618. Alice was baptized on March 27, 1618. She reached 80 years of age and died in Stratford, Fairfield, Connecticut, United States, on January 25, 1698. Alice was buried in Stratford, Fairfield County, Connecticut.

Daughter of Henry Tomlinson and Alice Johnson:

+ 1166 i. Margaret[23] Tomlinson was born in Derby, New Haven, Connecticut, United States, in 1642.

Family of Rachel Gardner and Thomas Noble

1016. Rachel[22] Gardner was born in 1608 in Aldington, Kent, England. She was the daughter of Thomas Gardner (880) and Elizabeth White.

Rachel died in Westfield, Hampden, Massachusetts, United States, in 1636 at the age of 28.

Rachel married Thomas Noble in 1620 in Somerset, England.

Thomas was baptized in St Leonard, Shoreditch, Middlesex, England, on July 11, 1602. Thomas Noble was born in St Giles, London, England, in 1606. He was the son of Thomas Noble and Jane ?.

Thomas reached 26 years of age and died in Westfield, Hampden, Massachusetts, United States, in 1632.

Son of Rachel Gardner and Thomas Noble:

+ 1167 i. Thomas[23] Noble was born in Westfield, Hampden, Massachusetts, United States, in 1632.

Family of Edward Bagot and Frances Wagstaffe

1017. Sir Edward[22] Bagot, 4th Baronet was born on July 21, 1673, in Blithfield Hall, Staffordshire. He was the son of Sir Walter Bagot 3rd Baronet (881) and Jane Salesbury.

Sir died in Blithfield Hall, Staffordshire, in May 1712 at the age of 38.

He married Frances Wagstaffe.

Frances Wagstaffe was born in Tachbrook, Warwickshire, on April 15, 1697. Frances reached 17 years of age and died in Tachbrook, Warwickshire, on May 20, 1714.

Son of Sir Edward Bagot, 4th Baronet and Frances Wagstaffe:

+ 1168 i. Sir Walter Wagstaffe[23] Bagot, 5th Baronet Bagot was born in Staffordshire, England, on August 23, 1702.

Family of George Walker and Mary Brown

1018. George[22] Walker was born in 1715 in Brompton by, Yorkshire, England. He was the son of Thomas Walker (882) and Anne Peele.

He married Mary Brown.

Mary Brown was born in Brompton by, Yorkshire, England, in 1715.

Daughter of George Walker and Mary Brown:

+ 1169 i. Margaret[23] Walker was born in Brompton by Sawdon, Yorkshire, in 1740.

Family of Marie Judith Messier and Joseph Bousquet

1019. Marie Judith[22] Messier was born on September 8, 1737, in Varennes, Quebec, Canada. She was the daughter of Francois Michel Messier (883) and Marie Josephe Guyon.

Marie died in Québec, Quebec, Canada, on April 8, 1805, at the age of 67.

She married Joseph Bousquet.

Joseph Bousquet was born in Verchères, Quebec, Canada, on March 28, 1734. He was the son of Jean Baptiste Bousquet and Marguerite Provost.

Joseph reached 50 years of age and died in Richelieu, Quebec, Canada, on March 17, 1785.

Son of Marie Judith Messier and Joseph Bousquet:

+ 1170 i. Joseph Marie^{23} Bousquet was born in Richelieu, Quebec, Canada, on September 9, 1766.

Family of Solomon Townsend and Lydia Tillinghast

1020. Solomon^{22} Townsend was born in April 1701. He was the son of Solomon Townsend (884) and Catherine Almy.

Solomon died in Newport, Rhode Island or Jamaica?, in 1756 at the age of 54.

He married Lydia Tillinghast.

Lydia Tillinghast was born in Providence, Providence, Rhode Island, United States, on October 16, 1708. Lydia reached 39 years of age and died at Age: 40 in Newport, Newport, Rhode Island, United States, on January 31, 1748. She was buried in Newport, Newport County, Rhode Island.

Son of Solomon Townsend and Lydia Tillinghast:

+ 1171 i. William^{23} Townsend was born in Newport, Newport, Rhode Island, United States, in October 1745.

Family of Isabella MacLean and Donald MacLean

1021. Isabella^{22} MacLean was born about 1695. She was the daughter of Allan MacLean (885) and Anne Cameron.

She married Donald MacLean.

Donald MacLean was born in Brolass, Mull, Scotland, in 1671. He was the son of Lachlan MacLean (916) and Isabella Maclean (921).

Donald was known by the title of 3rd Laird of Brolass. Donald reached 54 years of age and died in Scotland on April 23, 1725.

Children of Isabella MacLean and Donald MacLean:

+ 1172 i. Allan^{23} MacLean was born about 1710.
+ 1173 ii. Catherine Maclean was born about 1712.
+ 1174 iii. Isabel MacLean was born about 1715.
+ 1175 iv. Anne MacLean was born about 1720.

Family of John MacLean and Margery MacLachlan

1022. John[22] MacLean was born about 1700. He was the son of Allan MacLean (885) and Anne Cameron.

John was known by the title of 11th MacLean of Ardgour. He died on March 2, 1739, at the age of 39.

John married Margery MacLachlan on December 25, 1735. She was the daughter of Allan MacLachlan and Margaret MacLean (887).

Margery died in March 1770.

Children of John MacLean and Margery MacLachlan:

+ 1176 i. Hugh[23] MacLean was born about 1736.
    ii. Allan MacLean.
    iii. Sarah MacLean.

Family of Margaret MacLean and Angus Maclean

1023. Margaret[22] MacLean was born about 1702. She was the daughter of Allan MacLean (885) and Anne Cameron.

She married Angus Maclean. Angus Maclean was born about 1690. He was the son of Hector Maclean (1067) and Jannet MacLean (922).

Angus was known by the title of 4th MacLean of Kinlochaline. Angus reached 45 years of age and died on May 8, 1735.

Family of Mary MacLean and John MacLean

1024. Mary[22] MacLean was born in 1715 in Inverchaolain, Argyll. She was the daughter of Allan MacLean (885) and Anne Cameron.

Mary married John MacLean about 1735 in Inverchaolain, Argyll.

John MacLean was born in Inverchaolain, Argyll, on May 20, 1716. He was the son of Charles MacLean (907) and a daughter of Archibald MacLean.

Sons of Mary MacLean and John MacLean:

   i. John[23] MacLean was born about 1742.
   ii. Laughlan McLean was born in Coll, Argyll, Scotland, in 1744. He died in Scotland in 1819 at the age of 75.

Family of Margery MacLachlan and John MacLean

1025. Margery[22] MacLachlan. She was the daughter of Allan MacLachlan and Margaret MacLean (887).

Margery died in March 1770.

Margery married John MacLean on December 25, 1735.

John MacLean was born about 1700. John reached 39 years of age and died on March 2, 1739.

Children of Margery MacLachlan and John MacLean:

+ 1176   i.   Hugh[23] MacLean was born about 1736.
-          ii.   Allan MacLean.
-          iii.   Sarah MacLean.

Family of Anna MacLean and Angus MacLean

1026. Anna[22] MacLean. She is the daughter of Allan MacLean (888).

She married Angus MacLean. Angus MacLean was born about 1691. He was the son of Donald MacLean (781) and Catherime MacQuarrie.

Family of Marjory MacLean and Allan McLean

1027. Marjory[22] MacLean. She is the daughter of Allan MacLean (888).

She married Allan McLean.

Lachlan Maclean

1028. Lachlan[22] Maclean was born about 1722. He was the son of Charles Maclean (890) and an unknown woman.

Lachlan died on April 16, 1746, at the age of 24. killed at the Battle of Culloden.

Son of Lachlan Maclean:

         i.   Allan[23] Maclean was born about 1749.

Family of Allan MacLean and Anne MacLean

1029. Allan[22] MacLean was born in 1724 in Scotland. He was the son of Charles Maclean (890) and Isabella Cameron.

Allan was known by the title of 5th MacLean of Drimnin, 6th MacLean of Kinlochaline, 8th MacLean of Morvern. He died in Scotland on September 17, 1792, at the age of 68.

He married Anne MacLean.

Anne MacLean was born about 1720. Anne reached 35 years of age and died about 1755.

Allan MacLean married Mary MacLaine.

Mary MacLaine was born in 1740. She was the daughter of Lachlan MacLaine (1196) and Katherine Macdougall.

Mary reached 91 years of age and died in 1831.

Children of Allan MacLean and Anne MacLean:

+ 1327   i.   Charles[23] MacLean was born about 1754.

        ii.   Una Maclean.

Children of Allan MacLean and Mary MacLaine:

+ 1177   i.   Donald Roy Maclean was born in Kinlochleven, Mull, Scotland, about 1770.

        ii.   John MacLean. John died in Martinique.

+ 1178   iii.   Mary MacLean.

        iv.   Louisa MacLean.

+ 1179   v.   Catherine MacLean.

Family of John Maclean and Margaret Campbell

1030.   John[22] Maclean was born about 1726. He was the son of Charles Maclean (890) and Isabella Cameron.

John is deceased. drowned in the Sound of Mull.

He married Margaret Campbell. They had three sons.

Sons of John Maclean and Margaret Campbell:

        i.   Donald[23] Maclean was born about 1752. He died in Nova Scotia, Canada.

        ii.   Charles Maclean was born about 1754. He died in Nova Scotia, Canada.

+ 1180   iii.   Colin Maclean was born about 1756.

Family of Alexander Maclean and Mary MacLean

1031. Alexander[22] Maclean was born about 1705. He was the son of Donald Maclean (891) and Susanna Campbell.

Alexander was known by the title of 3rd McLean of Calgary.

He married Mary MacLean. They had three sons. She is the daughter of John MacLean.

Sons of Alexander Maclean and Mary MacLean:

+ 1181   i.   Donald A[23] McLean was born in Scotland in 1735.
- ii.   Charles Maclean was born about 1735.
- iii.   Duncan Maclean.

Family of Donald Maclean and Anne MacLean

1032. Donald[22] Maclean was born about 1685. He was the son of Allan Maclean (1073) and Margaret MacLean (894).

Donald was using a title in of Raodel.

He married Anne MacLean.

Anne MacLean was born about 1690. She was the daughter of Donald Maclean (1064) and Mary Campbell.

Children of Donald Maclean and Anne MacLean:

+ 1182   i.   Hector[23] Maclean was born about 1715.
- ii.   George Maclean.
+ 1183   iii.   Marion Maclean.

Family of Hector Maclean and Catherine MacLean

1033. Hector[22] Maclean was born about 1700. He was the son of Lachlan Maclean (897) and Janet MacLeod.

Hector was known by the title of 3rd MacLean of Grulin. He died about 1784 at the age of 84.

He married Catherine MacLean. He or she is a child of Donald MacLean (1059) and Marian MacLeod.

Daughter of Hector Maclean and Catherine MacLean:

- i.   Mary[23] Maclean was born about 1730. She died in 1826 at the age of 96.

Family of Una Maclean and Alexander MacGillvray

1034. Una[22] Maclean. She is the daughter of Lachlan Maclean (897) and Janet MacLeod.

She married Alexander MacGillvray.

Family of Allan the elder Maclean and Isabella Campbell

1035. Allan the elder[22] Maclean was born about 1700. He was the son of Charles Maclean (898) and Marian MacLean.

He married Isabella Campbell. She is the daughter of Donald Campbell.

Sons of Allan the elder Maclean and Isabella Campbell:

  i. Charles[23] Maclean was born about 1730. He died in 1754 at the age of 24. killed in the war with Hyder Ali.

  ii. Allan Maclean was born about 1732. He died in Jamaica in 1754 at the age of 22.

Family of Hector Maclean and Julian MacLean

1036. Hector[22] Maclean was born about 1702. He was the son of Charles Maclean (898) and Marian MacLean.

Hector was known by the title of of Torranbeg. He died in Torranbeg about 1798 at the age of 96.

He married Julian MacLean.

Julian MacLean was born about 1725. She was the daughter of Allan MacLean.

Children of Hector Maclean and Julian MacLean:

  i. Allan[23] Maclean was born about 1748.

+ 1184 ii. Anne Maclean was born about 1750.

+ 1185 iii. Mary Maclean was born about 1752.

  iv. John Maclean was born about 1754. He was known by the title of of Grulin.

  v. Alexander Maclean was born about 1756.

+ 1186 vi. Archibald Maclean was born in Torrenberg, Isle of Mull, Argyll, Scotland, in 1758.

+ 1187 vii. Alice Maclean was born about 1760.

+ 1188 viii. Catherine Maclean.

Family of Donald Maclean and Mary Mean

1037. Donald[22] Maclean was born about 1704. He was the son of Charles Maclean (898) and Marian MacLean.

He married Mary Mean.

Children of Donald Maclean and Mary Mean:

        i.   James[23] Maclean.

        ii.   John Maclean.

        iii. Christopher MacLean.

        iv. Mary MacLean.

        v.   Catherine MacLean.

Family of Alexander Maclean and Una MacGillivray

1038. Alexander[22] Maclean was born about 1709. He was the son of Charles Maclean (898) and Marian MacLean.

Alexander was known by the title of 1st MacLean of Pennycross. He died in 1800 at the age of 91.

Alexander married Una MacGillivray in 1760. She was the daughter of Alexander MacGillvray.

Children of Alexander Maclean and Una MacGillivray:

+ 1189 i. Archibald[23] Maclean was born in 1761.

+ 1190 ii. Catherine Maclean.

Family of Donald MacLean and Ann MacLean

1039. Donald[22] MacLean was born about 1700 in Isle of Mull, Argyll, Scotland. He was the son of John MacLean (899) and Isabella Campbell.

Donald was known by the title of 2nd MacLean of Pennygoun.

He married Ann MacLean.

Ann MacLean was born about 1705. She was the daughter of Lachlan MacLean.

Children of Donald MacLean and Ann MacLean:

+ 1191 i. Lachlan[23] MacLean was born about 1730.

		ii.	John MacLean was born about 1732.
		iii.	Hector MacLean was born about 1734. He died in 1799 at the age of 65.
		iv.	Donald MacLean was born about 1736.
+	1192	v.	Alexander MacLean was born about 1737.
		vi.	Ann MacLean.
		vii.	Margaret MacLean.
		viii.	Mary MacLean.

Family of Una MacLean and Allan MacLean

1040. Una[22] MacLean was born about 1714. She was the daughter of John MacLean (899) and Isabella Campbell.

She married Allan MacLean. They had three daughters.

Allan MacLean was born about 1710. Allan reached 73 years of age and died on December 10, 1783.

Daughters of Una MacLean and Allan MacLean:

+	1324	i.	Maria[23] MacLean was born about 1750.
+	1325	ii.	Sibella Maclean.
		iii.	Ann Maclean.

Family of Janet MacLean and Duncan MacArthur

1041. Janet[22] MacLean was born about 1716. She was the daughter of John MacLean (899) and Isabella Campbell.

She married Duncan MacArthur.

Family of Catherine MacLean and Donald MacDonald

1042. Catherine[22] MacLean was born about 1718. She was the daughter of John MacLean (899) and Isabella Campbell.

She married Donald MacDonald.

Family of Hector MacLean and Marion MacQuarrie

1043. Hector[22] MacLean was born about 1720 in Isle of Mull, Argyll, Scotland. He was the son of Charles MacLean (904) and Jean Campbell.

He married Marion MacQuarrie.

Son of Hector MacLean and Marion MacQuarrie:

> i. John[23] MacLean was born in Scotland about 1745. He died in New York.

Hector MacLean

1044. Hector[22] MacLean. He is the son of Allan MacLean (906).

Son of Hector MacLean:

> i. Lachlan[23] MacLean.

Family of Allan MacLean and Margory MacLean

1045. Allan[22] MacLean was born about 1700. He was the son of Charles MacLean (907) and a daughter of Donald Cameron.

Allan was known by the title of 6th MacLean of Inverscadell.

He married Margory MacLean. Margory MacLean was born in Torloisk, Argyll, Scotland. She is the daughter of Allan MacLean.

Family of John MacLean and Mary MacLean

1046. John[22] MacLean was born on May 20, 1716, in Inverchaolain, Argyll. He was the son of Charles MacLean (907) and a daughter of Archibald MacLean.

John was known by the title of of Kinlochaline.

John married Mary MacLean about 1735 in Inverchaolain, Argyll.

Mary MacLean was born in Inverchaolain, Argyll, in 1715.

Sons of John MacLean and Mary MacLean:

> i. John[23] MacLean was born about 1742.
>
> ii. Laughlan McLean was born in Coll, Argyll, Scotland, in 1744. He died in Scotland in 1819 at the age of 75.

Family of Murdock MacLaine and Anne Campbell

1047. Murdock[22] MacLaine. He was the son of Hector MacLaine (909) and Margaret Campbell.

Murdock was known by the title of 13th MacLean of Lochbuie. He died after 1729.

He married Anne Campbell. They had three daughters. She is the daughter of Hugh Campbell.

Daughters of Murdock MacLaine and Anne Campbell:

+ 1193 i. Margaret[23] MacLaine.

+ 1194 ii. Elizabeth MacLaine.

+ 1195 iii. Isabella MacLaine.

Family of John MacLaine and Isabelle MacDougall

1048. John[22] MacLaine was born about 1670. He was the son of Hector MacLaine (909) and Margaret Campbell.

John was known by the title of 14th MacLean of Lochbuie.

He married Isabelle MacDougall.

Isabelle MacDougall was born about 1678. She was the daughter of Duncan MacDougall.

Sons of John MacLaine and Isabelle MacDougall:

+ 1196 i. Lachlan[23] MacLaine was born in Lochbuie, Isle of Mull, Argyle, Scotland, in 1695.

         ii. Allan MacLaine.

Family of Allan MacLaine and Julian MacLean

1049. Allan[22] MacLaine was born about 1675. He was the son of Hector MacLaine (909) and Margaret Campbell.

He married Julian MacLean.

Julian MacLean was born in Torloisk, Mull, Scotland. She is the daughter of Lachlan Og MacLean (691) and Marian MacDonald.

Children of Allan MacLaine and Julian MacLean:

+ 1197 i. John[23] MacLaine was born in 1724.

+ 1198 ii. Julian MacLaine was born about 1700.

+ 1199 iii. Finvola MacLaine.

Family of Margaret MacLaine and Lachlan McQuarrie

1050. Margaret[22] MacLaine. She is the daughter of Hector MacLaine (909) and Margaret Campbell.

She married Lachlan McQuarrie.

Family of Mary MacLaine and Lachlan MacLean

1051. Mary[22] MacLaine. She was the daughter of Hector MacLaine (909) and Margaret Campbell.

Mary married Lachlan MacLean on May 21, 1722.

Family of Lachlan MacLaine and Flora MacQuarrie

1052. Lachlan[22] MacLaine. He is the son of Hector MacLaine (909) and Margaret Campbell.

He married Flora MacQuarrie. They had four sons. She is the daughter of Lachlan MacQuarrie and Catherine MacLean (914).

Sons of Lachlan MacLaine and Flora MacQuarrie:

+ 1200   i.   Murdoch[23] MacLaine was born in 1730.
+ 1201   ii.   Allan MacLaine.
         iii. Donald MacLaine.
+ 1202   iv.   John MacLaine.

Family of John MacLean 4th. Baronet and Mary MacPherson

1053. John[22] MacLean 4th. Baronet was born about 1670 in Isle of Mull, Argyll, Scotland. He was the son of Allan Maclean (913) and Julian Macleod.

John was known by the title of 19th Chief MacLean, 4th Baronet Morvern. He was known by the title of Sir.

John died at he died of Consumption in Gordon Castle in the vicinity of Fochabers on March 12, 1716, at the age of 46.

More facts and events for John MacLean 4th. Baronet:

John married Mary MacPherson about 1702 in Eskay, Scotland.

Mary MacPherson was born in Isle Of Skye, Scotland, in 1670. Mary was christened in Edinburgh Parish, Edinburgh, Midlothian, Scotland, on April 30, 1678. She reached 49 years of age and died in 1719.

Son of John MacLean 4th. Baronet:

+ 1203   i.   John[23] McLean was born in Scotland about 1692.

Children of John MacLean 4th. Baronet and Mary MacPherson:

    i.   Hector[23] Maclean was born in Calais, France, in 1703. He was known by the title of 20th Chief MacLean.

           Hector died in Rome, Italy, in 1750 at the age of 47.

    ii.   Louisa Maclean.

    iii.   Isabel Maclean.

    iv.   Mary Maclean.

    v.   Ann Maclean.

    vi.   Beatrix Maclean.

Family of Flora MacQuarrie and Lachlan MacLaine

1054. Flora[22] MacQuarrie. She is the daughter of Lachlan MacQuarrie and Catherine MacLean (914).

    She married Lachlan MacLaine. They had four sons.

Sons of Flora MacQuarrie and Lachlan MacLaine:

+ 1200   i.   Murdoch[23] MacLaine was born in 1730.

+ 1201   ii.   Allan MacLaine.

           iii.   Donald MacLaine.

+ 1202   iv.   John MacLaine.

Family of John Hector Og MacLean and Finvola MacLaine

1055. John Hector Og[22] MacLean was born about 1660. He was the son of Hector Og MacLean (915) and Janet McNeil.

    John is deceased. drown crossing in a small boat to Mull.

    He married Finvola MacLaine. They had three sons.

Sons of John Hector Og MacLean and Finvola MacLaine:

+ 1340   i.   Donald[23] MacLean was born about 1685.

           ii.   Hector MacLean was born about 1690. He is deceased. left no issue.

+ 1341   iii.   John MacLean was born about 1700.

Family of Donald MacLean and Isabella MacLean

1056. Donald[22] MacLean was born in 1671 in Brolass, Mull, Scotland. He was the son of Lachlan MacLean (916) and Isabella Maclean (921).

Donald was known by the title of 3rd Laird of Brolass. He died in Scotland on April 23, 1725, at the age of 54.

He married an unknown woman.

an unknown woman was born about 1700.

Donald MacLean married an unknown woman.

Donald MacLean married Isabella MacLean.

Isabella MacLean was born about 1695.

Son of Donald MacLean and an unknown woman:

+ 1204 i. James[23] Maclean was born about 1698.

Son of Donald MacLean and an unknown woman:

      i. Gillean[23] Maclean was born about 1700.

Children of Donald MacLean and Isabella MacLean:

+ 1172 i. Allan[23] MacLean was born about 1710.
+ 1173 ii. Catherine Maclean was born about 1712.
+ 1174 iii. Isabel MacLean was born about 1715.
+ 1175 iv. Anne MacLean was born about 1720.

Allan MacLean

1057. Allan[22] MacLean was born about 1684. He was the son of Lachlan MacLean (916) and Isabella Maclean (921).

Allan died in Stirling, Scotland, in 1722 at the age of 38.

Child of Allan MacLean:

+ 1205 i. Christina[23] MacLean was born in 1718.

Family of Lachlan MacLean and Marian MacDonald

1058. Lachlan[22] MacLean was born about 1652 in Coll, Argyll, Scotland. He was the son of Hector Roy MacLean (931) and Marion MacLean (917).

Lachlan was known by the title of 9th MacLean of Coll. He died at he drowned in Lochy in Lochaber in August 1687 at the age of 35.

He married Marian MacDonald. She is the daughter of John Dubh MacDonald.

Children of Lachlan MacLean and Marian MacDonald:

    i.   John Garbh[23] MacLean was born in Coll, Argyll, Scotland, about 1680. He was known by the title of 10th MacLean of Coll.

        John died in 1698 at the age of 18.

    ii.   Florence MacLean.

    iii.   Catherine MacLean.

Family of Donald MacLean and Isabel MacLeod

1059. Donald[22] MacLean was born in 1656 in Coll, Argyll, Scotland. He was the son of Hector Roy MacLean (931) and Marion MacLean (917).

Donald was known by the title of 11th MacLean of Coll. He died in Coll, Argyll, Scotland, in April 1729 at the age of 73.

Donald married Isabel MacLeod about 1678.

Isabel MacLeod was born about 1660. She was the daughter of Rory MacLeod.

Donald MacLean married Marian MacLeod. She is the daughter of Norman MacLeod.

Son of Donald MacLean and Isabel MacLeod:

+   1206   i.   Hector[23] MacLean was born in Coll, Argyll, Scotland, about 1686.

Children of Donald MacLean and Marian MacLeod:

+   1207   i.   Hugh[23] MacLean was born in Isle od Coll, Scotland, about 1692.

+   1208   ii.   Lachlan MacLean was born in Isle of Mull, Argyll, Scotland, in 1693.

+   1209   iii.   John Ardfinaig MacLean was born in Isle of Mull, Argyll, Scotland, in 1696.

        iv.   Neil MacLean.

+   1210   v.   Catherine MacLean.

Family of Catherine MacLean and Hector MacLean

1060. Catherine[22] MacLean was born about 1665. She was the daughter of Hector Roy MacLean (931) and Marion MacLean (917).

She married Hector MacLean.

Hector MacLean was born about 1645. He was the son of Hector MacLean (808) and Julian MacLean (698).

Hector was known by the title of 2nd MacLean of Muck.

Children of Catherine MacLean and Hector MacLean:

+ 1211 i. Lachlan[23] MacLean was born in Isle of Muck, Argyll, Scotland, about 1670.

+ 1212 ii. Hector MacLean was born about 1672.

       iii. Julian MacLean.

Family of Jannet MacLean and Hector Maclean

1061. Jannet[22] MacLean was born about 1666. She was the daughter of Hector Roy MacLean (931) and Marion MacLean (917).

She married Hector Maclean. They had four sons.

Hector Maclean was born about 1647.

Sons of Jannet MacLean and Hector Maclean:

       i. John[23] Maclean was born about 1675. He is deceased. unmarried.

       ii. Donald Maclean was born about 1676. He is deceased. left no issue.

       iii. Mary Maclean was born about 1678. He is deceased. unmarried.

       iv. Lachlan Maclean. Lachlan is deceased. died young.

Family of Margaret MacLean and Donald MacLean

1062. Margaret[22] MacLean. She is the daughter of Hector Roy MacLean (931) and Marion MacLean (917).

She married Donald MacLean.

Family of Una MacLean and John MacLean

1063. Una[22] MacLean. She is the daughter of Hector Roy MacLean (931) and Marion MacLean (917).

She married John MacLean.

Family of Donald Maclean and Mary Campbell

1064. Donald[22] Maclean was born about 1672 in Torloisk, Mull, Scotland. He was the son of John Maclean (920) and Catherine Campbell.

Donald was known by the title of 5th MacLean of Torloisk, 2nd MacLean of Tarbert. He died on August 20, 1748, at the age of 76.

He married Mary Campbell. She is the daughter of Archibald Campbell.

Children of Donald Maclean and Mary Campbell:

+ 1213 i. Anne[23] MacLean was born about 1690.

       ii. Hector Maclean was born in Torloisk, Mull, Scotland, about 1692. He was known by the title of 6th MacLean of Torloisk.

       Hector died in Glasgow, Scotland, on May 29, 1765, at the age of 73.

+ 1214 iii. Christianna Maclean was born about 1700.

+ 1215 iv. Lachlan Maclean was born about 1710.

+ 1216 v. Allan Maclean was born about 1725.

+ 1217 vi. Archibald Maclean.

       vii. Mary Maclean.

+ 1218 viii. Alicia Maclean.

       ix. Betty Maclean.

+ 1219 x. Elizabeth Maclean.

Family of Marion Maclean and Charles MacLean

1065. Marion[22] Maclean was born about 1678. She was the daughter of John Maclean (920) and Catherine Campbell.

She married Charles MacLean. Charles was known by the title of of Kilunaig.

Family of Angus Maclean and Anne MacDonald

1066. Angus[22] Maclean was born about 1690. He was the son of Hector Maclean (1067) and Jannet MacLean (922).

Angus was known by the title of 4th MacLean of Kinlochaline. He died on May 8, 1735, at the age of 45.

He married Margaret MacLean. Margaret MacLean was born about 1702.

Angus Maclean married Anne MacDonald. She is the daughter of Ronald MacDonald.

Family of Hector Maclean and Jannet MacLean

1067. Hector[22] Maclean was born about 1660. He was the son of John Maclean (923) and Mary Campbell.

Hector was known by the title of 3rd MacLean of Kinlochaline.

He married Jannet MacLean.

Jannet MacLean was born about 1647.

Son of Hector Maclean and Jannet MacLean:

+ 1066 i. Angus[23] Maclean was born about 1690.

Family of William McLean and Irene

1068. William[22] McLean was born in 1670 in Scotland. He was the son of John Maclean (923) and Mary Campbell.

William died in Scotland in 1752 at the age of 82.

He married Irene.

Irene was born in Scotland in 1670. Irene is deceased.

Son of William McLean and Irene:

+ 1220 i. William[23] McLean was born in Edinburg, Scotland, in 1690.

Family of Allan MacLean and Catherine Stewart

1069. Allan[22] MacLean was born about 1655. He was the son of Charles MacLean (924) and Marian MacLean (938).

Allan was known by the title of 3rd MacLean of Drimnin. He died on November 13, 1715, at the age of 60. Battle of Sheriffmuir.

He married Catherine Stewart.

Family of Charles MacLean and a daughter of Hector MacQuarrie

1070. Charles[22] MacLean was born about 1655. He was the son of Hector MacLean (926) and Florence McLean (1092).

He married a daughter of Hector MacQuarrie. She is the daughter of Hector MacQuarrie.

Son of Charles MacLean and a daughter of Hector MacQuarrie:

      i.   Lachlan[23] MacLean was born about 1685. He died in Spain.

Family of Janet MacLean and Lachlan Maclean

1071. Janet[22] MacLean was born about 1670. She was the daughter of Hector MacLean (926) and Florence McLean (1092).

She married Lachlan Maclean.

Lachlan Maclean was born about 1665. He was the son of Donald Maclean (929) and a daughter of MacGillvray.

Sons of Janet MacLean and Lachlan Maclean:

      i.   Donald[23] Maclean was born about 1695. He died in Ireland.

     ii.   Hector Maclean. Hector died in Ireland.

Family of John MacLean and Florence MacLean

1072. John[22] MacLean. He is the son of Hector MacLean (926) and Florence McLean (1092).

He married Florence MacLean. She is the daughter of Lachlan MacLean.

Family of Allan Maclean and Margaret MacLean

1073. Allan[22] Maclean was born about 1660. He was the son of Donald Maclean (929) and a daughter of MacGillvray.

He married Margaret MacLean.

Margaret MacLean was born about 1665.

Children of Allan Maclean and Margaret MacLean:

+ 1032   i.   Donald[23] Maclean was born about 1685.

          ii.   John Maclean. John is deceased. left no issue.

         iii.   Florence Maclean.

Family of Lachlan Maclean and Janet MacLean

1074. Lachlan[22] Maclean was born about 1665. He was the son of Donald Maclean (929) and a daughter of MacGillvray.

He married Janet MacLean.

Janet MacLean was born about 1670.

Sons of Lachlan Maclean and Janet MacLean:

      i.   Donald^{23} Maclean was born about 1695. He died in Ireland.

      ii.   Hector Maclean. Hector died in Ireland.

Family of John Mclean and Isabel MacLean

1075. John^{22} Mclean was born in 1680 in Treshnish, Isle of Mull, Argyll, Scotland. He was the son of Ewen McLean (930) and an unknown woman.

John was known by the title of Minister of Kilninian. He died in Isle of Mull, Argyll, Scotland, on March 12, 1756, at the age of 76.

He married Isabel MacLean.

Isabel MacLean was born about 1683. She was the daughter of Charles MacLean.

Children of John Mclean and Isabel MacLean:

		i.	John^{23} McLean was born about 1704.
+	1221	ii.	Anne Maclean was born in Isle of Mull, Argyll, Scotland, in 1707.
+	1222	iii.	Mary MacLean was born in Isle of Mull, Argyll, Scotland, in 1709.
+	1223	iv.	Catherine Maclean was born in Argylleshire, Scotland, in 1714.
+	1224	v.	Alexander Maclean was born in Isle of Mull, Argyll, Scotland, in 1722.

Family of Lachlan McLean and Mary MacArthur

1076. Lachlan^{22} McLean was born about 1685 in Coll, Argyll, Scotland. He was the son of Ewen McLean (930) and an unknown woman.

Lachlan died in Scotland in 1755 at the age of 70.

He married Mary MacArthur.

Mary MacArthur was born in Old Solas, Scotland, in 1682. Mary died in Scotland.

Son of Lachlan McLean and Mary MacArthur:

+   1225 i.   Hugh^{23} McLean was born in Kilmaluaig Tyree Scotland in 1715.

Family of Hector McLean and Jennet MacLean

1077. Hector[22] McLean was born in 1696 in Isle of Mull, Argyll, Scotland. He was the son of Ewen McLean (930) and Margaret MacLean (937).

Hector was baptized at : Argyll: Tyree - Register of Baptisms and Marriages, 1766-1774 in Argylleshire, Scotland. He died in Coll Parrish, Argyle, Scotland, on April 10, 1775, at the age of 79.

Hector married Jennet MacLean on June 22, 1743.

Jennet MacLean was born in Knock, Coll, Scotland. She was the daughter of Hector MacLean and Margaret Fowler.

Jennet died in on Coll on August 2, 1791.

Children of Hector McLean and Jennet MacLean:

+   1226   i.   Margaret[23] Mclean was born on May 22, 1745.
+   1227   ii.   Florence Mclean was born on October 15, 1747.
                iii.   Allan Mclean was born on April 23, 1751.
                iv.   Margaret McLean was born on July 28, 1752.

Family of John McLean and Mary MacLean

1078. John[22] McLean was born about 1699. He was the son of Ewen McLean (930) and Margaret MacLean (937).

John was known by the title of 10th MacLean of Treshnish.

John married Mary MacLean on July 16, 1705, in Isle of Mull, Argyll, Scotland.

Mary MacLean was born in Boreray, Inverness-shire, Scotland, about 1690.

Sons of John McLean and Mary MacLean:

+   1228   i.   Hugh[23] McLean was born about 1730.
                ii.   Neil McLean.

Family of John MacLean and ? Campbell

1079. John[22] MacLean was born about 1660. He was the son of Lachlan MacLean (935).

He married ? Campbell.

Sons of John MacLean and ? Campbell:

- i. Lachlan[23] MacLean was born about 1690. He is deceased. drowned at age 22.
- + 1229 ii. Alexander MacLean.

Family of Allan MacLean and Susanna Beauchamp

1080. Allan[22] MacLean was born on August 1, 1715, in Grishispol, Argyll, Scotland. He was the son of Allan MacLean (939) and Catherine MacLean.

Children of Allan MacLean and Mary Loomis:

- i. Mary[23] McLean was born in Vernon, Tolland, Connecticut, United States, after 1744. She died in East Windsor, Hartford, Connecticut, United States, on May 15, 1819.
- ii. Jabez McLean was born in 1746. He died in 1747 at the age of 1.
- iii. Susanna McLean was born in 1747. She died in 1748 at the age of 1.
- + 1230 iv. Alexander McLean was born in Vernon, Tolland, Connecticut, United States, on July 18, 1747.
- v. Dudley B. McLean was born after 1748. He died in 1749.
- vi. Jabez Maclean was born in Vernon, Tolland, Connecticut, United States, in 1750.

Family of John MacLean and Anne MacLean

1081. John[22] MacLean. He is the son of Allan MacLean (939) and Catherine MacLean.

John was known by the title of 2nd MacLean of Grishipol.

He married Anne MacLean. They have two sons. She is the daughter of John MacLean.

Sons of John MacLean and Anne MacLean:

- i. John[23] MacLean.
- ii. Archibald MacLean.

Family of Florence MacLean and Donald MacLean

1082. Florence[22] MacLean. She is the daughter of Allan MacLean (939) and Catherine MacLean.

She married Donald MacLean.

Family of Mary MacLean and John MacLean

1083. Mary[22] MacLean. She is the daughter of Allan MacLean (939) and Catherine MacLean.

She married John MacLean.

Family of Lachlan MacLean and Susanna MacLean

1084. Lachlan[22] MacLean was born in 1730. He was the son of Charles MacLean and Janet MacLean (940).

Lachlan was known by the title of 3rd MacLean of Gallanach. He died in 1802 at the age of 72.

He married Susanna MacLean.

Susanna MacLean was born about 1735. She was the daughter of John MacLean.

Son of Lachlan MacLean and Susanna MacLean:

    i.   Charles[23] MacLean was born in 1760. He was known by the title of 4th MacLean of Gallanach.

Family of Lachlan MacLean and Margaret MacDonald

1085. Lachlan[22] MacLean. He is the son of Hector MacLean (941) and Florence MacLean.

Lachlan was known by the title of 3rd MacLean of Drimnacross.

He married Margaret MacDonald. They have one daughter.

Daughter of Lachlan MacLean and Margaret MacDonald:

    i.   Marjory[23] MacLean.

Family of Angus MacLean and Elizabeth Campbell

1086. Angus[22] MacLean was born about 1657 in Argylleshire, Scotland. He was the son of Duncan McLean (709) and Christian Nikeich.

He married Elizabeth Campbell.

Elizabeth Campbell was born in Scotland about 1670.

Children of Angus MacLean and Elizabeth Campbell:

+   1231   i.   Duncan[23] MacLean was born about 1690.

ii. Marion MacLean.

iii. Catherine MacLean.

iv. Mary MacLean.

Family of Alexander MacLean and Una MacGillvray

1087. Alexander[22] MacLean. He is the son of Charles Maclean (945) and Marianna ?.

Alexander was known by the title of 1st MacLean of Pennycross.

He married Una MacGillvray. She is the daughter of Alexander MacGillvray.

Son of Alexander MacLean and Una MacGillvray:

i. Archibald[23] MacLean was born in 1761. He was known by the title of 2nd MacLean of Pennycross.

Archibald died on February 17, 1830, at the age of 69.

Family of Hugh MacLean and Flora MacLean

1088. Hugh[22] MacLean was born in 1738 in Guirdil, Isle of Rum, Scotland. He was the son of John MacLean (946) and Marion MacQueen.

He married Flora MacLean.

Flora MacLean was born about 1735.

Children of Hugh MacLean and Flora MacLean:

i. Hugh[23] MacLean.

ii. Hector MacLean.

iii. Flora MacLean.

iv. Marion MacLean.

+ 1232 v. John MacLean was born in Isle of Rum, Scotland, about 1770.

Family of Mary MacLean and John MacLean

1089. Mary[22] MacLean. She is the daughter of Donald MacLean (947) and Anne MacLean.

She married John MacLean. John was known by the title of of Langamull.

Family of Mary MacLean and John MacLean

1090. Mary[22] MacLean. She is the daughter of Donald MacLean (947) and Mary MacLean.

She married John MacLean. John was using a title in og Langamull.

Family of Hector McLean and Margaret MacLean

1091. Hector[22] McLean was born about 1630 in Isle of Mull, Argyll, Scotland. He was the son of Ewen McLean (948) and Catherine MacLean (563).

Hector was known by the title of 8th MacLean of Treshnish. He died in Argylleshire, Scotland, in 1693 at the age of 63.

He married Margaret MacLean.

Margaret MacLean was born about 1620.

Hector McLean married Catherine McLean in 1650 in Argylleshire, Scotland.

Catherine McLean was born in Bunessan, Argyll, Scotland, in 1625. Catherine reached 35 years of age and died in Isle of Mull, Argyll, Scotland, in 1660.

Son of Hector McLean and Margaret MacLean:

+ 930   i.   Ewen[23] McLean was born in Isle of Mull, Argyll, Scotland, about 1655.

Children of Hector McLean and Catherine McLean:

     i.   Lachlan[23] McLean was born in Scotland in 1652.

     ii.   Donald McLean was born in Scotland in 1654. He died in Scotland.

     iii.   Archibald McLean was born in Scotland in 1658. He is deceased. died young.

     iv.   Janet McLean was born in Scotland in 1658.

     v.   Flora MacLean was born in Isle of Mull, Argyll, Scotland, in 1660. She died in Minginish, Inverness-shire, Scotland, in 1702 at the age of 42.

Family of Florence McLean and Hector MacLean

1092. Florence[22] McLean was born about 1635. She was the daughter of Ewen McLean (948) and Catherine MacLean (563).

She married Hector MacLean.

Hector MacLean was born about 1630.

Children of Florence McLean and Hector MacLean:

+ 1070   i.   Charles[23] MacLean was born about 1655.

+ 1071   ii.   Janet MacLean was born about 1670.

+ 1072   iii.   John MacLean.

             iv.   Hugh MacLean.

             v.   Florence MacLean.

Farquhar McLean

1093. Farquhar[22] McLean was born about 1701. He was the son of Farquhar McLean (949).

Son of Farquhar McLean:

+ 1233   i.   Farquhar[23] McLean was born in 1743.

Family of Hector McLean and Elizabeth McHutcheon

1094. Hector[22] McLean was born about 1706 in Cameron, Mull, Scotland. He was the son of Farquhar McLean (949).

Hector died about 1796 at the age of 90.

At the age of 24, Hector married Elizabeth McHutcheon on May 23, 1730, in Luss, Dunbartonshire, Scotland, when she was 20 years old.

Elizabeth McHutcheon was born in Luss, Dunbartonshire, Scotland, on July 17, 1709. She was the daughter of William McHutcheon.

Elizabeth reached 59 years of age and died in Argyll, Scotland, in 1769.

Children of Hector McLean and Elizabeth McHutcheon:

             i.   Catherine[23] McLean was born in Luss, Dunbartonshire, Scotland, on September 26, 1730.

             ii.   Duncan McLean was born in Luss, Dunbartonshire, Scotland, on April 4, 1733.

             iii.   Robert McLean was born in Luss, Dunbartonshire, Scotland, on June 16, 1735.

+ 1234   iv.   Donald McLean was born in Luss, Dunbartonshire, Scotland, on November 27, 1737.

v. William McLean was born in Luss, Dunbartonshire, Scotland, on January 30, 1741.

vi. Helen McLean was born in Luss, Dunbartonshire, Scotland, on March 27, 1743.

+ 1235 vii. John McLean was born in Luss, Dunbartonshire, Scotland, on January 31, 1746.

viii. Ann McLean was born in Luss, Dunbartonshire, Scotland, on October 19, 1747.

ix. Hector McLean was born in Luss, Dunbartonshire, Scotland, on August 1, 1750.

x. Sarah McLean was born in Luss, Dunbartonshire, Scotland, on February 18, 1756.

Family of Lachlan McLean and Margaret Black

1095. Lachlan[22] McLean was born on February 19, 1735, in Inveraray, Argyll, Scotland. He was the son of Donald McLean (950) and Catherine Stewart.

Lachlan died in Bunessan, Kilfinichen, Argyllshire, Scotland, on February 17, 1819, at the age of 83.

Lachlan married Margaret Black on Wednesday, February 2, 1763, in Inverchaolain, Argyll, Scotland, UK. They had nine children.

Margaret Black was born in Argylleshire, Scotland, about 1741.

Children of Lachlan McLean and Margaret Black:

+ 1236 i. John[23] McLean was born in Inverchaolain, Argyllshire, Scotland, on February 8, 1765.

ii. Archibald McLean was born in Inverchaolain, Argyllshire, Scotland, on February 28, 1767. He was baptized in , Inverchaolain, Argyll, Scotland, on March 1, 1767.

iii. Donald McLean was born in Inverchaolain, Argyllshire, Scotland, on August 5, 1769.

iv. Elizabeth McLean was born in Inverchaolain, Argyll, Scotland, on October 6, 1771.

v. Lachlan McLean was born in Inverchaolain, Argyllshire, Scotland, on April 27, 1774.

vi. Patrick McLean was born in Inverchaolain, Argyllshire, Scotland, on November 16, 1776.

vii. Catherine McLean was born in Inverchaolain, Argyllshire, Scotland, on May 9, 1779.

viii. Alexander McLean was born in Inverchaolain, Argyllshire, Scotland, on June 23, 1781.

ix. Margaret McLean was born in Inverchaolain, Argyllshire, Scotland, on August 21, 1783.

Family of Duncan McLean and Agnes McDongal

1096. Duncan[22] McLean was born about 1739. He was the son of Donald McLean (950) and Catherine Stewart.

He married Agnes McDongal.

Daughter of Duncan McLean and Agnes McDongal:

    i. Mary[23] McLean was born in Lochgoilhead, Argyleshire, Scotland, on February 16, 1771.

John MacLean

1097. John[22] MacLean was born about 1735. He was the son of Charles MacLean (951).

Son of John MacLean:

+ 1237   i. Allan[23] MacLean was born about 1760.

Lachlan MacLean

1098. Lachlan[22] MacLean. He is the son of Charles MacLean (951).

Lachlan was known by the title of 7th MacLean of Hynish.

Sons of Lachlan MacLean:

+ 1238   i. Charles[23] MacLean.
      ii. Archibald MacLean.

Charles MacLean

1099. Charles[22] MacLean was born about 1720. He was the son of Neil Ban MacLean (959).

Son of Charles MacLean:

+ 1239 i. John^{23} MacLean was born about 1740.

Rory Mor MacLean

1100. Rory Mor^{22} MacLean. He is the son of Angus MacLean (964).

Son of Rory Mor MacLean:

+ 1240 i. John^{23} MacLean.

Family of John Mor MacLean and Marion MacLean

1101. John Mor^{22} MacLean was born about 1743 at Page 400 Clan Gillean in Kilmory Isle of Rum. He was the son of John MacLean (966) and Margaret MacLean (965).

John died in Kilmory Isle of Rum in 1798 at the age of 55. He was buried in Kilmory, Isle of Rum.

John married Marion MacLean about 1764. They had four sons.

Marion MacLean was born in Kilmory, Isle of Rum, about 1744. She was the daughter of Murdock MacLean.

Marion died in Kilmory, Isle of Rum. She was buried in Kilmory, Isle of Rum.

John Mor MacLean married Christy MacLean. She is the daughter of Neil MacLean.

Sons of John Mor MacLean and Marion MacLean:

    i. John Og^{23} MacLean.

    ii. Neil MacLean.

    iii. Hector MacLean.

    iv. Murdoch Mor MacLean.

Children of John Mor MacLean and Christy MacLean:

    i. Mary MacLean. Mary died in May 1838.

    ii. Christy MacLean.

    iii. Flora MacLean.

    iv. Marion MacLean.

    v. Margaret MacLean.

vi. Donald MacLean.

Donald MacLean

1102. Donald^{22} MacLean. He is the son of Charles MacLean (967).

Son of Donald MacLean:

+ 1241   i.   Angus^{23} MacLean.

Family of John McLean and Anna Margaretha Crist

1103. John^{22} McLean was born on May 28, 1727, in Kingston, Ulster, New York. He was the son of Cornelius McLean (968) and Sarah Schoonmaker.

John died in Montgomery Precinct, Ulster, New York, United States, on October 21, 1785, at the age of 58.

He married Anna Margaretha Crist.

Anna Margaretha Crist was born in New York in 1727.

Son of John McLean and Anna Margaretha Crist:

+ 1242   i.   Jonas^{23} McLean was born in Montgomery, Orange, New York, United States, on September 3, 1772.

Family of Murdoch MacLean and Christina Maclean

1104. Murdoch^{22} MacLean. He was the son of John MacLean (969) and Finvola MacLean.

Murdoch died in 1867.

He married Christina Maclean.

Family of William MacLean and Elizabeth MacLean

1105. William^{22} MacLean was born on Tuesday, July 20, 1762. He was the son of Charles MacLean (971) and Marjory MacIntosh.

William was known by the title of 10th MacLean of Dochgarroch. He died in 1841 at the age of 78.

William married Elizabeth MacLean on Thursday, May 28, 1789. They had three sons. She was the daughter of LachLan MacLean and Christian Cameron.

Sons of William MacLean and Elizabeth MacLean:

        i.   Allan[23] MacLean was born on March 22, 1790. He was known by the title of 11th MacLean od Dochgarroch.

            Allan died on October 26, 1876, at the age of 86.

+ 1243 ii.   Charles Maxwell MacLean was born on December 11, 1791.

+ 1244 iii. William MacLean was born on November 4, 1793.

Family of Jannet MacLean and Alexander MacIntosh

1106. Jannet[22] MacLean was born in January 1756. She was the daughter of Charles MacLean (971) and Marjory MacIntosh.

Jannet married Alexander MacIntosh in 1779.

Family of Marjory MacLean and Alexander Lee

1107. Marjory[22] MacLean was born in November 1763. She was the daughter of Charles MacLean (971) and Marjory MacIntosh.

Marjory died on May 29, 1820, at the age of 56.

She married Alexander Lee. Alexander died on February 15, 1807.

Family of Charles MacLean and Mary MacIntosh

1108. Charles[22] MacLean was born about 1712. He was the son of John MacLean (972) and Christina Dallas.

Charles was known by the title of 10th MacLean of Dochgarroch. He died in 1778 at the age of 66.

He married Mary MacIntosh.

Children of Charles MacLean and Mary MacIntosh:

        i.   John[23] MacLean. John was known by the title of 11th MacLean of Dochgarroch.

        ii.   Phineas MacLean. Phineas is deceased. died young.

        iii. Angus MacLean.

+ 1245 iv. William MacLean.

        v.   Jannet MacLean.

        vi. Marjory MacLean.

        vii. Barbara MacLean.

Family of William Mclean and Elizabeth Rule

1109. William[22] Mclean was born in 1702 in Isle of Mull, Argyll, Scotland. He was the son of Alexander MacLean (973) and Mary Campbell.

He was buried in Gettysburg, Adams County, Pennsylvania in 1785. William died in Gettysburg, Adams, Pennsylvania on June 13, 1785, at the age of 83.

He married Elizabeth Rule.

Elizabeth Rule was born on October 15, 1707. She was buried in Gettysburg, Adams County, Pennsylvania in 1784. Elizabeth reached 76 years of age and died in Hyland, York, Pennsylvania on July 17, 1784.

Son of William Mclean and Elizabeth Rule:

+ 1246 i. Moses[23] McLean was born in 1737.

Family of Robert MacLean and ? Fraser

1110. Robert[22] MacLean was born about 1710. He was the son of Alexander MacLean (973) and Mary Campbell.

He married ? Fraser.

Son of Robert MacLean and ? Fraser:

+ 1247 i. Hugh[23] MacLean was born about 1735.

Family of William MacLean and ? Fraser

1111. William[22] MacLean was born about 1712. He was the son of Alexander MacLean (973) and Mary Campbell.

He married ? Fraser.

Sons of William MacLean and ? Fraser:

    i. Aleander[23] MacLean.

    ii. Hugh MacLean.

Family of Alexander MacLean and Mary Grant

1112. Alexander[22] MacLean was born in 1720 in Dochgarroch, Inverness, Scotland. He was the son of David MacLean (974) and Anna Gordon.

Alexander died in Scotland about 1780 at the age of 60.

Alexander married Mary Grant in 1747 in Inverness Co., Scotland.

Children of Alexander MacLean and Mary Grant:

    i.   David^{23} McLean was born in Dores, Inverness-shire, Scotland, on March 22, 1760. He died in Lorne, 1654157, Nova Scotia, Canada.

    ii.   Anne McLean was born in Kinchyle, Inverness, Scotland, on April 9, 1762.

    iii.   Janet McLean was born in Kinchyle, Inverness, Scotland, on April 2, 1765.

    iv.   Margaret McLean was born in Kinchyle, Inverness, Scotland, on August 13, 1767.

    v.   William McLean was born in Kinchyle, Inverness, Scotland, on January 21, 1769.

    vi.   Donald McLean was born in Inverness, Scotland, on March 2, 1771.

Sons of Alexander MacLean:

    i.   Robert Mc Lean was born in Inverness Co, Scotland, in 1748. He died in Inverness, Inverness, Scotland, on May 29, 1828, at the age of 80.

    ii.   Robert McLean was born in Inverness Co, Scotland, in 1748. He died in Inverness, Inverness, Scotland, on May 29, 1828, at the age of 80.

John MacLean

1113.   John^{22} MacLean was born about 1722 in Dochgarroch, Inverness, Scotland. He was the son of David MacLean (974) and Anna Gordon.

Son of John MacLean:

    i.   Robert^{23} MacLean.

Family of Lachlan MacLean and Jane MacLean

1114.   Lachlan^{22} MacLean was born about 1720. He was the son of Donald MacLean (975) and ? Campbell.

He married Jane MacLean. They had five sons.

Jane was known by the title of of Kingerloch.

Sons of Lachlan MacLean and Jane MacLean:

      i. Donald^{23} MacLean was born about 1745.

      ii. Murdock MacLean.

      iii. Allan MacLean.

      iv. Hector MacLean.

      v. Charles MacLean.

Lachlan MacLean

1115. Lachlan^{22} MacLean was born about 1690. He was the son of Donald MacLean (978).

Lachlan was known by the title of 9th MacLean of Kingerloch. He died in 1756 at the age of 66.

Sons of Lachlan MacLean:

+ 1248 i. Hugh^{23} MacLean was born about 1725.

      ii. John MacLean.

      iii. Lachlan MacLean.

Family of Thomas Borthwick and Bessie Notman

1116. Thomas^{22} Borthwick was born in 1645 in , Midlothian, Scotland. He was the son of Baron John Borthwick (979) and Lady Mary Elizabeth Kerr.

Thomas died in Saltcoats, Midlothia, Scotland, on May 1, 1673, at the age of 28. He was buried in Saltcoats, Midlothia, Scotland, on August 13, 1673.

He married Bessie Notman.

Bessie Notman was born in Scotland in 1645. Bessie died in Scotland.

Daughter of Thomas Borthwick and Bessie Notman:

+ 1249 i. Elizabeth^{23} Borthwick was born in Inveresk, East Lothian, Scotland, on November 12, 1676.

Family of Robert Warren and Judith Anderson

1117. Robert^{22} Warren was born on January 11, 1700, in Surry, Surry, Virginia. He was the son of Robert Warren (980) and Anne ?.

Robert died in Northampton, North Carolina, United States, on July 3, 1793, at the age of 93.

Robert married Judith Anderson in 1730 in Virginia.

Judith Anderson was born in Virginia in 1705. Judith reached 90 years of age and died in North Carolina in October 1795.

Son of Robert Warren and Judith Anderson:

+ 1250 i. Hinchey^{23} Warren was born in Virginia in 1727.

Family of John Hardy and Mary Frances Jackman

1118. John^{22} Hardy was born in 1646 in Ipswich, Essex, Massachusetts Bay, British Colonial America. He was the son of Joseph Hardy (981).

John died in Bradford, Essex, Massachusetts Bay, British Colonial America. He was buried in Bradford, Essex, Massachusetts Bay, British Colonial America.

He married Mary Frances Jackman.

Mary Frances Jackman was born in Newbury, Essex, Massachusetts Bay, British Colonial America. She was buried in Bradford, Essex, Massachusetts Bay, Birtish Colonial America, in December 1689. Mary died in Bradford, Essex, Massachusetts Bay, British Colonial America, on December 2, 1689.

Son of John Hardy and Mary Frances Jackman:

+ 1251 i. Joseph^{23} Hardy was born about 1670.

Family of John Haskell and Patience Soule

1119. John^{22} Haskell was born in 1648 in Salem, Essex, Massachusetts. He was the son of Roger Haskell and Elizabeth Hardy (982).

John died in Middleboro, Plymouth, Massachusetts on May 15, 1706, at the age of 58.

He married Patience Soule. They had nine children.

Patience Soule was born in Duxbury, Plymouth, Massachusetts in 1648. Patience reached 58 years of age and died in Middleboro, Plymouth, Massachusetts on March 11, 1706.

Children of John Haskell and Patience Soule:

    i. John^{23} Haskell was born in Middleboro, Plymouth, Massachusetts on June 11, 1670. He died in Killingly, Windham, Connecticut on February 17, 1728, at the age of 57.

ii. Elizabeth Haskell was born in Middleboro, Plymouth, Massachusetts on July 2, 1672. She died in Middleboro, plymouth, massachuets in June 1715 at the age of 42.

iii. William Haskell was born in Plymouth, Plymouth, Massachusetts, United States, on June 11, 1674. He died in Plymouth, Plymouth, Massachusetts, United States, on May 27, 1740, at the age of 65.

iv. Patience Haskell was born in Plymouth, Plymouth, Massachusetts, United States, on February 1, 1679. She died in Plymouth, Plymouth, Massachusetts, United States, on February 14, 1705, at the age of 26.

v. Bethiah Haskell was born in Plymouth, Plymouth, Massachusetts, United States, on January 15, 1681. She died in Plymouth, Plymouth, Massachusetts, United States, in March 1738 at the age of 57.

vi. Mary Haskell was born in Middleboro, Plymouth, Massachusetts on July 4, 1684. She died in Harwich, Barnstable, Massachusetts, United States, in 1741 at the age of 56.

vii. Josiah Haskell was born in Plymouth, Plymouth, Massachusetts, United States, in 1686. He died in Freetown, Bristol, Massachusetts, United States, in 1745 at the age of 59.

+ 1252 viii. Josiah Haskell was born in Plymouth, Plymouth, Massachusetts, United States, on June 18, 1686.

ix. Susanna Haskell was born in Plymouth, Plymouth, Massachusetts, United States, on January 15, 1691. She died in Freetown, Bristol, Massachusetts, United States, in 1723 at the age of 31.

Family of Patience Dudley and Daniel Dennison

1120. Patience[22] Dudley was born in February 1618. She was the daughter of Thomas Dudley (983) and Dorothy Yorke.

Patience died on February 8, 1690, at the age of 72.

She married Daniel Dennison. Daniel Dennison was born about 1612.

Daniel reached 70 years of age and died on September 9, 1682.

Family of Mercy Dudley and John Woodbridge

1121. Mercy[22] Dudley was born in 1621 in Northampton, England. She was the daughter of Thomas Dudley (983) and Dorothy Yorke.

Mercy died in Newbury, MA, on July 1, 1691, at the age of 70.

Mercy married John Woodbridge in 1641. They had eleven children.

John Woodbridge was born in Stanton, England, in 1613. He was the son of John Woodbridge and Sarah Parker.

John reached 82 years of age and died in Newbury, MA, on March 17, 1695.

Children of Mercy Dudley and John Woodbridge:

		i.	Sarah[23] Woodbridge was born on June 7, 1640. She died about 1690 at the age of 49.
+	1253	ii.	Lucy Woodbridge was born on March 13, 1641.
+	1254	iii.	John Woodbridge was born in 1644.
+	1255	iv.	Benjamin Woodbridge was born in 1645.
+	1256	v.	Thomas Woodbridge was born in 1648.
+	1257	vi.	Dorothy Woodbridge was born in October 1649.
		vii.	Anne Woodbridge was born about 1653. She died on February 28, 1700, at the age of 47.
+	1258	viii.	Timothy Woodbridge was born in Barford, St Martins, Wiltshire, England, on January 13, 1656.
+	1259	ix.	Joseph Woodbridge was born about 1657.
+	1260	x.	Martha Woodbridge was born about 1660.
+	1261	xi.	Mary Woodbridge was born in 1662.

Family of Samuel Dudley and Mary Winthrop

1122. Samuel[22] Dudley. He is the son of Thomas Dudley (983) and Dorothy Yorke.

He married Mary Winthrop. She is the daughter of John Winthrop and Margaret Tyndall.

Family of Anne Dudley and Simon Bradstreet

1123. Anne[22] Dudley. She is the daughter of Thomas Dudley (983) and Dorothy Yorke.

She married Simon Bradstreet.

Anne Dudley married Simon Bradstreet.

Family of Sarah Dudley and Benjamin Keayne

1124. Sarah[22] Dudley. She is the daughter of Thomas Dudley (983) and Dorothy Yorke.

She married Benjamin Keayne.

Family of Joseph Dudley and Rebecca Tyng

1125. Joseph[22] Dudley. He is the son of Thomas Dudley (983) and Dorothy Yorke.

He married Rebecca Tyng.

Family of Paul Dudley and Mary Leverett

1126. Paul[22] Dudley. He is the son of Thomas Dudley (983) and Dorothy Yorke.

He married Mary Leverett.

Family of Mehitable King and Benjamin Marsh

1127. Mehitable[22] King was born on October 15, 1705, in Salem, Essex, MA. She was the daughter of William King and Hannah Cook (984).

At the age of 23, Mehitable married Benjamin Marsh on January 3, 1729, when he was 24 years old.

Benjamin Marsh was born in Salem, Essex, Massachusets, on October 10, 1704. He was the son of Ebenezer Marsh and Alice Booth.

Daughter of Mehitable King and Benjamin Marsh:

+ 1262 i. Mehitable[23] Marsh was born in Sutton, Worchester, Massachusets, on May 8, 1731.

Family of Noah Merrill and Esther Gillett

1128. Noah[22] Merrill was born on May 8, 1707, in Hartford, CT. He was the son of Isaac Merrill and Sarah Cook (985).

Noah died in New Hartford, Litchfield, Conn., in 1739 at the age of 31.

Noah married Esther Gillett about 1727 in West Hartford, Conn..

Children of Noah Merrill and Esther Gillett:

+ 1263 i. Noah[23] Merrill was born in Haverhill, Essex, MA, about 1726.
+ 1264 ii. Ichabod Merrill was born before September 15, 1728.
+ 1265 iii. Esther Merrill was born in West Hartford, Hartford, CT, before March 8, 1730.

+	1266	iv.	Joseph Merrill was born in West Hartford, Hartford, CT, before January 30, 1732.
+	1267	v.	Mehitable Merrill was born in Hartford, Hartford, CT, before May 26, 1734.
		vi.	Unknown Merrill was born in 1739.

Family of Timothy Merrill and Mary Kellog

1129. Timothy[22] Merrill was born on March 22, 1709, in Hartford, CT. He was the son of Isaac Merrill and Sarah Cook (985).

Timothy died in November 1788 at the age of 79.

Timothy married Mary Kellog on November 9, 1738, in West Hartford, Conn..

Timothy Merrill married Mary Griswold on Thursday, March 23, 1758, in Farmington, Hartford, Conn..

Mary Griswold was born in 1726. Mary reached 71 years of age and died on April 9, 1797.

Children of Timothy Merrill and Mary Kellog:

+	1268	i.	Timothy[23] Merrill was born in West Hartford, Hartford, CT, on July 21, 1741.
+	1269	ii.	Mary Merrill was born in West Hartford, Hartford, CT, on September 28, 1743.
		iii.	Lucy Merrill was born in West Hartford, Hartford, CT, on January 14, 1746. She died in West Hartford, Hartford, CT, on June 11, 1752, at the age of 6.
+	1270	iv.	Isaac Merrill was born on January 19, 1748.
+	1271	v.	James Merrill was born on September 25, 1751.

Children of Timothy Merrill and Mary Griswold:

+	1272	i.	Rhoda Merrill was born on December 8, 1758.
+	1273	ii.	Jonathan Merrill was born in West Hartford, Hartford, CT, on November 28, 1760.
+	1274	iii.	Ashbel Merrill was born in West Hartford, Hartford, CT, on September 7, 1762.
		iv.	Lucy Merrill was born on December 20, 1763.

	1275	v.	Ruby Merrill was born on November 25, 1765.
+	1276	vi.	Enos Merrill was born in Hartford, Hartford, CT, on November 1, 1768.

Family of Eliakim Merrill and Sarah Watson

1130. Eliakim[22] Merrill was born before August 8, 1714 in Hartford, CT. He was the son of Isaac Merrill and Sarah Cook (985).

Eliakim was baptized in Hartford, CT, on August 8, 1714.

Eliakim married Sarah Watson before 1741. They had eleven children.

Children of Eliakim Merrill and Sarah Watson:

	1277	i.	Eliakim[23] Merrill was born in New Hartford, Litchfield, CT, before February 14, 1742.
+	1278	ii.	Elias Merrill was born before June 14, 1744.
		iii.	George Merrill was born before March 30, 1746.
		iv.	Mary Merrill was born before December 20, 1747.
+	1279	v.	Bildad Merrill was born in New Hartford, Litchfield, CT, before January 28, 1750.
		vi.	Sarah Merrill was born in Canton, CT, in 1752.
+	1280	vii.	Martin Merrill was born in New Hartford, Litchfield, CT, before April 21, 1754.
		viii.	Zelinda Merrill was born in New Hartford, Litchfield, CT, before November 23, 1755.
		ix.	Esther Merrill was born in New Hartford, Litchfield, CT, before February 12, 1758.
		x.	Isaac Merrill was born in New Hartford, Litchfield, CT, before January 27, 1760.
		xi.	Betty Merrill was born in New Hartford, Litchfield, CT, before December 13, 1761.

Family of Joseph Merrill and Mary Jewel

1131. Joseph[22] Merrill was born before December 2, 1716 in Hartford, CT. He was the son of Isaac Merrill and Sarah Cook (985).

Joseph died before 1749.

Joseph married Mary Jewel on January 15, 1740, in Amesbury, Essex, Mass.. Mary Jewel was born on December 1, 1717.

[Copy of Hebron.FTW]

[Merrill full 2.FTW]

Mary Jewell, daughter of Samuel and Sarah (Ring) Jewel of Amesbury was born 8 Apr 1718.
Mary Jewell, daughter of Joseph and Anna (Quimby) Jewel of Amesbury was born 1 Dec 1717.
It is not known which of these Mary Jewel's married Joseph(4) Merrill.

Family of Sarah Merrill and Matthew Clark Jr.

1132. Sarah^{22} Merrill was born before May 24, 1719. She was the daughter of Isaac Merrill and Sarah Cook (985).

Sarah married Matthew Clark Jr. on May 8, 1746, in Farmington, Hartford, Conn..

Family of Esther Merrill and Lot Norton

1133. Esther^{22} Merrill was born before November 19, 1721 in West Hartford, CT. She was the daughter of Isaac Merrill and Sarah Cook (985).

Esther married Lot Norton on Thursday, December 2, 1756, in Farmington, Hartford, Conn..

Family of Daniel Durland and Sarah De Motte

1134. Daniel^{22} Durland was born about 1737 in Long Island City, Queens, New York. He was the son of John Gerret Dorlandt and Mary Birdsall (986).

Daniel died in Hanley Mtn, Annapolis, Nova Scotia, Canada, after 1794.

Daniel married Sarah De Motte on Thursday, September 22, 1763, in Hempstead, Nassau, New York.

Sarah De Motte was born in Newburgh, Ulster, New York in 1740. Sarah reached 52 years of age and died in Mount Hanley, Annapolis, Nova Scotia, Canada, in 1792.

Sons of Daniel Durland and Sarah De Motte:

+ 1281 i. Daniel^{23} Durland was born in Wilmot, Annapolis Co., Nova Scotia, Canada, in 1772.

ii. Charles E Durland was born in Flatbush, Kings, New York, United States, in 1773. He died in Roxbury, Annapolis, Nova Scotia, Canada, after 1871.

Family of Katherine Whiting and John Lane

1135. Katherine[22] Whiting. She is the daughter of Samuel Whiting (987) and Elizabeth Read.

She married John Lane. They have one daughter.

Daughter of Katherine Whiting and John Lane:

+ 1282 i. Susanna[23] Lane.

Family of Ephraim Spalding and Abigail Bullard

1136. Ephraim[22] Spalding. He is the son of Edward Spalding (989) and Mary Adams.

He married Abigail Bullard. They have one son.

Son of Ephraim Spalding and Abigail Bullard:

+ 1283 i. Erastus[23] Spalding.

23rd Generation

Family of Ann Winn and Moses Cleveland

1137. Ann[23] Winn was born on September 26, 1626, in Woburn, Middlesex, Massachusetts. She was the daughter of Edward Winn (991) and Joanna Sargent.

Ann died in Woburn, Middlesex, Massachusetts, on May 6, 1682, at the age of 55.

She married Moses Cleveland.

Moses Cleveland was born in Ipswich, Suffolk, England, on February 2, 1620. He was the son of Isaac Samuel Cleveland and Alice ?.

Moses immigrated to Plymouth, Massachusetts in 1635. Moses reached 81 years of age and died in Woburn, Middlesex, Massachusetts, on January 9, 1702.

Son of Ann Winn and Moses Cleveland:

+ 1284 i. Samuel[24] Cleaveland was born in Woburn, Middlesex, Massachusetts, on May 9, 1657.

Family of Catherine Bulkeley and Richard Treat

1138. Catherine[23] Bulkeley was born in 1660 in Wethersfield, Hartford, Connecticut. She was the daughter of Gershom Bulkeley (992) and Sarah Chauncey.

Catherine died in Wethersfield, Hartford, Connecticut, United States, in 1712 at the age of 52.

Catherine married Richard Treat on November 23, 1704, in Wethersfield, Hartford, Connecticut.

Richard Treat was born in Wethersfield, Hartford, Connecticut, United States, in 1675. He was the son of James Treat and Rebecca Lattimer.

Richard reached 38 years of age and died in Wethersfield, Hartford, Connecticut, United States, on May 7, 1713.

Daughter of Catherine Bulkeley and Richard Treat:

i. Catharine[24] Treat was born in Wethersfield, Hartford, Connecticut, United States, on August 26, 1706. She died in Wethersfield, Hartford, Connecticut, United States, on September 14, 1778, at the age of 72.

Family of Dorothy Bulkeley and Thomas Treat

1139. Dorothy[23] Bulkeley was born in 1662. She was the daughter of Gershom Bulkeley (992) and Sarah Chauncey.

Dorothy died in Glastonbury, Conn., in 1757 at the age of 95.

At the age of 31, Dorothy married Thomas Treat on July 5, 1693, when he was 24 years old.

Thomas Treat was born in Wethersfield, CT, on December 12, 1668. He was the son of Richard Treat and Sarah Coleman.

Thomas reached 43 years of age and died in Glastonbury, CT, on January 28, 1712.

Thomas Treat (12/12/1668-1/28/1712) was the son of Richard Treat and Sarah Coleman. He was born in Wethersfield, Conn. He died in Glastonbury, Conn. He married on 7/5/1693 Dorothy Bulkeley* (1662-

1757) the daughter of Rev. Gershom Bulkeley and Sarah Chauncey. Thomas was one of the petitioners for the incorporation of Glastonbury. From the "Treat Genealogy": "The inventory of Mr. Treat's estate, taken April 3, 1713, amounted to 700 pounds, 6s. He was commonly called "Thomas Treat of Nayaug", and inherited from his father in 1693 the large farm left by his grandfather Richard. His name was sometimes spelled Trat." Thomas and Dorothy eight children.

CH: 1. Richard (5/14/1694-1759)
2. Charles (b 2/28/1695) who married Sarah Gardiner on 10/12/1727
3. Thomas (5/3/1699-1/15/1780) who married Mary Hopson on 5/10/1726
4. Isaac (8/15/1701-8/29/1763) who married Rebecca Bulkeley on 12/10/1730
5. Dorothy (b 8/28/1704)
6. Dorotheus (b 8/28/1704) (twin of Dorothy)
7. Sarah (b 1/21/1706) who married Joseph Tryon, Jr.
8. Mary (1/9/1709-2/12/1735) who married Joseph Stevens on 1/1/1732

Thomas' gravestone in the Old Burying Ground on the Green, Glastonbury reads: :

> HERE LIES BVRIED
> THE BODY OF Mr
> THOMAS TREAT WHO
> DIED JANVARY THE 17th
> ANNO DOM 1712
> ETATIS AB VT 44
> YEARS

Children of Dorothy Bulkeley and Thomas Treat:

+	1285	i.	Richard[24] Treat was born in Glastonbury, CT, on May 14, 1694.
+	1286	ii.	Charles Treat was born on February 28, 1695.
+	1287	iii.	Thomas Treat was born in Glastonbury, Hartford County, Connecticut, United States, on May 3, 1699.
+	1288	iv.	Isaac Treat was born on August 15, 1701.
		v.	Dorothy Treat was born on August 28, 1704.
		vi.	Dorotheus Treat was born on August 28, 1704.
+	1289	vii.	Sarah Treat was born on January 21, 1706.
+	1290	viii.	Mary Treat was born on January 9, 1709.

Family of Peter Bukeley and Rachel Talcott

1140. Peter[23] Bukeley was born in 1664. He was the son of Gershom Bulkeley (992) and Sarah Chauncey.

Peter died in 1701 at the age of 37.

He married Rachel Talcott.

Charles Bulkeley

1141. Charles[23] Bulkeley. He is the son of Gershom Bulkeley (992) and Sarah Chauncey.

Daughter of Charles Bulkeley:

+ 1291 i. Hannah[24] Bulkeley was born in New London, New London, Connecticut, on April 17, 1692.

Family of John Ferris and Mary Jackson

1142. John[23] Ferris was born in 1634 in Leicester, England. He was the son of Jeffery Ferris and Mary Anne Howard (993).

He married Mary Jackson.

Mary Jackson was born in Hempstead, Nassau, New York in 1644. Mary reached 60 years of age and died in Westchester, New York in 1704.

Daughter of John Ferris and Mary Jackson:

+ 1292 i. Phebe[24] Ferris was born in Nassau, Queens (Long Island), New York in 1667.

Family of Peter Bulkeley and Rebecca Wheeler

1143. Peter[23] Bulkeley was born on January 3, 1641, in Concord, Middlesex, Massachusetts. He was the son of Edward Bulkeley (994) and Lucien ?.

Peter died in Concord, Middlesex, Massachusetts, United States, on May 24, 1688, at the age of 47.

At the age of 26, Peter married Rebecca Wheeler on April 16, 1667, in Concord, Middlesex, Massachusetts, United States, when she was 21 years old.

Rebecca Wheeler was born in Concord, Middlesex, Massachusetts, United States, on September 6, 1645. She was the daughter of Joseph Wheeler and Sarah Goldstone.

Rebecca reached 72 years of age and died in Concord, Middlesex, Massachusetts, United States, on February 20, 1718.

Children of Peter Bulkeley and Rebecca Wheeler:

  i. Grace[24] Bulkley was born in Fairfield, Fairfield, Connecticut, United States, in 1670. She died in Weathersfield, Hartford, Connecticut, United States, in 1712 at the age of 42.

  ii. Joseph Bulkeley was born in Concord, Middlesex, Massachusetts, United States, on September 7, 1670. He died in Littleton, Middlesex, Massachusetts, United States, on September 24, 1748, at the age of 78.

  iii. Rebecca Bulkeley was born in Concord, Middlesex, Massachusetts, United States, on August 24, 1681. She died in Concord, Middlesex, Massachusetts, United States, in 1747 at the age of 65.

+ 1293 iv. Rebecca Bulkeley.

Family of Peter Bulkeley and Rebecca Wheeler

1144. Peter[23] Bulkeley. He is the son of Edward Bulkeley (994) and Lucien ?.

He married Rebecca Wheeler.

Rebecca Wheeler was born in Concord, Middlesex, Massachusetts, United States, on September 6, 1645. She was the daughter of Joseph Wheeler and Sarah Goldstone.

Rebecca reached 72 years of age and died in Concord, Middlesex, Massachusetts, United States, on February 20, 1718.

Daughter of Peter Bulkeley and Rebecca Wheeler:

+ 1293 i. Rebecca[24] Bulkeley.

Family of Elizabeth Bulkeley and Joseph Emerson

1145. Elizabeth[23] Bulkeley was born in Concord, MA. She was the daughter of Edward Bulkeley (994) and Lucien ?.

Elizabeth married Joseph Emerson in 1665.

Joseph Emerson was born in Ipswich, MA, in 1620. He was the son of Thomas Emerson.

Joseph reached 60 years of age and died in 1680.

Son of Elizabeth Bulkeley and Joseph Emerson:

+ 1294 i. Edward[24] Emerson was born in Concord, MA, in 1670.

Family of Prince Allen and Deborah Butler

1146. Prince[23] Allen was born about 1720 in Dartmouth, Bristol, Massachusetts. He was the son of James B Allen (995) and Mary Akin.

Prince died in Dartmouth, Bristol, MASSECHUSETTS USA, on October 9, 1778, at the age of 58.

He married Deborah Butler.

Deborah Butler was born in Dartmouth, Bristol, Massachusetts, in 1723. Deborah was known by the title of Mrs.

She reached 91 years of age and died on November 30, 1814.

Daughter of Prince Allen and Deborah Butler:

+ 1295 i. Elizabeth[24] Allen was born in Dartmouth, Bristol, Mass., on November 28, 1751.

Family of John Knowles and Jemima Austin (Asten)

1147. John[23] Knowles was born in 1625 in Hampton, Rockingham, New Hampshire. He was the son of John Knowles (996) and Jemima Aster.

John served in the military in New Hampshire. He died at Age at Death: 73 in Hampton, Rockingham, New Hampshire, United States, on December 5, 1705, at the age of 80. John was buried in Hampton, Rockingham County, New Hampshire.

He married Jemima Austin (Asten).

Jemima Austin (Asten) was born in Hampton, Rockingham, New Hampshire, United States, on January 24, 1641. She was the daughter of Francis Austin and Isabell Bland Smith.

Jemima reached 64 years of age and died in Hampton, Rockingham, New Hampshire, United States, on December 5, 1705. She was buried in Hampton, Rockingham County, New Hampshire.

Son of John Knowles and Jemima Austin (Asten):

+ 1296 i. John[24] Knowles was born in Hampton, Rockingham, New Hampshire, United States, on February 6, 1661.

Family of Richard Knowles and Ruth Bowers

1148. Richard^{23} Knowles was born on September 17, 1614, in Bolton, Lancashire, England. He was the son of John Knowles (996) and Elizabeth Willis.

Richard died in Plymouth, Plymouth, Massachusetts on February 1, 1682, at the age of 67.

He married Ruth Bowers.

Ruth Bowers was born in Lincolnshire, of Lincolnshire, England, in 1616. Ruth reached 71 years of age and died in Eastham, Barnstable, Massachusetts in 1687.

Son of Richard Knowles and Ruth Bowers:

+ 1297 i. Samuel^{24} Knowles was born in Plymouth, Plymouth, Massachusetts, United States, on September 17, 1651.

Family of John Hutchinson and Anne Tow

1149. John^{23} Hutchinson was born on September 6, 1641, in Nottingham, Nottinghamshire, England. He was the son of John Hutchinson and Lady Lucy Apsley (997).

John died in Nottingham, Nottinghamshire, England, on August 28, 1677, at the age of 35.

He married Anne Tow.

Anne Tow was born in 1635. Anne reached 45 years of age and died in 1680.

Son of John Hutchinson and Anne Tow:

+ 1298 i. John^{24} Hutchinson was born in Hexham, Northumberland, England, about 1665.

Family of Richard Whittington Wright and Anne Mottrom

1150. Richard Whittington^{23} Wright was born in 1633 in London, Middlesex, England. He was the son of Francis Wright and Anne Merriton (998).

Richard died in Chicacoan, Northumberland, Virginia, United States, on December 10, 1663, at the age of 30.

He married Anne Mottrom.

Anne Mottrom was born in London, England, in 1639. Anne reached 68 years of age and died in Cople, Westmoreland, Virginia, United States, in 1707.

Son of Richard Whittington Wright and Anne Mottrom:

+ 1299 i. Francis[24] Wright was born in Chickacone, Northumberland, Virginia, about 1660.

Family of Francis Stiles and Sarah Mary Birdseye

1151. Francis[23] Stiles was born on August 1, 1602, in Milbrook, Bedfordshire, England. He was the son of Thomas Stiles (999) and Maria ?.

Francis immigrated in 1635. Came to this country in 1635 on the pinnace "Christian", a citizen of London and a master carpenter. He immigrated in 1635. Came to this country in 1635 on the pinnace "Christian", a citizen of London and a master carpenter.

Francis died in Stratford, Fairfield, Connecticut, United States, on June 4, 1662, at the age of 59.

He married Sarah Mary Birdseye.

Sarah Mary Birdseye was born in Milbrook, Bedfordshire, England, in 1600. Sarah reached 82 years of age and died in New Haven, New Haven, Connecticut, United States, in 1682.

Daughter of Francis Stiles and Sarah Mary Birdseye:

+ 1300 i. Hannah[24] Stiles was born in Stratford, Fairfield, Connecticut, United States, in October 1631.

Family of John Gerrish and Elizabeth Waldron

1152. John[23] Gerrish was born on February 12, 1646, in Newbury, Essex, Massachusetts. He was the son of William Gerrish and Joanna Percival Lowell (1000).

John worked as a Judge. He was known by the title of Captain.

John died in Newbury, Essex, Massachusetts, United States, on December 19, 1714, at the age of 68.

More facts and events for John Gerrish:

He married Elizabeth Waldron.

Elizabeth Waldron was born in Dover, Strafford, New Hampshire, United States, on October 18, 1645. Elizabeth was christened in Strafford. She reached 79 years of age and died in Dover, Strafford, New Hampshire, United States, on December 7, 1724.

Son of John Gerrish and Elizabeth Waldron:

+ 1301 i. Paul[24] Gerrish was born in Dover, Strafford, New Hampshire, United States, on January 13, 1674.

Family of Joshua Gray and Jennat Elliot

1153. Joshua[23] Gray was born on November 17, 1714, in York, York, Maine. He was the son of Robert Gray (1001) and Elizabeth Freethy (990).

Joshua died in Sedgwick, Hancock, Maine on October 30, 1781, at the age of 66.

Joshua married Jennat Elliot in 1750 in York, York County, Maine.

Jennat Elliot was born in Portsmouth, Rockingham, New Hampshire in 1714. She was the daughter of Richard Elliot and Abigail Wilson.

Jennat reached 95 years of age and died in , Hancock, Maine in 1809.

Sons of Joshua Gray and Jennat Elliot:

i. Reuben[24] Gray was born in Brunswick, Cumberland, ME, on May 7, 1743. He died in Brooksville, Hancock, ME buried @ Walkers Cemty, on March 11, 1832, at the age of 88.

+ 1302 ii. James Gray was born in Hancock County, Maine on August 20, 1745.

Family of James Jordan and Elizabeth Ratcliffe

1154. James[23] Jordan was born on November 23, 1665, in Nansemond, Virginia. He was the son of Thomas Jordan (1002) and Margaret Brasseur.

James died at Age: 66 in Isle of Wight, Virginia on October 13, 1732, at the age of 66.

He married Elizabeth Ratcliffe.

Elizabeth Ratcliffe was born in Travescore Neck, Nansemond, Virginia, United States, on July 21, 1668. She was the daughter of Richard Ratcliffe and Elizabeth Parr.

Elizabeth reached 26 years of age and died in Chuckatuck, Nansemond, Virginia, United States, on June 30, 1695.

Daughter of James Jordan and Elizabeth Ratcliffe:

+ 1303 i. Elizabeth[24] Jordan was born in Chuckatuck, New Kent, Virginia, United States, in 1690.

Family of John Coddington and Mary Ann Robinson

1155. John[23] Coddington was born on Tuesday, April 14, 1778, in Hector, Schuyler, New York. He was the son of Benjamin Coddington and Phoebe Conger (1003).

John died in Hector, Schuyler, New York on August 12, 1845, at the age of 67.

John married Mary Ann Robinson in 1797 in Ulysses, Tompkins, New York.

Mary Ann Robinson was born in Ireland in 1779. She was the daughter of Barzilla Robinson and Rebecca Loomis.

Mary reached 66 years of age and died in Exeter, Otsego, New York, United States, on March 15, 1845.

Children of John Coddington and Mary Ann Robinson:

      i.   James Harvey[24] Coddington was born in Howard, Steuben, New York on May 3, 1798. He died in Hector, Schuyler, New York in 1870 at the age of 71.

+ 1304 ii.   Calvin Coddington was born in Ulysses, Tompkins Co., New York in 1800.

      iii. Samuel Coddington was born in Ulysess, Tompkins, New York on April 27, 1802. He died in Howard, Steuben, New York on May 17, 1875, at the age of 73.

      iv. Julia Ann Coddington was born in Ulysses, Tompkins, New York in 1804.

      v.   Aaron Coddington was born in Ulysses, Tompkins, New York in 1806. He died in London, Ontario, Canada, on March 6, 1884, at the age of 78.

      vi. Alvah Coddington was born in Ulysses, Tompkins, New York on April 22, 1808. He died in Tecumseh, Lenawee, Michigan on June 18, 1882, at the age of 74.

      vii. John Coddington was born in Hector, Schuyler, New York in 1810. He died in Seneca, Lenawee, Michigan on October 17, 1851, at the age of 41.

      viii. Maria Coddington was born in Hector, Schuyler, New York in 1814.

Family of John Thompson and Margaret Cook

1156. John^{23} Thompson was born in 1736 in New York. He was the son of Ebenezer Thompson (1004) and Esther Stevens.

John died in Berne, Albany, New York, United States, in 1790 at the age of 54.

He married Margaret Cook.

Margaret Cook was born in New York in 1730. Margaret reached 46 years of age and died in Mecklenburg, North Carolina, United States, in August 1776.

Son of John Thompson and Margaret Cook:

+ 1305 i. William^{24} Thompson was born in Albany, Albany, New York, United States, in 1760.

Family of Recompense Thomas and Elizabeth ?

1157. Recompense^{23} Thomas was born on November 2, 1709, in New Haven, New Haven, Connecticut. He was the son of John Thomas (1005) and Mary Ford.

Recompense died in Ridgefield, Fairfield, Connecticut, United States, on April 18, 1793, at the age of 83.

Recompense married Elizabeth ? on July 26, 1731, in Ridgefield, Fairfield, Connecticut.

Elizabeth ? was born in Ridgefield, Fairfield, Connecticut, United States, in 1711. Elizabeth reached 45 years of age and died at died in childbirth in Ballston Spa, Saratoga, New York, United States, in 1756.

Son of Recompense Thomas and Elizabeth ?:

+ 1306 i. Recompense^{24} Thomas was born in Ridgefield, Fairfield, Connecticut on January 28, 1735.

Family of Lois Thomas and Joseph Collins

1158. Lois^{23} Thomas was born on June 27, 1727, in New Haven, CT. She was the daughter of Israel Thomas (1006) and Sarah Humphreville.

Lois died in Woodbridge, New Haven, Connecticut, United States, on February 19, 1788, at the age of 60.

At the age of 20, Lois married Joseph Collins on October 28, 1747, in Congregational, Woodbridge, CT, when he was 18 years old. They had nine children.

Joseph Collins was born in New Haven, CT, on March 7, 1729. He was the son of Joseph Collins and Patience Brown.

Joseph reached 77 years of age and died in Woodbridge, CT, on January 27, 1807.

Children of Lois Thomas and Joseph Collins:

		i.	Eunice[24] Collins was born on December 8, 1747.
		ii.	Joel Collins was born on March 16, 1750.
+	1307	iii.	Mehitabel Collins was born on July 14, 1752.
+	1308	iv.	Amos Collins Sr. was born in New Haven, CT, on April 25, 1757.
+	1309	v.	Anna Collins was born on April 25, 1757.
		vi.	Joseph Collins was born in New Haven, New Haven, Connecticut, United States, in 1759. He died in Cheshire, New Hampshire, United States, in 1810 at the age of 51.
+	1310	vii.	Sarah Collins was born about 1765.
		viii.	Benjamin Minot Collins was born in New Haven, New Haven, Connecticut, United States, in 1767. He died in Berkshire, Berkshire, Massachusetts, United States, on April 7, 1850, at the age of 83.
		ix.	Thankful Collins was born in New Haven, New Haven, Connecticut, United States, in 1769.

Family of John Merriam and Rebecca Sharp

1159. John[23] Merriam was born on April 25, 1671, in Lynn, Essex, Massachusetts. He was the son of William Merriam (1008) and Elizabeth Breed.

John died at Age: 83 in Meriden, New Haven, Connecticut on October 11, 1754, at the age of 83.

He married Rebecca Sharp.

Rebecca Sharp was born at Age: 0 in Lynn, Essex, Massachusetts on March 26, 1671. She was the daughter of Nathaniel Sharpe and Rebecca Marshall.

Rebecca reached 80 years of age and died at Age: 80 in Lynn, Essex, Massachusetts on April 30, 1751.

Son of John Merriam and Rebecca Sharp:

+	1311	i.	William[24] Merriam was born in Lynn, Essex, Massachusetts, United States, on April 9, 1700.

Family of Elizabeth Benat and William Hobbs

1160. Elizabeth[23] Benat was born on June 4, 1653, in Hambledon, Buckinghamshire, England. She was the daughter of John Bennett (1009) and Anne Quaint.

Elizabeth was baptized in St Olave, Bermondsey, Surrey, England, on December 31, 1652. She died in England.

At the age of 20, Elizabeth married William Hobbs on December 11, 1673, in Hambledon, Buckinghamshire, England, when he was 20 years old.

William was baptized in St Olave, Bermondsey, Surrey, England, on December 31, 1652. William Hobbs was born in Hambleden, Buckinghamshire, England, on April 25, 1653. He was the son of Thomas Hobbs and Mary ?.

William reached 102 years of age and died in Hambleden, Buckinghamshire, England, on July 14, 1755.

Son of Elizabeth Benat and William Hobbs:

+ 1312　i.　William[24] Hobbs was born in Hambleden, Buckinghamshire, England, on February 23, 1674.

Family of Richard Bennett and Anne Alice Pierce

1161. Richard[23] Bennett was born in 1645 in Upper Parish, Isle of Wight, Virginia. He was the son of Richard Bennett (1010) and Anne Barham.

Richard died in Upper, Isle of Wight, Virginia, United States, on March 30, 1720, at the age of 75.

He married Anne Alice Pierce.

Anne Alice Pierce was born in Virginia, United States, in 1660. Anne reached 50 years of age and died in Upper Parish, Isle of Wight, Virginia, United States, in 1710.

Son of Richard Bennett and Anne Alice Pierce:

+ 1313　i.　James[24] Bennett was born in York, Virginia, United States, in 1680.

Family of Elizabeth Harwood and Isaac Dicken

1162. Elizabeth[23] Harwood was born in 1694 in Tuckahoe, Talbot, Maryland. She was the daughter of Peter Harwood (1011) and Elizabeth Taylor.

Elizabeth died in Virginia, United States, in 1735 at the age of 41.

Elizabeth married Isaac Dicken on June 25, 1710, in Gloucester, Gloucester, Virginia.

Isaac Dicken was born in Walton, Staffordshire, England, in 1690. He was the son of Christopher Dicken and Agnes Britian.

Isaac reached 45 years of age and died in Kingston Parish, Gloucester, Virginia, United States, in 1735.

Children of Elizabeth Harwood and Isaac Dicken:

    i.   James[24] Dickens was born in Middlesex, Connecticut, United States, in 1710. He died in Baltimore, Baltimore, Maryland, United States, on July 21, 1763, at the age of 53.

    ii.   Christopher Dickens was born in Culpepper, Virginia, United States, in 1712. He died in Culpeper, Culpeper, Virginia, United States, on August 12, 1778, at the age of 66.

    iii.   Susanna Dickens was born in St George Parish, Spotsylvania, Virginia, United States, on June 14, 1714. She died in Culpeper, Culpeper, Virginia, United States, on May 17, 1784, at the age of 69.

+   1314 iv.   John Dicken was born in Philadelphia, Pennsylvania, United States, in 1720.

Family of Edward Harrington and Mary Ocington

1163. Edward[23] Harrington was born on March 2, 1668, in Watertown, MA. He was the son of Robert Harrington (1012) and Susanna George.

Edward died in Waltham, MA, on January 21, 1736, at the age of 67.

At the age of 24, Edward married Mary Ocington on March 30, 1692, in Watertown, Middlesex, Massachusetts when she was 22 years old.

Mary Ocington was born in Watertown, Middlesex, Massachusetts on September 7, 1669. Mary reached 56 years of age and died in Waltham, Middlesex, Massachusetts on October 23, 1725.

Son of Edward Harrington and Mary Ocington:

+   1315 i.   Samuel[24] Harrington was born in Watertown, Mass, on August 3, 1704.

Family of Elizabeth Bronson and Samuel Stanley

1164. Elizabeth[23] Bronson was born on August 12, 1682, in Lyme, New London, Connecticut. She was the daughter of Abraham Bronson and Anna Griswold (1013).

Elizabeth died in Watertown, Litchfield, Connecticut on October 9, 1767, at the age of 85.

At the age of 19, Elizabeth married Samuel Stanley on July 15, 1702, in Lyme, New London, Connecticut when he was 25 years old.

Samuel Stanley was born in Farmington, Hartford, Connecticut on June 7, 1677. He was the son of John Stanley and Esther Newell.

Son of Elizabeth Bronson and Samuel Stanley:

+ 1316   i.   Abraham[24] Stanley was born in Waterbury, New Haven, Connecticut on April 13, 1705.

Family of Joshua Prescott and Sarah Clifford

1165. Joshua[23] Prescott was born on March 1, 1669, in Hampton, Norfolk, NH. He was the son of James Prescott (1014) and Mary Boulter.

Joshua died in East Kingston, Rockingham, New Hampshire, United States, in 1769 at the age of 99.

At the age of 41, Joshua married Sarah Clifford on October 12, 1710, in Hampton, Rockingham, New Hampshire, United States, when she was 19 years old.

Sarah Clifford was born in Hampton, Rockingham, New Hampshire, United States, on May 10, 1691. Sarah reached 21 years of age and died in Hampton, Rockingham, New Hampshire, United States, in 1713.

Children of Joshua Prescott and Sarah Clifford:

       i.   Nathan[24] Prescott was born in Hampton, Norfolk, New Hampshire, United States, in 1711. He died in Kingston, Rockingham, New Hampshire, United States, in 1764 at the age of 53.

+ 1317   ii.   Joshua Prescott was born in Hampton, New Hampshire in 1713.

       iii.   Edward Prescott was born in Hampton, Norfolk, NH in 1717. He died in Chester, Rockingham, New Hampshire, United States, in 1804 at the age of 87.

- iv. Annie Prescott was born in Hampton, Norfolk, New Hampshire, United States, in 1719. She died in Gilmanton, Belknap, New Hampshire, United States, on August 31, 1799, at the age of 80.
- v. Reuben Prescott was born in Hampton, Norfolk, New Hampshire, United States, in 1721.
- vi. Patience Prescott was born in Hampton, Rockingham, New Hampshire, in 1724. She died in December 1793 at the age of 69.
- vii. John Prescott was born in Hampton, Rockingham, New Hampshire, in 1726. He died in Epping, Rockingham, New Hampshire, on May 2, 1785, at the age of 59.
- viii. Abram Prescott was born in Kingston, Rockingham, New Hampshire, United States, in 1728. He died on July 19, 1733, at the age of 5.

Family of Margaret Tomlinson and Jabez Harger

1166. Margaret[23] Tomlinson was born in 1642 in Derby, New Haven, Connecticut. She was the daughter of Henry Tomlinson (1015) and Alice Johnson.

Margaret died in Derby, New Haven, Connecticut, United States, on March 17, 1698, at the age of 56.

At the age of 20, Margaret married Jabez Harger on November 5, 1662, in Stratford, Fairfield, Connecticut, United States, when he was 20 years old.

Jabez Harger was born in Stratford, Fairfield, CT on February 24, 1642. He was the son of Jabez Harger and Hannah Rose.

Jabez reached 35 years of age and died in Derby, New Haven, Connecticut, United States, in 1678.

Children of Margaret Tomlinson and Jabez Harger:

- i. Abigail[24] Harger was born in Stratford, Fairfield, Connecticut, United States, on March 2, 1672. She died in Connecticut, United States, on December 25, 1733, at the age of 61.
- + 1318 ii. Jabez Harger was born in Stratford, Connecticut, in 1678.

Family of Thomas Noble and Hannah Warriner

1167. Thomas[23] Noble was born in 1632 in Westfield, Hampden, Massachusetts. He was the son of Thomas Noble and Rachel Gardner (1016).

Thomas was known by the title of Deacon. He died in Westfield, Hampden, Massachusetts, United States, on January 20, 1704, at the age of 72.

At the age of 28, Thomas married Hannah Warriner on November 1, 1660, in Springfield, Hampden, Massachusetts, United States, when she was 17 years old.

Hannah Warriner was born in Springfield, Hampden, Massachusetts, United States, on August 17, 1643. Hannah reached 77 years of age and died in Westfield, Hampden, Massachusetts, United States, on May 12, 1721.

Children of Thomas Noble and Hannah Warriner:

+ 1319 i. John[24] Noble was born in Springfield, Hampden, Massachusetts, United States, on March 6, 1662.

ii. Hannah Noble was born in Springfield, Hampden, Massachusetts, United States, on February 24, 1664. She died in Hadley, Hampshire, Massachusetts, United States, on October 13, 1741, at the age of 77.

iii. Thomas Noble was born in Westfield, Hampden, Massachusetts, United States, on January 14, 1665. He died in Westfield, Hampden, Massachusetts, United States, in 1727 at the age of 61.

iv. Matthew Noble was born in Westfield, Hampden, Massachusetts, United States, in February 1668. He died in Sheffield, Berkshire, Massachusetts, United States, in 1744 at the age of 75.

v. Mark Noble was born in West, Nimba, Liberia, on May 16, 1677. He died in Westfield, Hampden, Massachusetts on April 16, 1741, at the age of 63.

vi. James Noble was born in Westfield, Hampden, Massachusetts, United States, on October 1, 1677. He died in Westfield, Hampden, Massachusetts, United States, on January 18, 1711, at the age of 33.

Family of Walter Wagstaffe Bagot and Barbara Legge

1168. Sir Walter Wagstaffe[23] Bagot, 5th Baronet Bagot was born on August 23, 1702, in Staffordshire, England. He was the son of Sir Edward Bagot, 4th Baronet Bagot (1017) and Frances Wagstaffe.

He died in Blithfield Hall, Staffordshire, on January 20, 1768, at the age of 65.

He married Lady Barbara Legge.

Lady Barbara Legge was born in Devon, England, on October 3, 1701. Lady reached 64 years of age and died in Staffordshire, England, on October 29, 1765.

Daughter of Sir Walter Wagstaffe Bagot and Lady Barbara Legge:

+ 1320 i. Barbara[24] Bagot was born in Blithfield, Staffordshire, England, on March 29, 1725.

Family of Margaret Walker and David Morley

1169. Margaret[23] Walker was born in 1740 in Brompton by Sawdon, Yorkshire. She was the daughter of George Walker (1018) and Mary Brown.

Margaret died in Middleton by Pickering, Yorkshire, England, in 1821 at the age of 81.

Margaret married David Morley on Tuesday, April 21, 1761, in Brompton by, Yorkshire, England.

David Morley was born in Danby, Yorkshire, in 1739. He was the son of David Morley and Ann Towlson.

David reached 76 years of age and died in Middleton by Pickering in April 1815.

Children of Margaret Walker and David Morley:

+ 1321 i. David[24] Morley was born in Middleton by Pickering, Yorkshire, England, on October 17, 1764.

  ii. George Morley was born in Pickering, Yorkshire, England, in 1767.

  iii. John Morley was born in Middleton by Pickering, Yorkshire, in 1769. He died in Pickering Workhouse, Pickering, Yorkshire - North Riding, England, in 1849 at the age of 80.

  iv. Ann Morley was born in Pickering, Yorkshire, England, in 1773.

  v. Isaac Morley was born in Pickering, Yorkshire, England, in 1773.

  vi. Christopher Morley was born in Pickering, Yorkshire, England, in 1775.

  vii. Moses Morley was born in Pickering, Yorkshire, England, on February 5, 1777.

  viii. Aaron Morley was born in Pickering, Yorkshire, England, on February 23, 1779. He died in 1863 at the age of 83.

  ix. Hannah Morley was born in Pickering, Yorkshire, England, on April 5, 1781.

  x. Mary Morley was born in Pickering, Yorkshire, England, in 1785.

Family of Joseph Marie Bousquet and Elisabeth Chenet

1170. Joseph Marie[23] Bousquet was born on Tuesday, September 9, 1766, in Richelieu, Quebec, Canada. He was the son of Joseph Bousquet and Marie Judith Messier (1019).

Joseph was baptized in St-Antoine-Sur-Richelieu, Québec, in 1766. He died in Richelieu, Quebec, Canada, on September 19, 1828, at the age of 62.

He married Elisabeth Chenet.

Elisabeth Chenet was born in St-Denis sur Richelieu, Quebec, Canada, on Monday, September 12, 1774. Elisabeth reached 85 years of age and died in St Denis Sur Richelieu, Quebec, Canada, on 6, 1860.

Son of Joseph Marie Bousquet and Elisabeth Chenet:

+ 1322 i. Joseph[24] Bousquet was born in Richelieu, Quebec, Canada, on January 21, 1817.

Family of William Townsend and Hanna Lyon

1171. William[23] Townsend was born in October 1745 in Newport, Newport, Rhode Island. He was the son of Solomon Townsend (1020) and Lydia Tillinghast.

William died in Shipwreck on east coast of Kinsale, Ireland, in October 1781 at the age of 36.

At the age of 31, William married Hanna Lyon on Thursday, July 31, 1777, in New Bedford, Bristol, Massachusetts, United States, when she was 19 years old.

Hanna Lyon was born in Newport, Newport, Rhode Island, United States, on Tuesday, March 21, 1758. She was the daughter of Uriel Lyon and Patience Heath.

Hanna reached 84 years of age and died in Providence co, Rhode Island, on April 1, 1842.

Son of William Townsend and Hanna Lyon:

+ 1323 i. Solomon Townsend[24] was born in Providence, Providence, Rhode Island, United States, on March 29, 1779.

Family of Allan MacLean and Una MacLean

1172. Allan[23] MacLean was born about 1710. He was the son of Donald MacLean (1056) and Isabella MacLean (1021).

Allan was known by the title of 4th Laird of Brolass, 22nd Chief MacLean, 6th Baronet of Morvern. He died on December 10, 1783, at the age of 73.

He married Una MacLean. They had three daughters.

Una MacLean was born about 1714. She was the daughter of John MacLean (899) and Isabella Campbell.

Daughters of Allan MacLean and Una MacLean:

+ 1324   i.   Maria[24] MacLean was born about 1750.
+ 1325   ii.   Sibella Maclean.
        iii.   Ann Maclean.

Family of Catherine Maclean and Lachlan MacLean

1173. Catherine[23] Maclean was born about 1712. She was the daughter of Donald MacLean (1056) and Isabella MacLean (1021).

She married Lachlan MacLean. Lachlan MacLean was born in Isle of Mull, Argyll, Scotland, in 1693. He was the son of Donald MacLean (1059) and Marian MacLeod.

Lachlan was known by the title of 12th MacLean of Coll. Lachlan reached 51 years of age and died on December 31, 1744.

Family of Isabel MacLean and John MacLaine

1174. Isabel[23] MacLean was born about 1715. She was the daughter of Donald MacLean (1056) and Isabella MacLean (1021).

She married John MacLaine.

John MacLaine was born in 1724. He was the son of Allan MacLaine (1049) and Julian MacLean (804).

John was known by the title of 17th MacLean of Lochbuie. John reached 64 years of age and died on February 4, 1788.

Children of Isabel MacLean and John MacLaine:

+ 1326   i.   Archibald[24] MacLaine.
        ii.   Isabel MacLaine.

iii. Catherine MacLaine.

iv. Margaret MacLaine.

Family of Anne MacLean and Allan MacLean

1175. Anne[23] MacLean was born about 1720. She was the daughter of Donald MacLean (1056) and Isabella MacLean (1021).

Anne died about 1755 at the age of 35.

She married Allan MacLean.

Allan MacLean was born in Scotland in 1724. He was the son of Charles Maclean (890) and Isabella Cameron.

Allan was known by the title of 5th MacLean of Drimnin, 6th MacLean of Kinlochaline, 8th MacLean of Morvern. Allan reached 68 years of age and died in Scotland on September 17, 1792.

"Allan, fifth of Drimnin and sixth of Kinlochaline, was the eighth chieftain of the Macleans of Morvern. He was born in 1724. He was wounded in the battle of Culloden. He was served heir male special, in 1749, to John Maclean of Kinlochaline in Knock in Morvern, Killean in Mull, and Scarinish in Tiree." Sinclair, pp. 439

Children of Anne MacLean and Allan MacLean:

+ 1327 i. Charles[24] MacLean was born about 1754.

      ii. Una Maclean.

Family of Hugh MacLean and Elizabeth Houston

1176. Hugh[23] MacLean was born about 1736. He was the son of John MacLean (1022) and Margery MacLachlan (1025).

Hugh was known by the title of 12th MacLean of Ardgour. He died on September 4, 1768, at the age of 32.

Hugh married Elizabeth Houston in 1763.

Children of Hugh MacLean and Elizabeth Houston:

+ 1328 i. Alexander[24] MacLean was born in Ardgour, Argyll, Scotland, on April 16, 1764.

+ 1329 ii. Anna MacLean was born on November 11, 1765.

Family of Donald Roy Maclean and Lillias Grant

1177. Donald Roy[23] Maclean was born about 1770 in Kinlochleven, Mull, Scotland. He was the son of Allan MacLean (1029) and Mary MacLaine (1338).

Donald died in 1853 at the age of 83.

Donald married Lillias Grant in 1793. They had sixteen children.

Lillias Grant was born about 1773. Lillias reached 60 years of age and died in Scotland in 1833.

Children of Donald Roy Maclean and Lillias Grant:

		i.	Allan[24] Maclean was born about 1797. He died in 1818 at the age of 21.
+	1330	ii.	Charles Maclean was born in Edinburgh Parish, Edinburgh, Midlothian, Scotland, on October 11, 1806.
+	1331	iii.	Andrew Maclean was born in Edinburgh, Scotland, in 1812.
		iv.	Fitzroy Jeffries Grafton Maclean was born in 1813. He died in 1858 at the age of 45.
+	1332	v.	Christina Maclean.
		vi.	Colquhoun Maclean. Colquhoun died in off the coast of Africa in 1822.
		vii.	Mary Maclean.
		viii.	Lillian Maclean.
		ix.	Anne Maclean.
		x.	Hector Maclean. Hector died in in the West Indies in 1818.
		xi.	Margaret Maclean.
		xii.	Isabella Maclean.
		xiii.	John Maclean.
		xiv.	Jane Maclean. Jane died in 1822.
		xv.	Alexander Maclean. Alexander died in 1818.
		xvi.	Archibald Maclean.

Family of Mary MacLean and Hector MacLean

1178. Mary[23] MacLean. She is the daughter of Allan MacLean (1029) and Mary MacLaine (1338).

She married Hector MacLean.

Family of Catherine MacLean and John Campbell

1179. Catherine[23] MacLean. She is the daughter of Allan MacLean (1029) and Mary MacLaine (1338).

She married John Campbell.

Family of Colin Maclean and Helen Cameron

1180. Colin[23] Maclean was born about 1756. He was the son of John Maclean (1030) and Margaret Campbell.

Colin died in Jamaica.

He married Helen Cameron.

Family of Donald A McLean and Barbara McLean

1181. Donald A[23] McLean was born in 1735 in Scotland. He was the son of Alexander Maclean (1031) and Mary MacLean.

Donald died in Ontario, Canada, in 1809 at the age of 74.

He married Barbara McLean.

Barbara McLean was born in Scotland in 1740. Barbara reached 63 years of age and died in Ontario, Canada, in 1803.

Children of Donald A McLean and Barbara McLean:

    i.   Donald Watson[24] Mclean was born in Scotland in 1765. He died in Lancaster, Ontario, Canada.

    ii.   Mary Ross was born in Scotland in 1768. She died in Lancaster, Ontario, Canada, on March 11, 1855, at the age of 87.

    iii.   Allan McLean was born in New York in 1776. He died in Lancaster, Ontario, Canada, in 1864 at the age of 88.

Family of Hector Maclean and Helen Campbell

1182. Hector[23] Maclean was born about 1715. He was the son of Donald Maclean (1032) and Anne MacLean (1213).

Hector died in 1796 at the age of 81.

He married Helen Campbell.

Hector Maclean married Ann Campbell.

Son of Hector Maclean and Ann Campbell:

    i.   George^{24} Maclean.

Family of Marion Maclean and Hugh MacLean

1183. Marion^{23} Maclean. She is the daughter of Donald Maclean (1032) and Anne MacLean (1213).

She married Hugh MacLean.

Daughter of Marion Maclean and Hugh MacLean:

+   1333 i.   Flora^{24} MacLean was born in Gribun, Scotland, in August 1784.

Family of Anne Maclean and Alexander MacKinnon

1184. Anne^{23} Maclean was born about 1750. She was the daughter of Hector Maclean (1036) and Julian MacLean.

She married Alexander MacKinnon.

Family of Mary Maclean and Lachlan Ban MacLean

1185. Mary^{23} Maclean was born about 1752. She was the daughter of Hector Maclean (1036) and Julian MacLean.

She married Lachlan Ban MacLean. Lachlan Ban MacLean was born in Kilfinichen, Argyll, Scotland, in 1750.

Lachlan was known by the title of of Bunessan. He reached 69 years of age and died in Bunessan, Kilfinichen, Argyllshire, Scotland, on February 17, 1819.

Family of Archibald Maclean and Prudence French

1186. Archibald^{23} Maclean was born in 1758 in Torrenberg, Isle of Mull, Argyll, Scotland. He was the son of Hector Maclean (1036) and Julian MacLean.

Archibald was employed in Soldier, Magistrate, Member of the House of Assembly. He served in the military at New York Volunteers in New York in 1783.

Archibald was known by the title of Captain. Archibald was buried in MacLean Cemetery in the Flats in February 1830. He died in Nashwaak, New Brunswick, Canada, on February 18, 1830, at the age of 72.

He married Prudence French.

Prudence French was born in Fredericton, New Brunswick, Canada, in 1772. She was buried in New Brunswick, Canada, in October 1800. Prudence reached 28 years of age and died at d. Saturday 11th Oct., St. Marys, York Co., Prudence w/o Archiald McLEAN, age 28. NBRG in St Mary's Parish, York Co., New Brunswick, Canada, on October 11, 1800.

Archibald Maclean married Susan Drummond.

Children of Archibald Maclean and Prudence French:

    i.   Allan^{24} Maclean was born in 1792. He died in 1871 at the age of 79.

+ 1334 ii.   Salome Maclean was born in Nova Scotia, Canada.

Sons of Archibald Maclean and Susan Drummond:

    i.   Archibald Maclean.

    ii.   John Maclean.

Family of Alice Maclean and Archibald Maclean

1187. Alice^{23} Maclean was born about 1760. She was the daughter of Hector Maclean (1036) and Julian MacLean.

Alice died on August 31, 1840, at the age of 80.

She married Archibald Maclean. They had nine children.

Archibald Maclean was born in 1761. He was the son of Alexander Maclean (1038) and Una MacGillivray.

Archibald was known by the title of 2nd MacLean of Pennycross. Archibald reached 69 years of age and died on February 13, 1830.

"Archibald, only son of Dr. Alexander Maclean, was born in 1761, and was served heir to his father in 1800. He was for some time major of the 3d regiment of the Argyleshire Fencibles. He was the writer of the Pennycross MS." Sinclair, pp. 448

Children of Alice Maclean and Archibald Maclean:

+ 1335 i.   Alexander^{24} Maclean was born in Kilfinichen, Argyll, on May 3, 1791.

+ 1336 ii. Allan Thomas Maclean was born in Scotland in May 1793.

iii. Charles James Maclean. Charles died in Calcutta, India, in May 1837.

iv. Mary Maclean.

v. John Maclean. John died in Nassau, Bahamas, in 1822.

vi. Julia Maclean.

vii. Hector Maclean. Hector died in London, England, in 1834.

viii. Lachlan Maclean. Lachlan died in Colombo in 1830.

ix. Archibald Donald Maclean.

Family of Catherine Maclean and Alexander Sinclair

1188. Catherine[23] Maclean. She is the daughter of Hector Maclean (1036) and Julian MacLean.

She married Alexander Sinclair.

Family of Archibald Maclean and Alice Maclean

1189. Archibald[23] Maclean was born in 1761. He was the son of Alexander Maclean (1038) and Una MacGillivray.

Archibald was known by the title of 2nd MacLean of Pennycross. He died on February 13, 1830, at the age of 69.

He married Alice Maclean. They had nine children.

Alice Maclean was born about 1760. Alice reached 80 years of age and died on August 31, 1840.

Children of Archibald Maclean and Alice Maclean:

+ 1335 i. Alexander[24] Maclean was born in Kilfinichen, Argyll, on May 3, 1791.

+ 1336 ii. Allan Thomas Maclean was born in Scotland in May 1793.

iii. Charles James Maclean. Charles died in Calcutta, India, in May 1837.

iv. Mary Maclean.

v. John Maclean. John died in Nassau, Bahamas, in 1822.

vi. Julia Maclean.

vii. Hector Maclean. Hector died in London, England, in 1834.

viii. Lachlan Maclean. Lachlan died in Colombo in 1830.

ix. Archibald Donald Maclean.

Family of Catherine Maclean and Donald MacLean

1190. Catherine[23] Maclean. She is the daughter of Alexander Maclean (1038) and Una MacGillivray.

She married Donald MacLean.

Lachlan MacLean

1191. Lachlan[23] MacLean was born about 1730. He was the son of Donald MacLean (1039) and Ann MacLean.

Lachlan died in Tennesee.

Children of Lachlan MacLean:

i. John[24] MacLean.

ii. Joshua MacLean.

iii. Gabriel MacLean.

iv. Charles-Durell MacLean.

v. Susan MacLean.

vi. Mary Ann MacLean.

vii. Isabel MacLean.

Family of Alexander MacLean and Chriatina MacLean

1192. Alexander[23] MacLean was born about 1737. He was the son of Donald MacLean (1039) and Ann MacLean.

Alexander died in Manitoba, Canada.

He married Chriatina MacLean. She is the daughter of John MacLean.

Family of Margaret MacLaine and Donald Campbell

1193. Margaret[23] MacLaine. She is the daughter of Murdock MacLaine (1047) and Anne Campbell.

She married Donald Campbell.

Family of Elizabeth MacLaine and Allan MacLaine

1194. Elizabeth[23] MacLaine. She is the daughter of Murdock MacLaine (1047) and Anne Campbell.

She married Allan MacLaine.

Family of Isabella MacLaine and John Scroyne

1195. Isabella[23] MacLaine. She is the daughter of Murdock MacLaine (1047) and Anne Campbell.

She married John Scroyne.

Family of Lachlan MacLaine and Katherine Macdougall

1196. Lachlan[23] MacLaine was born in 1695 in Lochbuie, Isle of Mull, Argyle, Scotland. He was the son of John MacLaine (1048) and Isabelle MacDougall.

Lachlan was known by the title of 15th MacLean of Lochbuie. He died on December 31, 1744, at the age of 49.

He married Katherine Macdougall.

Katherine Macdougall was born in of, Dunolly, Scotland, in 1702.

Children of Lachlan MacLaine and Katherine Macdougall:

- i. Hector[24] MacLaine was born in Lochbuie, Argyll, Scotland, United Kingdom, about 1727. He was known by the title of 16th MacLean of Lochbuie.

   Hector died about 1749 at the age of 22.

+ 1337 ii. Anne MacLaine.

+ 1338 iii. Mary MacLaine was born in 1740.

Family of John MacLaine and Isabel MacLean

1197. John[23] MacLaine was born in 1724. He was the son of Allan MacLaine (1049) and Julian MacLean (804).

John was known by the title of 17th MacLean of Lochbuie. He died on February 4, 1788, at the age of 64.

He married Isabel MacLean.

Isabel MacLean was born about 1715.

John MacLaine married ?.

Children of John MacLaine and Isabel MacLean:

+ 1326   i.   Archibald[24] MacLaine.

           ii.   Isabel MacLaine.

           iii.   Catherine MacLaine.

           iv.   Margaret MacLaine.

Son of John MacLaine and ?:

           i.   Gillean MacLean.

Family of Julian MacLaine and James Maclean

1198.   Julian[23] MacLaine was born about 1700. She was the daughter of Allan MacLaine (1049) and Julian MacLean (804).

        She married James Maclean.

        James Maclean was born about 1698. He was the son of Donald MacLean (1056) and an unknown woman.

Son of Julian MacLaine and James Maclean:

+ 1339   i.   John[24] Maclean was born about 1735.

Family of Finvola MacLaine and John Hector Og MacLean

1199.   Finvola[23] MacLaine. She is the daughter of Allan MacLaine (1049) and Julian MacLean (804).

        She married John Hector Og MacLean. They had three sons.

        John Hector Og MacLean was born about 1660. He was the son of Hector Og MacLean (915) and Janet McNeil.

        John is deceased. drown crossing in a small boat to Mull.

Sons of Finvola MacLaine and John Hector Og MacLean:

+ 1340   i.   Donald[24] MacLean was born about 1685.

           ii.   Hector MacLean was born about 1690. He is deceased. left no issue.

+ 1341   iii.   John MacLean was born about 1700.

Family of Murdoch MacLaine and Jane Campbell

1200.   Murdoch[23] MacLaine was born in 1730. He was the son of Lachlan MacLaine (1052) and Flora MacQuarrie (1054).

Murdoch was known by the title of 19th MacLaine of Lochbuie. He died on July 5, 1804, at the age of 74.

Murdoch married Jane Campbell on Tuesday, February 14, 1786. They had eleven children.

Jane died on August 18, 1824.

Children of Murdoch MacLaine and Jane Campbell:

+ 1342 i. Murdoch[24] MacLaine was born on August 1, 1791.
- ii. John MacLaine was born on August 22, 1792. He died at killed in action in a native riot in Ceylon on January 14, 1818, at the age of 25.
- iii. Jane MacLaine.
- iv. Flora MacLaine.
- v. Margaret MacLaine.
- vi. Phoebe MacLaine.
- vii. Elizabeth MacLaine.
- viii. Harriet MacLaine.
- ix. Catherine MacLaine.
- x. Mary MacLaine.
- xi. Jane Jarvis MacLaine.

Allan MacLaine

1201. Allan[23] MacLaine. He was the son of Lachlan MacLaine (1052) and Flora MacQuarrie (1054).

Allan died after 1776.

Sons of Allan MacLaine:

- i. Allan[24] MacLaine.
- ii. William MacLaine.

John MacLaine

1202. John[23] MacLaine. He is the son of Lachlan MacLaine (1052) and Flora MacQuarrie (1054).

Child of John MacLaine:

      i.   Flora Ann[24] MacLaine.

Family of John McLean and Mary Mckinnon

1203. John[23] McLean was born about 1692 in Scotland. He was the son of John MacLean (1053).

He was buried in Alfordsville Township, Robeson, North Carolina, United States, in 1787. John died in Alfordsville, Robeson, North Carolina, United States, on March 2, 1787, at the age of 95.

John married Mary Mckinnon in Robeson, North Carolina. They had three sons.

Mary Mckinnon was born in Isle Of Skye, Scotland, in 1715. Mary reached 105 years of age and died in Dillon, Dillon, South Carolina, United States, in 1820.

Sons of John McLean and Mary Mckinnon:

+ 1343   i.   Daniel[24] McLean was born in Skye, Argyllshire, Scotland, in 1736.

          ii.   John McLean was born in Skye Isle, Inverness-shire, Scotland, in 1749. He died in Robeson, North Carolina, in October 1815 at the age of 66. John was buried in Alfordsville Township, Robeson, North Carolina, United States, in October 1815.

          iii. Malcolm Mclean was born in Skye, Highland, Scotland, United Kingdom, about 1750. He died in Alfordsville, Robeson, North Carolina, United States, in October 1815 at the age of 65.

Family of James Maclean and Julian MacLaine

1204. James[23] Maclean was born about 1698. He was the son of Donald MacLean (1056) and an unknown woman.

He married Julian MacLaine.

Julian MacLaine was born about 1700.

Son of James Maclean and Julian MacLaine:

+ 1339   i.   John[24] Maclean was born about 1735.

Family of Christina MacLean and John MacLean

1205. Christina[23] MacLean was born in 1718. He or she was a child of Allan MacLean (1057).

Christina died in March 1808 at the age of 90.

He or she married John MacLean.

John MacLean was born in 1724. He was the son of Donald MacLean (723).

John reached 84 years of age and died in March 1808.

Children of Christina MacLean and John MacLean:

      i.   Allan[24] MacLean.

      ii.   Donald MacLean.

      iii. Marion MacLean.

Family of Hector MacLean and Mary Campbell

1206. Hector[23] MacLean was born about 1686 in Coll, Argyll, Scotland. He was the son of Donald MacLean (1059) and Isabel MacLeod.

Hector was known by the title of 12th MacLean of Coll. He died on November 6, 1756, at the age of 70.

He married Mary Campbell. They had five daughters.

Hector MacLean married Jean Campbell.

Daughters of Hector MacLean and Mary Campbell:

      i.   Isabella[24] MacLean.

      ii.   Margaret MacLean.

      iii. Mary MacLean.

      iv. Una MacLean.

      v.   Sibella MacLean.

Family of Hugh MacLean and Jannet MacLeod

1207. Hugh[23] MacLean was born about 1692 in Isle od Coll, Scotland. He was the son of Donald MacLean (1059) and Marian MacLeod.

Hugh was known by the title of 13th MacLean of Coll. He died in Coll, Argyll, Scotland, on May 4, 1786, at the age of 94.

He married Jannet MacLeod.

Jannet MacLeod was born in Tallisker, Isle os Skye, Scotland, in 1731. Jannet reached 49 years of age and died in Isle Skye, Inverness-shire, Scotland, on July 21, 1780.

Children of Hugh MacLean and Jannet MacLeod:

+ 1344 i. Alexander[24] MacLean was born in Coll, Argyll, Scotland, on July 14, 1753.

 ii. Donald MacLean. Donald died at drowned with eight others in in the Sound of Ulva on September 25, 1774.

 iii. Hector MacLean.

 iv. Norman MacLean.

 v. Roderick MacLean.

 vi. Allan MacLean.

 vii. Marian MacLean.

Family of Lachlan MacLean and Catherine Maclean

1208. Lachlan[23] MacLean was born in 1693 in Isle of Mull, Argyll, Scotland. He was the son of Donald MacLean (1059) and Marian MacLeod.

Lachlan was known by the title of 12th MacLean of Coll. He died on December 31, 1744, at the age of 51.

He married Catherine Maclean. Catherine Maclean was born about 1712.

Family of John Ardfinaig MacLean and Catherine McLean

1209. John Ardfinaig[23] MacLean was born in 1696 in Isle of Mull, Argyll, Scotland. He was the son of Donald MacLean (1059) and Marian MacLeod.

John died in 1756 at the age of 60.

He married Catherine McLean.

Catherine McLean was born in Isle of Mull, Argyll, Scotland, about 1696. Catherine reached 66 years of age and died in 1762.

Son of John Ardfinaig MacLean and Catherine McLean:

+ 1345 i. Lachlan[24] McLean was born in Glentarsin, Inverchoalain, Argyll, Scot., in 1714.

Family of Catherine MacLean and Hector Maclean

1210. Catherine[23] MacLean. He or she is a child of Donald MacLean (1059) and Marian MacLeod.

He or she married Hector Maclean.

Hector Maclean was born about 1700. Hector reached 84 years of age and died about 1784.

Daughter of Catherine MacLean and Hector Maclean:

      i.   Mary[24] Maclean was born about 1730. She died in 1826 at the age of 96.

Family of Lachlan MacLean and Mary MacDonald

1211. Lachlan[23] MacLean was born about 1670 in Isle of Muck, Argyll, Scotland. He was the son of Hector MacLean (936) and Catherine MacLean (1060).

Lachlan was known by the title of 3rd MacLean of Muck. He died on December 31, 1744, at the age of 74.

He married Mary MacDonald.

Mary MacDonald was born in Bellfinlay, Scotland, about 1695. Mary reached 84 years of age and died in Scotland in 1779.

Children of Lachlan MacLean and Mary MacDonald:

+ 1346 i.   Hector[24] MacLean was born about 1697.

+ 1347 ii.   Catherine MacLean was born in Isle of Muck, Argyll, Scotland, about 1705.

+ 1348 iii. Donald MacLean was born in Isle of Muck, Argyll, Scotland, about 1725.

            iv. Mary MacLean.

Family of Hector MacLean and Marian MacLean

1212. Hector[23] MacLean was born about 1672. He was the son of Hector MacLean (936) and Catherine MacLean (1060).

Hector is deceased. died young without children.

He married Marian MacLean. She is the daughter of Lachlan MacLean.

Family of Anne MacLean and Donald Maclean

1213. Anne[23] MacLean was born about 1690. She was the daughter of Donald Maclean (1064) and Mary Campbell.

She married Donald Maclean.

Donald Maclean was born about 1685.

Children of Anne MacLean and Donald Maclean:

+ 1182   i.   Hector[24] Maclean was born about 1715.

          ii.   George Maclean.

+ 1183   iii.   Marion Maclean.

Family of Christianna Maclean and Alexander MacLean

1214. Christianna[23] Maclean was born about 1700. She was the daughter of Donald Maclean (1064) and Mary Campbell.

She married Alexander MacLean.

Family of Lachlan Maclean and Margaret Smith

1215. Lachlan[23] Maclean was born about 1710. He was the son of Donald Maclean (1064) and Mary Campbell.

Lachlan was known by the title of 7th MacLean of Torloisk. He died in 1799 at the age of 89.

He married Margaret Smith.

Daughter of Lachlan Maclean and Margaret Smith:

+ 1349   i.   Marianne[24] Maclean was born in Torloisk, Mull, Argyllshire, Scotland, in 1765.

Daughter of Lachlan Maclean:

+ 1349   i.   Marianne[24] Maclean was born in Torloisk, Mull, Argyllshire, Scotland, in 1765.

Family of Allan Maclean and Janet MacLean

1216. Allan[23] Maclean was born about 1725. He was the son of Donald Maclean (1064) and Mary Campbell.

Allan was known by the title of General. He died in London, England, in March 1797 at the age of 72.

He married Janet MacLean. Janet MacLean was born about 1758. She was the daughter of Donald MacLean (1340) and Mary Dickson.

Janet reached 78 years of age and died in May 1836.

Archibald Maclean

1217. Archibald[23] Maclean. He was the son of Donald Maclean (1064) and Mary Campbell.

Archibald was buried about 1800.

Son of Archibald Maclean:

+ 1350   i.   John[24] Maclean.

Family of Alicia Maclean and Lachlan MacQuarrie

1218. Alicia[23] Maclean. She is the daughter of Donald Maclean (1064) and Mary Campbell.

She married Lachlan MacQuarrie.

Family of Elizabeth Maclean and Lachlan MacLean

1219. Elizabeth[23] Maclean. She is the daughter of Donald Maclean (1064) and Mary Campbell.

She married Lachlan MacLean. Lachlan was using a title in of Garmony.

Elizabeth Maclean married James Parke. They have one son.

Son of Elizabeth Maclean and James Parke:

     i.   James Allan[24] Parke.

Family of William McLean and Della Dolla Pittman

1220. William[23] McLean was born in 1690 in Edinburg, Scotland. He was the son of William McLean (1068) and Irene.

William died in Edinburgh, Midlothia, Scotland, on July 10, 1718, at the age of 28.

He married Della Dolla Pittman.

Della Dolla Pittman was born in Edinburgh, Midlothian, Scotland, in 1690. Della is deceased.

Son of William McLean and Della Dolla Pittman:

+ 1351 i. Andrew Francis[24] McLane was born in Edinburgh, Midlothian, Scotland, in 1710.

Family of Anne Maclean and John MacLean

1221. Anne[23] Maclean was born in 1707 in Isle of Mull, Argyll, Scotland. She was the daughter of John Mclean (1075) and Isabel MacLean.

She married John MacLean. John MacLean was born about 1700. He was the son of Allan MacLean.

John was using a title in of Grishipol.

Family of Mary MacLean and Alexander MacLean

1222. Mary[23] MacLean was born in 1709 in Isle of Mull, Argyll, Scotland. She was the daughter of John Mclean (1075) and Isabel MacLean.

She married Alexander MacLean. Alexander MacLean was born about 1705. He was the son of Donald MacLean.

Family of Catherine Maclean and John MacLean

1223. Catherine[23] Maclean was born in 1714 in Argylleshire, Scotland. She was the daughter of John Mclean (1075) and Isabel MacLean.

Catherine died in 1772 at the age of 58.

She married John MacLean. John MacLean was born about 1709. He was the son of Archibald Og MacLean.

Family of Alexander Maclean and Christy MacLean

1224. Alexander[23] Maclean was born in 1722 in Isle of Mull, Argyll, Scotland. He was the son of John Mclean (1075) and Isabel MacLean.

Alexander died in Isle of Mull, Argyll, Scotland, on January 28, 1765, at the age of 43.

Alexander married Christy MacLean in 1750. They had three sons.

Christy MacLean was born about 1728. She was the daughter of Donald MacLean.

Sons of Alexander Maclean and Christy MacLean:

  i. John[24] Maclean was born about 1757.

  ii. Donald Maclean was born about 1760.

iii. Lachlan Maclean was born about 1762.

Family of Hugh McLean and Catherine Cameron

1225. Hugh[23] McLean was born in 1715 in Kilmaluag Tyree Scotland. He was the son of Lachlan McLean (1076) and Mary MacArthur.

Hugh died in Morvern, Argyll, Scotland, in March 1784 at the age of 69.

Hugh married Catherine Cameron in 1756 in Tyree, Scotland.

Catherine Cameron was born in Tyree Scotland in 1716.

Son of Hugh McLean and Catherine Cameron:

+ 1352 i. John[24] McLean was born in Kilmaluaig Tyree Scotland in 1756.

Family of Margaret Mclean and Alexander MacLean

1226. Margaret[23] Mclean was born on May 22, 1745. She was the daughter of Hector McLean (1077) and Jennet MacLean.

Margaret died before 1752.

She married Alexander MacLean.

Family of Florence Mclean and Lachlan McLean

1227. Florence[23] Mclean was born on October 15, 1747. She was the daughter of Hector McLean (1077) and Jennet MacLean.

She married Lachlan McLean.

Family of Hugh McLean and Barbara MacLean

1228. Hugh[23] McLean was born about 1730. He was the son of John McLean (1078) and Mary MacLean.

He married Barbara MacLean. Barbara MacLean was born about 1732. She was the daughter of Archibald MacLean (828) and Susan Campbell.

Family of Alexander MacLean and Eunice Mackinnon

1229. Alexander[23] MacLean. He is the son of John MacLean (1079) and ? Campbell.

He married Eunice Mackinnon. They have six children.

Children of Alexander MacLean and Eunice Mackinnon:

i. Lachlan[24] MacLean.

ii. Donald MacLean.

iii. Malcolm MacLean.

iv. Christy MacLean.

v. Mary MacLean.

vi. Catherine MacLean.

Family of Alexander McLean and Johannah Smith

1230. Alexander[23] McLean was born on July 18, 1747, in Vernon, Tolland, Connecticut. He was the son of Allan MacLean (1080) and Mary Loomis.

Alexander served in the military between July 1778 and September 1778. Served as Boatswains Mate aboard the "Oliver Cromwell". He died at Age: 59 in Vernon, Connecticut, on June 30, 1806, at the age of 58. Alexander was buried in Vernon, Tolland County, Connecticut in July 1806.

At the age of 21, Alexander married Johannah Smith on Tuesday, December 27, 1768, when she was 20 years old.

Johannah Smith was born in N. Bolton, Connecticut, on July 19, 1748. Johannah reached 73 years of age and died at Age: 75 in Connecticut on May 29, 1822. She was buried in Vernon, Tolland County, Connecticut.

Children of Alexander McLean and Johannah Smith:

i. Hannah[24] McLean was born in N. Bolton, Tolland, Connecticut, on December 7, 1769. She died on February 20, 1841, at the age of 71.

ii. Alexander McLean was born in North Bolton, CT, on June 12, 1772. Alexander was buried at West Cemetery in Manchester, Connecticut in November 1843. He died at Age: 71 in Manchester, Hartford, Connecticut, on November 11, 1843, at the age of 71.

iii. Mary McLean was born on November 5, 1774. She died on October 18, 1776, at the age of 1.

iv. Francis McLean was born in S. Bolton, Tolland, Connecticut, on September 26, 1777. He died on November 6, 1861, at the age of 84.

v. Allen McLean was born on June 20, 1781. Allen was buried in Simsbury, Hartford County, Connecticut in March 1861. He died on March 19, 1861, at the age of 79.

vi. Mary McLean was born on January 15, 1785. Mary was buried in Vernon, Tolland County, Connecticut in December 1805. She died on December 27, 1805, at the age of 20.

vii. Rosannah McLean was born on August 14, 1789. She died on September 29, 1808, at the age of 19. Rosannah was buried in Vernon, Tolland County, Connecticut in October 1808.

Family of Duncan MacLean and Mary MacLean

1231. Duncan[23] MacLean was born about 1690. He was the son of Angus MacLean (1086) and Elizabeth Campbell.

Duncan died in Uisken, Argyll, Scotland, in 1770 at the age of 80.

He married Mary MacLean. They had four sons. She is the daughter of John MacLean.

Sons of Duncan MacLean and Mary MacLean:

    i. Alexander[24] MacLean was born about 1715.

    ii. John MacLean.

    iii. Archibald MacLean.

    iv. Duncan MacLean. Duncan died in 1770.

Family of John MacLean and Mary MacAulay

1232. John[23] MacLean was born about 1770 in Isle of Rum, Scotland. He was the son of Hugh MacLean (1088) and Flora MacLean.

He married Mary MacAulay.

Mary MacAulay was born about 1775.

Son of John MacLean and Mary MacAulay:

+ 1353 i. John[24] MacLean was born in Stornoway, Ross-shire, Scotland, in 1802.

Family of Farquhar McLean and Elizabeth McQuarrie

1233. Farquhar[23] McLean was born in 1743. He was the son of Farquhar McLean (1093).

Farquhar died in 1822 at the age of 79.

Farquhar married Elizabeth McQuarrie in 1771.

Elizabeth McQuarrie was born in Scotland, United Kingdom. She was the daughter of Lachlan McQuarrie.

Children of Farquhar McLean and Elizabeth McQuarrie:

    i.   Murdock[24] McLean was born in Kilninian, Argyll, Scotland, United Kingdom, on September 19, 1774. He is deceased.

    ii.   Mary Mclean. Mary is deceased.

Family of Donald McLean and Janet Robertson

1234. Donald[23] McLean was born on November 27, 1737, in Luss, Dunbartonshire, Scotland. He was the son of Hector McLean (1094) and Elizabeth McHutcheon.

He married Janet Robertson.

Janet Robertson was born in Cairnie, Aberdeenshire, Scotland, on September 28, 1740. Janet was baptized in Cairnie By Huntly, Aberdeen, Scotland, on September 29, 1740. She reached 32 years of age and died about 1773.

Son of Donald McLean and Janet Robertson:

+   1354   i.   Willian[24] McLean was born about 1768.

Family of John McLean and Catherine Blair

1235. John[23] McLean was born on January 31, 1746, in Luss, Dunbartonshire, Scotland. He was the son of Hector McLean (1094) and Elizabeth McHutcheon.

At the age of 19, John married Catherine Blair on Wednesday, April 24, 1765, in Strathlachlan, Argyll, Scotland, when she was 21 years old.

Catherine Blair was born in Port Glasgow, Renfrew, Scotland, on September 10, 1743. She was the daughter of David Blair and Margaret Yuill.

Catherine reached 76 years of age and died in Lochgoilhead, Argyleshire, Scotland, about 1820.

Children of John McLean and Catherine Blair:

+   1355   i.   Hector[24] McLean was born in Strathlachlan, Argyll, Scotland, in January 1765.

+   1356   ii.   Malcolm McLean was born in Lochgoilhead, Argyleshire, Scotland, on January 26, 1771.

- iii. Mary McLean was born in Lochgoilhead, Argyleshire, Scotland, in August 1773.
- iv. Margaret McLean was born in Lochgoilhead, Argyleshire, Scotland, in February 1776.
- v. Catherine McLean was born in Lochgoilhead, Argyleshire, Scotland, in May 1778.
- vi. Donald McLean was born in Lochgoilhead, Argyleshire, Scotland, in December 1780.

Family of John McLean and Mary McPherson

1236. John[23] McLean was born on Friday, February 8, 1765, in Inverchaolain, Argyllshire, Scotland. He was the son of Lachlan McLean (1095) and Margaret Black.

John worked as a weaver in Inverchaolain, Argyll, Scotland, UK. He died in Inverchaolain, Argyll, Scotland, UK, on August 28, 1844, at the age of 79. John was buried in Inverchaolain, Argyll, Scotland, UK.

John married Mary McPherson on Thursday, January 17, 1793, in Inverchaolain, Argyll, Scotland, UK.

Mary McPherson was born in Argyll, Scotland, UK, about 1769. Mary died after 1841.

Children of John McLean and Mary McPherson:
- i. Catherine[24] McLean was born in Inverchaolain, Argyll, Scotland, UK, on August 30, 1794. She died in Inverchaolain, Argyll, Scotland, UK, about 1816 at the age of 21. Catherine was buried in Inverchaolain, Argyll, Scotland, UK.
- ii. John McLean was born in Inverchaolain, Argyll, Scotland, UK, on April 23, 1796. He died in Inverchaolain, Argyll, Scotland, UK, about 1826 at the age of 29. John was buried in Inverchaolain, Argyll, Scotland, UK.
- iii. Lachlan McLean was born in Inverchaolain, Argyll, Scotland, UK, on August 4, 1798. He died in Inverchaolain, Argyll, Scotland, UK, about 1823 at the age of 24. Lachlan was buried in Inverchaolain, Argyll, Scotland, UK.
- iv. Peter McLean was born in Inverchaolain, Argyll, Scotland, UK, on February 14, 1802. He died at Acute pneumonia in Dunoon

and Kilmun, Argyll, Scotland, UK, on March 7, 1877, at the age of 75.

Family of Allan MacLean and Margaret MacFadyen

1237. Allan[23] MacLean was born about 1760. He was the son of John MacLean (1097).

He married Margaret MacFadyen. She is the daughter of Neil MacFadyen.

Children of Allan MacLean and Margaret MacFadyen:

- \+ 1357   i.   John[24] MacLean was born in Caolas, Tiree, on January 8, 1787.
- \+ 1358   ii.   Donald Cubair MacLean.
- \+ 1359   iii.   Charles MacLean.
-          iv.   Neil MacLean.
-          v.   Mary MacLean.

Charles MacLean

1238. Charles[23] MacLean. He is the son of Lachlan MacLean (1098).

Son of Charles MacLean:

- \+ 1360   i.   Donald[24] MacLean.

John MacLean

1239. John[23] MacLean was born about 1740. He was the son of Charles MacLean (1099).

John died in 1760 at the age of 20.

Children of John MacLean:

- \+ 1361   i.   Hector[24] MacLean.
-          ii.   Isabel MacLean.

Family of John MacLean and Ann MacLean

1240. John[23] MacLean. He is the son of Rory Mor MacLean (1100).

He married Ann MacLean. They had four sons.

Sons of John MacLean and Ann MacLean:

-          i.   James[24] MacLean. James died about 1828.
-          ii.   Hector MacLean. Hector died about 1828.

iii. Neil MacLean. Neil died about 1830.

iv. John MacLean. John died about 1830.

Angus MacLean

1241. Angus[23] MacLean. He is the son of Donald MacLean (1102).

Sons of Angus MacLean:

      i. Donald[24] MacLean.

      ii. Gillespick Mor MacLean.

      iii. John MacLean.

Family of Jonas McLean and Mary Trumpour

1242. Jonas[23] McLean was born on Thursday, September 3, 1772, in Montgomery, Orange, New York. He was the son of John McLean (1103) and Anna Margaretha Crist.

Jonas died in NY, Orange, California.

He married Mary Trumpour.

Mary Trumpour was born in Montgomery, Orange, New York, United States, on Sunday, February 14, 1773. Mary died in Dryden, Tompkins, New York, United States, in 1774.

Son of Jonas McLean and Mary Trumpour:

+ 1362   i. Harvey[24] McLean was born in Montgomery, Orange, New York, United States, on June 25, 1797.

Family of Charles Maxwell MacLean and Sarah Amelia Marshall

1243. Charles Maxwell[23] MacLean was born on Sunday, December 11, 1791. He was the son of William MacLean (1105) and Elizabeth MacLean.

Charles died on December 16, 1864, at the age of 73.

Charles married Sarah Amelia Marshall in 1823.

Sarah died on March 21, 1837.

Daughter of Charles Maxwell MacLean and Sarah Amelia Marshall:

      i. Charlotte Amelia[24] MacLean was born in 1824. She died in Inverness, Scotland, on November 1, 1910, at the age of 86.

Family of William MacLean and Elizabeth Henderson

1244. William[23] MacLean was born on Monday, November 4, 1793. He was the son of William MacLean (1105) and Elizabeth MacLean.

William died on June 19, 1872, at the age of 78.

William married Elizabeth Henderson on Monday, June 6, 1825. They had nine children. She was the daughter of Thomas Henderson.

Elizabeth died on July 6, 1880.

Children of William MacLean and Elizabeth Henderson:

    i. William Thomas Henderson[24] MacLean was born on April 9, 1826. He was known by the title of 12th MacLean of Dochgarroch.

    William died on March 15, 1892, at the age of 65.

+ 1363 ii. Allan MacLean was born on May 29, 1827.

    iii. Jessie MacLean was born on December 19, 1835. She died on February 4, 1870, at the age of 34.

    iv. Marian MacLean was born on July 29, 1837. She died on March 29, 1909, at the age of 71.

    v. Thomas Henderson MacLean.

    vi. Eliza MacLean.

    vii. Helen MacLean.

    viii. Annie MacLean.

    ix. Isabella MacLean.

Family of William MacLean and Mary MacIntosh

1245. William[23] MacLean. He was the son of Charles MacLean (1108) and Mary MacIntosh.

William died in 1759. killed at the storming of Guadaloupe.

William married Mary MacIntosh on November 6, 1751.

Family of Moses McLean and Sarah Charlesworth

1246. Moses[23] McLean was born in 1737. He was the son of William Mclean (1109) and Elizabeth Rule.

Moses was known by the title of Col. Moses was buried in Chillicothe, Ross County, Ohio in 1810. He died in Chillicothe, Ross, Ohio on September 10, 1810, at the age of 73.

At the age of 26, Moses married Sarah Charlesworth on Thursday, April 14, 1763, in Abington, Montgomery, Pennsylvania, United States, when she was 20 years old.

Sarah Charlesworth was born on December 13, 1742. Sarah reached 35 years of age and died in Marsh Creek Settlement, York, Pennsylvania, United States, in 1778.

Moses McLean married Susanne Dick.

Son of Moses McLean and Sarah Charlesworth:

+   1364   i.   Samuel D.[24] McLean was born in Pennsylvania about 1780.

Family of Hugh MacLean and ? Manicol

1247.   Hugh[23] MacLean was born about 1735. He was the son of Robert MacLean (1110) and ? Fraser.

He married ? Manicol. They had three sons.

Sons of Hugh MacLean and ? Manicol:

         i.   Malcolm[24] MacLean was born about 1770.

         ii.   Robert MacLean.

         iii.   Peter MacLean.

Family of Hugh MacLean and Mary Stewart

1248.   Hugh[23] MacLean was born about 1725. He was the son of Lachlan MacLean (1115).

Hugh was known by the title of 10th MacLean of Kingerloch. He died in 1784 at the age of 59.

He married Mary Stewart.

Family of Elizabeth Borthwick and James Tweedie

1249.   Elizabeth[23] Borthwick was born on November 12, 1676, in Inveresk, East Lothian, Scotland. She was the daughter of Thomas Borthwick (1116) and Bessie Notman.

Elizabeth died in North Leith, Midlothian, Scotland.

She married James Tweedie.

James Tweedie was born in Leith, Midlothian, Scotland, in 1675. James reached 19 years of age and died in Hamilton, Midlothian, Scotland, in 1694.

Daughter of Elizabeth Borthwick and James Tweedie:

+ 1365 i. Mary[24] Tweedie was born in Leith, Midlothian, Scotland, on March 16, 1698.

Family of Hinchey Warren and Rachel Anderson

1250. Hinchey[23] Warren was born in 1727 in Virginia. He was the son of Robert Warren (1117) and Judith Anderson.

Hinchey died in Georgia in 1803 at the age of 76.

Hinchey married Rachel Anderson in 1749 in Northampton, North Carolina.

Rachel Anderson was born in North Carolina in 1728. Rachel reached 58 years of age and died in North Carolina in 1786.

Son of Hinchey Warren and Rachel Anderson:

+ 1366 i. Josiah[24] Warren was born in Virginia on February 18, 1759.

Family of Joseph Hardy and Mary Burbank

1251. Joseph[23] Hardy was born about 1670. He was the son of John Hardy (1118) and Mary Frances Jackman.

Joseph died in Bradford, Essex, Massachusetts Bay, British Colonial America. He was buried in Groveland, Essex County, Massachusetts, United States of America.

He married Mary Burbank.

Mary Burbank was born on November 26, 1675. Mary reached 86 years of age and died in Bradford, Essex County, Massachusetts, United States of America, on September 3, 1762. She was buried in Groveland, Essex County, Massachusetts, United States of America.

Sons of Joseph Hardy and Mary Burbank:

+ 1367 i. James[24] Hardy was born in Bradford, Essex, Massachusetts on April 14, 1699.

+ 1368 ii. David Hardy.

Family of Josiah Haskell and Sarah Canady

1252. Josiah[23] Haskell was born on June 18, 1686, in Plymouth, Plymouth, Massachusetts. He was the son of John Haskell (1119) and Patience Soule.

Josiah died in Freetown, Bristol, Massachusetts, United States, in 1733 at the age of 46.

He married Sarah Canady.

Sarah Canady was born in Plymouth, Plymouth, Massachusetts on November 11, 1693. Sarah reached 34 years of age and died in Freetown, Bristol, Massachusetts on March 29, 1728.

Son of Josiah Haskell and Sarah Canady:

+ 1369 i. Benjamin[24] Haskell was born in Plymouth, Plymouth, Massachusetts, United States, on March 8, 1719.

Family of Lucy Woodbridge and Daniel Epps

1253. Lucy[23] Woodbridge was born on March 13, 1641. She was the daughter of John Woodbridge and Mercy Dudley (1121).

She married Daniel Epps.

Lucy Woodbridge married Simon Bradstreet. Simon died in 1683.

Lucy Woodbridge married Simon Bradstreet. Simon died in 1683.

Family of John Woodbridge and Abigail Leete

1254. John[23] Woodbridge was born in 1644. He was the son of John Woodbridge and Mercy Dudley (1121).

John died in 1691 at the age of 47.

He married Abigail Leete. Abigail Leete was born about 1648.

Abigail reached 62 years of age and died in 1710.

Family of Benjamin Woodbridge and Mary Ward

1255. Benjamin[23] Woodbridge was born in 1645. He was the son of John Woodbridge and Mercy Dudley (1121).

Benjamin died in 1709 at the age of 64.

He married Mary Ward. Mary Ward was born in 1649.

Mary reached 36 years of age and died in 1685.

Family of Thomas Woodbridge and Mary Jones

1256. Thomas[23] Woodbridge was born in 1648. He was the son of John Woodbridge and Mercy Dudley (1121).

Thomas died in 1681 at the age of 33.

He married Mary Jones. Mary died in 1714.

Family of Dorothy Woodbridge and Nathaniel Fryer

1257. Dorothy[23] Woodbridge was born in October 1649. She was the daughter of John Woodbridge and Mercy Dudley (1121).

She married Nathaniel Fryer. Nathaniel died in 1705.

Family of Timothy Woodbridge and Mehitabel Wyllis

1258. Timothy[23] Woodbridge was born on January 13, 1656, in Barford, St Martins, Wiltshire, England. He was the son of John Woodbridge and Mercy Dudley (1121).

Timothy died in Hartford, CT, on April 30, 1732, at the age of 76.

He married Mehitabel Wyllis. She is the daughter of Hezekiah Wyllis.

Timothy Woodbridge married Mary Bryan in 1702.

Mary Bryan was born about 1652. She was the daughter of Richard Bryan and Mary Pantry.

Mary died before 1713.

Timothy Woodbridge married Abigail Warren.

Abigail Warren was born in 1676.

Children of Timothy Woodbridge and Mehitabel Wyllis:

+ 1370 i. Timothy[24] Woodbridge was born about 1686.
- ii. Mary Woodbridge was born about 1692. She died in 1766 at the age of 74.
- iii. Ruth Woodbridge was born about 1695. She died in 1731 at the age of 36.
- iv. John Woodbridge was born about 1697. He died in 1697.

Children of Timothy Woodbridge and Mary Bryan:

+ 1371 i. Susanna Woodbridge was born in Hartford, CT, about 1703.

+ 1372 ii. Ashbel Woodbridge was born about 1704.

Son of Timothy Woodbridge and Abigail Warren:

   i. Theodore Woodbridge was born about 1717. He died about 1747 at the age of 30.

Family of Joseph Woodbridge and Martha Rogers

1259. Joseph[23] Woodbridge was born about 1657. He was the son of John Woodbridge and Mercy Dudley (1121).

Joseph died in 1726 at the age of 69.

He married Martha Rogers. Martha Rogers was born about 1661.

Family of Martha Woodbridge and Samuel Ruggles

1260. Martha[23] Woodbridge was born about 1660. She was the daughter of John Woodbridge and Mercy Dudley (1121).

Martha died in 1738 at the age of 78.

She married Samuel Ruggles. Samuel Ruggles was born in January 1658. He was the son of Samuel Ruggles.

Samuel reached 57 years of age and died in February 1715.

Family of Mary Woodbridge and Samuel Appleton

1261. Mary[23] Woodbridge was born in 1662. She was the daughter of John Woodbridge and Mercy Dudley (1121).

Mary died on June 9, 1712, at the age of 50.

She married Samuel Appleton. Samuel died in 1693.

Family of Mehitable Marsh and Arthur Daggett

1262. Mehitable[23] Marsh was born on May 8, 1731, in Sutton, Worchester, Massachusets. She was the daughter of Benjamin Marsh and Mehitable King (1127).

Mehitable died in Y.

At the age of 19, Mehitable married Arthur Daggett on January 28, 1751, in Sutton, Worchester, Massachusets, when he was 20 years old.

Arthur Daggett was born in Sutton, Worchester, Massachusets, on January 30, 1730. He was the son of Ebenezer Daggett and Hannah Sibley.

Arthur reached 45 years of age and died in Sutton, Worchester, Massachusets, on August 23, 1775.

[Comp02.FTW]

!History of the Town of Sutton Massachusetts, Benedict & Tracy, p 630.

Children of Mehitable Marsh and Arthur Daggett:

    i.   Arthur[24] Daggett Jr. was born in Sutton, Worchester, Massachusets, on April 23, 1751. He died in Montpelier, Washington, Vermont, on August 25, 1835, at the age of 84.

    ii.   Mehitable Daggett was born in Sutton, Worchester, Massachusets, on October 10, 1752. She died in Y.

    iii.   Simoen Daggett was born in Sutton, Worchester, Massachusets, on March 7, 1757. He died in Y.

+ 1373   iv.   Gideon Daggett was born in Sutton, Worchester, Massachusets, on December 21, 1759.

    v.   Betty Daggett was born in Sutton, Worchester, Massachusets, on February 3, 1763. She died in Y.

    vi.   Tamar Daggett was born in Sutton, Worchester, Massachusets, on March 24, 1767. She died in Y.

Family of Noah Merrill and Abigail Cooper

1263. Noah[23] Merrill was born about 1726 in Haverhill, Essex, MA. He was the son of Nathaniel Merrill and Mary Belknap.

Noah died in 1739 at the age of 13.

Noah married Abigail Cooper on Thursday, May 30, 1754.

Noah Merrill married Sarah Lee on Thursday, April 12, 1759.

Family of Ichabod Merrill and Mary Merrill

1264. Ichabod[23] Merrill was born before September 15, 1728. He was the son of Noah Merrill (1128) and Esther Gillett.

He married Mary Merrill.

Mary Merrill was born in New Hartford, Litchfield, CT, on March 28, 1743. She was the daughter of Joseph Merrill and Abigail Stone.

Children of Ichabod Merrill and Mary Merrill:

    i. Lucy[24] Merrill was born in Plaistow, NH, on March 21, 1760.

    ii. Jeremiah Merrill was born in West Hartford, Hartford, CT, before July 29, 1764.

    iii. Esther Merrill was born in Methuen, Essex, Mass., on March 16, 1765.

    iv. Noah Merrill was born in West Hartford, Hartford, CT, before September 8, 1765.

    v. Eli Merrill was born in New Hartford, Litchfield, CT, before October 4, 1772.

    vi. Mary Merrill was born in West Hartford, Hartford, CT, before April 30, 1775.

    vii. Diadama Merrill was born in West Hartford, Hartford, CT, before December 20, 1778.

    viii. Isaac Merrill was born in West Hartford, Hartford, CT, before April 16, 1780.

Family of Esther Merrill and Lot Norton

1265. Esther[23] Merrill was born before March 8, 1730 in West Hartford, Hartford, CT. She was the daughter of Noah Merrill (1128) and Esther Gillett.

Esther died on November 10, 1778.

Esther married Lot Norton on Thursday, December 2, 1756, in West Hartford, Hartford, CT.

Family of Joseph Merrill and Mary Merrill

1266. Joseph[23] Merrill was born before January 30, 1732 in West Hartford, Hartford, CT. He was the son of Noah Merrill (1128) and Esther Gillett.

Joseph died on March 20, 1817.

He married Mary Merrill.

Family of Mehitable Merrill and William Seymour

1267. Mehitable[23] Merrill was born before May 26, 1734 in Hartford, Hartford, CT. She was the daughter of Noah Merrill (1128) and Esther Gillett.

Mehitable died in Stillwater, Saratoga, NY, on June 29, 1810.

Mehitable married William Seymour on Thursday, December 27, 1753. William Seymour was born in Hartford, Hartford, CT, on August 18, 1728.

William reached 53 years of age and died in Norwalk, CT, in 1782.

Family of Timothy Merrill and ? Plumb

1268. Timothy[23] Merrill was born on July 21, 1741, in West Hartford, Hartford, CT. He was the son of Timothy Merrill (1129) and Mary Kellog.

He married ? Plumb.

Family of Mary Merrill and John Thompson Jr.

1269. Mary[23] Merrill was born on September 28, 1743, in West Hartford, Hartford, CT. She was the daughter of Timothy Merrill (1129) and Mary Kellog.

Mary died in 1810 at the age of 66.

Mary married John Thompson Jr. on Thursday, April 29, 1773, in Farmington, Hartford, Connecticut. John Thompson Jr. was born in 1739.

Family of Isaac Merrill and ??? Gillett

1270. Isaac[23] Merrill was born on January 19, 1748. He was the son of Timothy Merrill (1129) and Mary Kellog.

Isaac died after 1817.

He married ??? Gillett.

Family of James Merrill and Jerusha Seymour

1271. James[23] Merrill was born on September 25, 1751. He was the son of Timothy Merrill (1129) and Mary Kellog.

James died on March 16, 1807, at the age of 55.

At the age of 23, James married Jerusha Seymour on Thursday, November 24, 1774, in Farmington, CT, when she was 20 years old. They had seven sons.

Jerusha Seymour was born on Monday, August 12, 1754. Jerusha reached 73 years of age and died on October 14, 1827.

Sons of James Merrill and Jerusha Seymour:

    i.   Orsamus Cook[24] Merrill was born in Farmington, Hartford, CT, on June 16, 1775. He died in Bennington, VT, on April 12, 1869, at the age of 93.

ii. Uel Merrill was born in Farmington, Hartford, CT, on February 24, 1779. He died in Savannah, Georgia, on August 15, 1811, at the age of 32.

iii. Timothy Merrill was born in Farmington, Hartford, CT, in 1781. He died in Montpelier, VT, in 1836 at the age of 55.

iv. James Seymour Merrill was born in Farmington, Hartford, CT, on July 18, 1786. He died in Savannah, Georgia, on October 9, 1816, at the age of 30.

v. Erastus Merrill was born in Farmington, Hartford, CT, on January 12, 1790. He died in Bennington, VT, on September 5, 1809, at the age of 19.

vi. Ferrand Merrill was born in Farmington, Hartford, CT, on October 25, 1792. He died in Bennington, VT, on October 2, 1809, at the age of 16.

vii. Edwin Merrill was born in Farmington, Hartford, CT, on September 19, 1795. He died in Bennington, VT, on November 10, 1816, at the age of 21.

Family of Rhoda Merrill and Reuben Gillett

1272. Rhoda[23] Merrill was born on Friday, December 8, 1758. She was the daughter of Timothy Merrill (1129) and Mary Griswold.

Rhoda married Reuben Gillett about 1778.

Family of Jonathan Merrill and Anna Gillett

1273. Jonathan[23] Merrill was born on Friday, November 28, 1760, in West Hartford, Hartford, CT. He was the son of Timothy Merrill (1129) and Mary Griswold.

Jonathan died in Castleton, Rutland, VT, on August 21, 1836, at the age of 75.

He married Anna Gillett.

Anna Gillett was born in Bristol, VT, after 1760. Anna died in Castleton, Rutland, VT.

Children of Jonathan Merrill and Anna Gillett:

i. Enos[24] Merrill was born in Burlington, CT, on November 5, 1785. He died in Castleton, Rutland, VT, on April 10, 1858, at the age of 72.

ii. Malachi Merrill was born in Burlington, CT, about 1787. He died in Castleton, Rutland, VT, about 1850 at the age of 63.

iii. James Merrill was born in Burlington, CT, about 1789.

iv. Rhoda Merrill was born in Burlington, CT, about 1791. She died in April 1870 at the age of 79.

v. Margaret Merrill was born in Burlington, CT, about 1793.

vi. Mary G. Merrill was born in Burlington, CT, about 1795.

Family of Ashbel Merrill and Abigail Hart

1274. Ashbel[23] Merrill was born on Tuesday, September 7, 1762, in West Hartford, Hartford, CT. He was the son of Timothy Merrill (1129) and Mary Griswold.

Ashbel died in 1793 at the age of 30.

Ashbel married Abigail Hart before 1786.

Abigail Hart was born in 1762. Abigail reached 90 years of age and died on August 12, 1852.

Children of Ashbel Merrill and Abigail Hart:

i. Ashbel[24] Merrill was born in West Hartford, Hartford, CT, on December 17, 1786. He died in Castleton, Rutland, VT, on April 26, 1867, at the age of 80.

ii. Chester Merrill was born in 1789.

iii. Achsa Merrill was born in 1791. She died on September 26, 1817, at the age of 26.

iv. Hervey Merrill was born in West Hartford, Hartford, CT, in August 1793. He died on February 8, 1858, at the age of 64.

Family of Ruby Merrill and Darius Woodruff

1275. Ruby[23] Merrill was born on Monday, November 25, 1765. She was the daughter of Timothy Merrill (1129) and Mary Griswold.

Ruby died in Farmington, Hartford, CT, in July 1845 at the age of 79.

She married Darius Woodruff. Darius died in November 1841.

Family of Enos Merrill and Susan Noble Willard

1276. Enos[23] Merrill was born on Tuesday, November 1, 1768, in Hartford, Hartford, CT. He was the son of Timothy Merrill (1129) and Mary Griswold.

Enos died in Milton, Chittenden, VT, on August 9, 1858, at the age of 89.

At the age of 21, Enos married Delight Higley on Monday, November 23, 1789, in Vermont when she was 22 years old. They had four daughters.

Delight Higley was born in Simsbury, Hartford, CT, on Sunday, August 23, 1767. Delight reached 33 years of age and died in Castleton, Rutland, VT, on October 13, 1800.

At the age of 32, Enos Merrill married Jeanne Guernsey on Sunday, February 22, 1801, in Castleton, VT, when she was 19 years old.

Jeanne Guernsey was born on Friday, August 10, 1781. Jeanne reached 41 years of age and died on March 22, 1823.

At the age of 55, Enos Merrill married Susan Noble Willard on Friday, December 5, 1823, when she was 41 years old.

Susan Noble Willard was born on Monday, July 22, 1782. Susan reached 81 years of age and died on May 3, 1864.

Daughters of Enos Merrill and Delight Higley:

   i.   Lucy[24] Merrill was born in Castleton, VT, on May 14, 1791. She died on June 13, 1873, at the age of 82.

   ii. Allison Merrill was born in 1793.

   iii. Selah Higley Merrill was born in 1796.

   iv. Laura Merrill was born in Castleton, VT, on November 30, 1799. She died in 1838 at the age of 38.

Children of Enos Merrill and Jeanne Guernsey:

   i.   Emily Merrill was born in Castleton, VT, on February 8, 1802. She died on September 6, 1863, at the age of 61.

   ii. Lucas Guernsey Merrill was born in Castleton, VT, in 1804. He died in 1890 at the age of 86.

   iii. Jane Eliza Merrill was born in Castleton, VT, on November 7, 1818. She died on May 22, 1899, at the age of 80.

Son of Enos Merrill and Susan Noble Willard:

    i.   Timothy Noble Merrill was born in Castleton, VT, on February 1, 1825. He died in Republic, MO, in 1899 at the age of 73.

Family of Eliakim Merrill and Kegiah Loomis

1277. Eliakim[23] Merrill was born before February 14, 1742 in New Hartford, Litchfield, CT. He was the son of Eliakim Merrill (1130) and Sarah Watson.

Eliakim died in New Hartford, Litchfield, CT, on February 24, 1812.

Eliakim married Kegiah Loomis about 1763.

Children of Eliakim Merrill and Kegiah Loomis:

    i.   Zelinda[24] Merrill was born in New Hartford, Litchfield, CT, in 1765.

    ii.   Charles Merrill was born in New Hartford, Litchfield, CT, in 1768.

    iii.   Isaac Merrill was born in New Hartford, Litchfield, CT, on March 11, 1770.

    iv.   Titus Merrill was born in New Hartford, Litchfield, CT, on May 12, 1771.

    v.   Salmon Merrill was born in New Hartford, Litchfield, CT, on October 10, 1773.

    vi.   Mary Merrill was born in New Hartford, Litchfield, CT, on August 17, 1777.

    vii.   Nancy Merrill was born in New Hartford, Litchfield, CT, on October 29, 1780.

    viii.   Sabra Merrill was born in New Hartford, Litchfield, CT, on October 27, 1785.

Family of Elias Merrill and Lydia Andrews

1278. Elias[23] Merrill was born before June 14, 1744. He was the son of Eliakim Merrill (1130) and Sarah Watson.

Elias married Lydia Andrews in January 1766 in New Hartford, Litchfield, CT.

Lydia Andrews was born after 1744.

Children of Elias Merrill and Lydia Andrews:

    i.   Hannah[24] Merrill was born in New Hartford, Litchfield, CT, before October 26, 1766.

    ii.   Lydia Merrill was born in 1768.

    iii.   Olive Merrill was born in 1771.

    iv.   Elias Merrill was born in 1773.

Family of Bildad Merrill and Damaris Mix

1279. Bildad[23] Merrill was born before January 28, 1750 in New Hartford, Litchfield, CT. He was the son of Eliakim Merrill (1130) and Sarah Watson.

Bildad died on November 21, 1815.

Bildad married Damaris Mix on Sunday, January 16, 1774.

Damaris Mix was born in West Hartford, Hartford, CT, on Monday, January 3, 1757. Damaris reached 37 years of age and died in January 1795.

Bildad Merrill married Hannah Lewis on Wednesday, February 24, 1796, in Whitestown, First Presbyterian Church Of Whitesboro, Oneida, NY.

Children of Bildad Merrill and Damaris Mix:

    i.   Irene[24] Merrill was born about December 1774. She died on September 28, 1776, at the age of 1.

    ii.   Bildad Merrill was born in New Hartford, Litchfield, CT, on September 9, 1777. He died in Holland Patent, NY, in September 1851 at the age of 73.

    iii.   Ira Merrill was born on October 29, 1779. He died in Geneva, Ontario County?, NY, on April 17, 1849, at the age of 69.

    iv.   Isaac Merrill was born in New Hartford, Litchfield, CT, on December 8, 1781. He died in Utica, NY, on May 7, 1860, at the age of 78.

    v.   Irene Merrill was born in New Hartford, Litchfield, CT, on January 8, 1784. She died on October 12, 1813, at the age of 29.

    vi.   Zelinda Merrill was born in New Hartford, Litchfield, CT, on January 16, 1786. She died on November 10, 1863, at the age of 77.

vii. Andrew Merrill was born in New Hartford, Litchfield, CT, on May 6, 1792. He died in Utica, NY, on January 25, 1826, at the age of 33.

viii. Sarah Merrill was born on April 7, 1794. She died on April 12, 1794.

Son of Bildad Merrill and Hannah Lewis:

i. Lewis Merrill was born on August 23, 1799. He died on April 27, 1823, at the age of 23.

Family of Martin Merrill and Rhoda Case

1280. Martin[23] Merrill was born before April 21, 1754 in New Hartford, Litchfield, CT. He was the son of Eliakim Merrill (1130) and Sarah Watson.

Martin died in New Hartford, Litchfield, CT, on March 11, 1812.

Martin married Rhoda Case before 1778.

Sons of Martin Merrill and Rhoda Case:

i. Nelson[24] Merrill was born in New Hartford, Litchfield, CT, on April 3, 1799. He died in Livonia, NY, on April 16, 1875, at the age of 76.

ii. Martin Merrill was born in New Hartford, Litchfield, CT, on December 29, 1801. He died in New Hartford, Litchfield, CT, on October 23, 1881, at the age of 79.

Family of Daniel Durland and Sarah Hawkesworth

1281. Daniel[23] Durland was born in 1772 in Wilmot, Annapolis Co., Nova Scotia, Canada. He was the son of Daniel Durland (1134) and Sarah De Motte.

Daniel died in Wilmot, Annapolis, Nova Scotia, Canada, in 1842 at the age of 70.

At the age of 26, Daniel married Sarah Hawkesworth on Monday, November 26, 1798, in Wilmot, Annapolis, Nova Scotia, Canada, when she was 23 years old.

Sarah Hawkesworth was born in Granville, Annapolis, Canada, on Tuesday, September 5, 1775. Sarah reached 101 years of age and died in Granville, Annapolis, Nova Scotia, Canada, in 1877.

Son of Daniel Durland and Sarah Hawkesworth:

+ 1374 i. Adam Easton[24] Durland was born in Hanley Mountain, Annapolis, Nova Scotia, Canada, on December 27, 1814.

Family of Susanna Lane and Nathaniel Davis

1282. Susanna[23] Lane. She is the daughter of John Lane and Katherine Whiting (1135).

She married Nathaniel Davis. They have one son.

Susanna Lane married Nathaniel Davis. They have one son.

Son of Susanna Lane and Nathaniel Davis:

+ 1375 i. Nathaniel[24] Davis.

Son of Susanna Lane and Nathaniel Davis:

+ 1376 i. Nathaniel[24] Davis.

Family of Erastus Spalding and Jennet Mack

1283. Erastus[23] Spalding. He is the son of Ephraim Spalding (1136) and Abigail Bullard.

He married Jennet Mack. They have one daughter.

Daughter of Erastus Spalding and Jennet Mack:

+ 1377 i. Martha Ann[24] Spalding.

Index of Individuals

Acheson
    Archibald 46
    Isabelle (1576–) 46, 85

Ackworth
    Catherine (1596–1616) 64

Adams
    Deborah 142
    Mary 154, 210
    Samuel 142

Adderley
    Catherine (1594–1622) 41, 75
    Humphrey (1568–) 41

Adelaide: 29

Akin
    Mary (–1787) 156, 215

Alabaster
    Elizabeth (1538–1638) 31, 66

Allen
    Ebenezer (1650–1725) 66, 107, 156
    Ebenezer (1727–1807) 156
    Edmund (1558–1616) 31
    Elizabeth (1565–1665) 32
    Elizabeth (1751–1830) 215
    George (1568–1648) 32, 66
    James B (1695–1771) 107, 156, 215
    Jane (1587–1626) 66, 106, 156
    John (1500–1558) 31
    John (1538–1558) 31, 66
    Mary (1568–1668) 32
    Prince (ca.1720–1778) 156, 215
    Ralph (1542–1648) 32
    Ralph (1621–1691) 32, 66, 107
    Thomas (1560–1635) 31, 66, 106

Allyn
    Richard (1564–1652) 32

Almy
    Catherine (1674–) 118, 170

Amiot
    Jean Baptiste (1658–1685) 41, 76
    Marie Anne (1685–1725) 42, 76, 117

Anderson
    Judith (1705–1795) 203, 256
    Rachel (1728–1786) 256

Andrews
    Lydia (>1744–) 266

Appleton
    Samuel (–1693) 259

Apsley
    Allen (1582–1630) 108, 157
    John (ca.1561–ca.1650) 108
    Lady Lucy (1620–1680) 216
    Lucy (1620–1680) 108, 157

Ardene
    Annie (1545–1624) 74, 115

Arundel
    Mary of (1540–1557) 31, 65

Ashton
    Frances (1533–1610) 30, 65

Aster
    Jemima 157, 215

Aston
    Edward (–1568) 30

Austin
    Francis (Austen) (1602–1642) 215
    Jemima (Asten) (1641–1705) 215

Bagot
    Barbara (1725–1796) 227
    Edward, 2nd Baronet (1616–1673) 75
    Edward, 2nd Baronet Bagot(1616–1673) 116
    Edward, 4th Baronet Bagot (1673–1712) 169, 226
    Edward, 4th Baronet Bagot(1673–1712) 116
    Hervey, 1st Baronet Bagot of Blithfield (1591–1660)40, 75
    Sir Edward 2nd Baronet (1616–1673) 41
    Sir Walter (1557–1623) 40
    Walter Wagstaffe, 5th Baronet Bagot (1702–1768) ..169, 226
    Walter, 3rd Baronet Bagot (1644–1704) 116, 169

Bagot 3rd Baronet
    Sir Walter (1644–1704) 75

Baker
    Frances (1580–1608) 69, 110

Baldwin
    Temperance Fowler (1622–1716) 63, 103
    V (–1067) 29

Barham
    Anne (1624–1682) 164, 222
    Robert (1598–1648) 164

Barker
    Elizabeth (1618–1688) 64, 104
    Robert (1580–1618) 64

Barton
    Elizabeth 102

Baudrey
    Bridget (1520–1548) 68, 109

Sir Thomas (1500–1534) 68

Beckwith
Grace (ca.1576–ca.1665) 158

Belconger
John (1589–1653) 35

Belknap
Mary 260

Benat
Elizabeth (1653–) 164, 222

Bennett
James (1680–1752) 222
John (1560–1625) 38, 71, 113
John (1606–1671) 113, 163, 222
Mary (1627–1700) 113
Richard (1528–1574) 37, 71
Richard (1609–1675) 113, 164, 222
Richard (1645–1720) 164, 222
Thomas (1503–1547) 37
Thomas (1580–1642) 72, 113, 164
William (1556–1597) 38, 71, 113
William (ca.1579–1645) 71, 113, 163

Berkeley
Mary Dorothy (1584–1608) 105, 154
Rowland (1552–1611) 105

Berney
John (1503–1557) 109
Mary (1528–1614) 109, 158

Bigod
Hugh (1186–1225) 4
Hugh (1215–1266) 5
Lady Isabel (1210–1239) 4, 5
Roger (–1270) 5
Roger (ca.1150–<1221) 4

Birdsall
Henry (1578–1651) 62, 63
Henry (1658–1699) 63, 103, 153
Judith (1619–1689) 62, 102
Mary (1690–1749) 103, 153, 209
Nathan (1620–1696) 63, 103

Birdseye
Sarah Mary (1600–1682) 217

Black
Margaret (ca.1741–) 195, 251

Blair
Catherine (1743–ca.1820) 250
David (1710–) 250

Blake
Annie (1561–1601) 73

Boleyn
Mary (1504–1543) 32

Booth
Alice (1678–) 206

Borthwick
Baron John (1615–1675) 101, 149, 202
Elizabeth (1676–) 202, 255
James (1570–1599) 60
John (1590–1623) 60, 100, 149
Lord James (1570–1599) 100
Thomas (1645–1673) 149, 202, 255
William (1539–1582) 60

Boulter
Mary (1648–1735) 167, 224

Bousquet
Jean Baptiste (1702–1777) 169
Joseph (1734–1785) 169, 228
Joseph (1817–1894) 228
Joseph Marie (1766–1828) 170, 228

Bowers
Ruth (1616–1687) 216

Bowles
Joan 30

Bradstreet
Simon 205
Simon (–1683) 257

Brashieur
Robert (1597–1665) 160

Brasseur
Margaret (1642–1708) 159, 218

Braye
Dorothy (1540–1605) 67, 107

Breed
Allen (1601–1692) 163
Elizabeth (1634–1676) 163, 221

Brigg
Elizabeth (1647–1703) 75, 116

Britian
Agnes (1650–1714) 223

Bronson
Abraham (1647–1719) 166, 224
Elizabeth (1682–1767) 167, 224

Brown
Mary (1715–) 169, 227
Patience (1694–1730) 221

Brownson
John (1602–1680) 166

Bryan
Mary (ca.1652–<1713) 258
Richard (1632–1689) 258

Bukeley
Edward (–1748) 155
John (–1731) 155
Peter (1664–1701) 155, 213

Bulkeley
- Benjamin (1624–) 107
- Catherine (1660–1712) 155, 211
- Charles 155, 213
- Danill (1625–) 107
- Dorothy (1640–) 105
- Dorothy (1662–1757) 155, 211
- Edward (1540–1621) 105
- Edward (1614–1696) 106, 156, 213, 214
- Eleazer (1638–) 105
- Elizabeth 156, 214
- Frances 64
- Gershom (1635–1713) 105, 155, 211, 213
- Hannah (1692–1720) 213
- Jabez (1626–1629) 107
- Jane (1531–1553) 29, 64
- John (1619–) 107
- Joseph (1623–) 107
- Joseph (1670–1748) 214
- Mary (1615–1616) 106
- Marye (1621–1624) 107
- Nathaniall (1618–1629) 106
- Peter 156, 214
- Peter (1583–1659) 105, 106, 155, 156
- Peter (1641–1688) 156, 213
- Peter (1643–) 106
- Rebecca 214
- Rebecca (1681–1747) 214
- Richard (1495–1547) 29
- Sarah (1574–1611) 63
- Thomas (1617–) 106

Bulkley
- Grace (1670–1712) 214

Bullard
- Abigail 210, 269

Burbank
- Mary (1675–1762) 256

Burges
- James (1529–1590) 37, 71
- Nicholas (1500–1556) 37
- Sarah (1559–1635) 37, 71, 112

Burte
- Agnes (1537–1564) 35

Butler
- Agnes (1523–1606) 39
- Deborah (1723–1814) 215

Buxton
- Anthony (ca.1616–) 102
- Elizabeth (ca.1642–) 102, 151

Byron
- Margaret (1593–1619) 157

Cambell
- John 83

Cameron
- a daughter of Donald 125, 178
- Anne 118, 170, 171
- Catherine (1716–) 247
- Catherine (ca.1590–1680) 42, 43, 44, 45
- Christian 198
- Ewen 118
- Helen 232
- Isabella 120, 172, 173, 230
- John 79
- Mary 78, 79, 121, 122

Campbell
- ? 54, 93, 94, 148, 189, 201, 247
- Angus 42
- Ann 122, 233
- Anne 126, 179, 236, 237
- Anne (ca.1615–) 42, 77, 78
- Archibald 185
- Catherine 85, 98, 128, 130, 131, 146, 185
- Colin 126
- Donald 59, 130, 175, 236
- Duncan 47
- Elizabeth (ca.1670–) 191, 249
- Florence (1595–1636) 45, 85, 89, 128, 132, 135, 136
- Helen 233
- Hugh 126, 179
- Isabel (ca.1650–) 54, 94
- Isabella 95, 123, 143, 175, 176, 177, 229
- Jane (–1824) 239
- Jean 124, 177, 241
- John 85, 98, 124, 132, 232
- John (ca.1620–) 54
- Julian 82
- Margaret 51, 126, 173, 178, 179, 180, 232
- Margaret (1545–1570) 48, 86
- Margaret (1552–1609) 46, 48
- Marian 47, 85
- Mary 174, 185, 241, 244, 245
- Mary (1625–) 131, 186
- Mary (ca.1687–) 148, 200
- Robert 82
- Sally (1605–) 53
- Sir Dugald 5th Lord of Auchinbreck (1561–1641) 89
- Susan 95, 144, 247
- Susanna (ca.1684–1715) 120, 174

Canady
- Sarah (1693–1728) 257

Capell
- Elizabeth (1572–) 41

Carey
- Sir William (1499–1528) 32

Cary
- Lady Mary Katherine (1524–1568) 32
- Mary Katherine (1524–1568) 66

Case
- Rhoda 268

Cave
- Lady Elizabeth (1553–1628) 40

Charles
    Tabitha (1618–1690) 111, 112, 163

Charlesworth
    Sarah (1742–1778) 255

Chauncey
    Charles (1592–1672) 155
    Sarah (1631–1699) 155, 211, 213

Chedder
    Joan (1451–) 34

Chenet
    Elisabeth (1774–1860) 228

Chester
    Dorcas 104, 153

Chetwood
    Grace (ca.1602–1669) 65, 105, 155
    Richard (ca.1530–) 65
    Richard (ca.1560–>1631) 65
    Sir Richard (ca.1560–>1631) 105

Chisholm
    Agnes (ca.1636–) 58
    Alexander 58

Chisolm
    Agnes (1634–) 59, 99

Clark
    Matthew Jr. 209

Clavell
    Grace (1570–1598) 107, 157
    John (1538–1609) 107

Cleaveland
    Samuel (1657–1736) 211

Cleveland
    Isaac Samuel (1584–1626) 210
    Moses (1620–1702) 210

Clifford
    Sarah (1691–1713) 224

Clinton
    Ann (1596–1632) 114, 165

Coddington
    Aaron (1806–1884) 219
    Alvah (1808–1882) 219
    Benjamin (1730–1792) 160, 219
    Benjamin (1762–1823) 160
    Benjamin Jr (1708–1750) 160
    Calvin (1800–1836) 219
    James Harvey (1798–1870) 219
    John (1778–1845) 161, 219
    John (1810–1851) 219
    Jonathan (1776–1855) 161
    Joseph (1763–1833) 160
    Julia Ann (1804–) 219
    Maria (1814–) 219
    Moses (1768–1853) 160

    Phoebe (1766–) 160
    Rhoda (1775–) 160
    Samuel (1802–1875) 219

Coleman
    Sarah (1542–1734) 211

Collins
    Amos Sr. (1757–1832) 221
    Anna (1757–1826) 221
    Benjamin Minot (1767–1850) 221
    Eunice (1747–) 221
    Joel (1750–) 221
    Joseph (1686–1734) 221
    Joseph (1729–1807) 220
    Joseph (1759–1810) 221
    Mehitabel (1752–1762) 221
    Sarah (ca.1765–) 221
    Thankful (1769–) 221

Conger
    Elizabeth (1678–1731) 36
    Elizabeth (1742–1796) 111
    Enos (1667–1689) 35
    Gershom (1685–1711) 36
    Joanna (1670–1742) 36
    John (1633–1712) 35, 69
    John (1674–1726) 36, 69, 110
    John (1702–1784) 70, 110, 160
    Jonathan (1683–1733) 36
    Lediah (1679–1692) 36
    Mary (1666–1666) 35
    Phoebe (1740–1813) 111, 160, 219
    Sarah (1668–1702) 35

Conqueror
    William The (1027–1087) 29

Constable
    Dorothy (1536–1589) 75, 116

Cook
    Abigail (1670–) 103
    Ebenezer (1677–1679) 103
    Edmund (ca.1568–1619) 62
    Elizabeth (1654–1654) 63
    Elizabeth (1665–) 102
    Hannah (1648–) 62
    Hannah (1658–) 63
    Hannah (1671–) 103, 151, 206
    Henry (1615–1661) 62, 102
    Henry (1648–) 62
    Henry (1652–1705) 63
    Henry (ca.1681–) 103
    Isaac (1640–1692) 62, 102, 151
    Isaac (1666–1671) 102
    Isaac (1674–1679) 103
    Isaac (1840–) 63
    John (1647–1716) 62
    John (1673–) 103
    John (1747–) 63
    Judith (1643–1869) 62
    Lydia (ca.1685–) 103
    Margaret (1730–1776) 220

    Martha (1649–) 62
    Mary (1649–) 62
    Mary (1668–) 102
    Rachel (1645–1740) 62
    Rachel (1675–1679) 103
    Samuel (1641–1703) 62
    Samuel (1679–1718) 103
    Sarah (1682–) 103, 152, 206, 207, 208, 209
    William 151

Cooke
    Margaret Ellen (1530–1602) 37

Cooper
    Abigail 260
    Alexander (1600–1682) 110
    Sarah (1656–1726) 110, 159

Copeland
    Mary (1643–1639) 115, 167

Corker
    Lucy (1604–1700) 110, 159
    William (1584–1677) 110

Council
    Olive (1595–1655) 101, 150

Crafford
    Anne (1581–1623) 60

Crist
    Anna Margaretha (1727–) 198, 253

Cross
    John (ca.1505–1577) 39

Crosse
    Agnes (–1623) 39, 73

Cubbage
    a daughter of James 57

Cunningham
    Margaret (1563–1595) 46, 47, 48, 83

Dacre
    Anne (1557–1630) 65, 106

Daggett
    Arthur (1730–1775) 259
    Arthur Jr. (1751–1835) 260
    Betty (1763–) 260
    Ebenezer (1696–1762) 259
    Gideon (1759–1838) 260
    Mehitable (1752–) 260
    Simoen (1757–) 260
    Tamar (1767–) 260

Dallas
    Alexander 147
    Christina 147, 199
    Jannet (1680–) 99, 146
    William 99

Davenport
    Jane (1525–1566) 40, 74

    William (1472–1541) 40

Davis
    Nathaniel 269

de Anjou
    Hamelin (1130–1202) 4

De Clare
    Isabel (1172–1220) 4

De Grey
    Margaret (1486–) 40

De Motte
    Sarah (1740–1792) 209, 268

De Wahull
    Alice (1542–1575) 65

de Warenne
    John (1231–1304) 5

De Warenne
    William (1166–1240) 4

Dennison
    Daniel (ca.1612–1682) 204

Devere
    Lady Frances (1517–1577) 31

DeWarenne
    Isabel (1137–1203) 4

DeWitt
    Marritje (1680–1733) 98, 145

Dick
    Susanne 255

Dicken
    Christopher (1644–1718) 223
    Isaac (1690–1735) 223
    John (1720–1763) 223

Dickens
    Christopher (1712–1778) 223
    James (1710–1763) 223
    Susanna (1714–1784) 223

Dickson
    Mary 245

Disney
    Emlyn (1478–1556) 33

dit Villeneuve
    Mathieu Amiot (1628–1688) 41

Dixon
    Daug (1626–1665) 104

Dorlandt
    John Gerret (1688–1744) 153, 209

Dormer
    Ann (1525–1640) 33, 67

Drummond
- Susan 234

Dudley
- Anne 151, 205
- Deborah 151
- Dorothy 151
- John 61, 102
- Joseph 151, 206
- Mercy (1621–1691) 151, 204, 257, 258, 259
- Patience (1618–1690) 151, 204
- Paul 151, 206
- Roger (ca.1552–1585) 61, 102, 151
- Samuel 151, 205
- Sarah 151, 206
- Simon 61
- Thomas 151
- Thomas (1576–1653) 102, 151, 204, 205, 206

Durland
- Adam Easton (1814–1895) 269
- Charles E (1773–>1871) 210
- Daniel (1772–1842) 209, 268
- Daniel (ca.1737–>1794) 153, 209, 268

Edwards
- Margaret (1564–1600) 36

Elliot
- Jennat (1714–1809) 218
- Richard (1679–1732) 218

Emerson
- Edward (1670–1743) 215
- Joseph (1620–1680) 214
- Thomas (ca.1591–1666) 214

Epps
- Daniel 257

Erskine
- Mary (1575–1613) 89

Evered
- Joane (1561–1621) 36

Eyre
- Catherine 155

Fairclough
- Mary (1550–1631) 66, 106

Farwell
- Henry 64, 104
- Olive 64, 104, 154

Fatmangle
- Maria 96

Ferris
- Jeffery (1610–1666) 155, 213
- John (1634–) 156, 213
- Phebe (1667–) 213

Filmer
- Katherine (1597–1662) 164

Fitch
- Mirable (1591–1690) 70, 112

Flanders
- Matilda of (1031–1083) 29

Ford
- Mary (1676–1712) 161, 220
- Samuel (1640–1712) 161

Foule
- Elinor (1587–1650) 150

Fowke
- Elizabeth Florence (1592–1665) 160

Fowler
- Ballie 58
- Margaret 189
- Margaret (1651–) 58, 99
- Margaret (1661–1734) 100, 147, 148, 149

Fraser
- ? 200, 255
- Agnes 58, 59
- Farquhar 79, 90, 139
- Florence (ca.1635–) 79, 90, 120, 139

Freathy
- Alexander (1580–) 64

Freeman
- Alice (1605–1664) 36, 70
- Henry (1560–1594) 36

Freethy
- Elizabeth (1680–1754) 105, 154, 159, 218
- James (1651–1690) 64, 104, 154, 159
- William (1612–1688) 64, 104

French
- Prudence (1772–1800) 234

Fryer
- Nathaniel (–1705) 258

Gardiner
- George (1510–1548) 40, 75
- George (1535–1589) 40, 75, 116
- Stephen (1483–1555) 40

Gardner
- Rachel (1608–1636) 116, 168, 225
- Thomas (1565–1635) 75, 116, 168

Garey
- Elizabeth (1633–1697) 113, 164

George
- Susanna (1632–1694) 165, 223

Gerrish
- Capt. William (1591–1687) 159
- John (1646–1714) 159, 217
- Paul (1674–1743) 218
- William (1617–1687) 159, 217

Gifert
  Alison (1608–) 69, 109
Gifford
  Millicent (1537–1571) 107
Gillett
  ??? 262
  Anna (>1760–) 263
  Esther 206, 260, 261
  Reuben 263
Goldstone
  John (1550–1605) 112
  Sarah (1602–1670) 112, 163
  Sarah (1602–1671) 213, 214
Goldthwaite
  Elizabeth 151
Goodale
  Rebecca Alice (1575–1645) 109, 158
Gookin
  Catherine (1599–1641) 61, 101
Gordon
  Anna 148, 200, 201
Grant
  Lillias (ca.1773–1833) 231
  Mary 200
Gray
  George (1625–1693) 69, 109, 159
  Gilbert (1543–1624) 34
  James (1606–>1625) 34, 69, 109
  James (1745–1821) 218
  John (1580–) 34, 69
  Joshua (1714–1781) 154, 159, 218
  Reuben (1743–1832) 218
  Robert (1680–1771) 110, 154, 159, 218
  Sarah (1675–1720) 162
Green
  Margaret (1550–1610) 65, 105
Greenham
  Elizabeth (1582–1603) 72
Griffith
  Catharine (1504–1540) 29
Griswold
  Anna (1651–1721) 115, 166, 224
  George (1548–1623) 115
  Mary (1726–1797) 207, 263, 264, 265
  Matthew (1620–1698) 114, 166
Guernsey
  Jeanne (1781–1823) 265
Guyon
  Geneviève (1666–1686) 41, 76
  Marie Josephe (1710–1762) 117, 169

Gyllyiott
  Isabel (1544–) 38
Hablett
  Alice (1513–1564) 71
Haney
  Susan 146
Harcourt
  Susanna (1654–1682) 76, 117
hardy
  Isabel (1620–1693) 101
Hardy
  David 256
  Elizabeth (ca.1617–1676) 101, 150, 203
  James (1699–1792) 256
  John (1646–) 150, 203, 256
  John (ca.1587–1652) 61, 101, 150
  Joseph (1615–1638) 101, 150, 203
  Joseph (ca.1670–) 203, 256
  Martha (1620–1688) 102
  Michael (1530–1595) 61
  Richard (1567–1645) 61, 101
  William 150
Harger
  Abigail (1672–1733) 225
  Jabez (1619–) 225
  Jabez (1642–1678) 225
  Jabez (1678–ca.1738) 225
Harrington
  Alexander (1496–1539) 38
  Edward (1584–1653) 73
  Edward (1668–1736) 166, 223
  Elizabeth (1559–) 39
  James (1565–1592) 39
  James (1592–1630) 73, 114, 165
  John (1525–1582) 38, 73
  John (1561–1612) 73
  John (1651–1741) 166
  Mary (1663–1716) 166
  Rebecca (1622–1680) 114
  Robert (1616–1707) 114, 165, 223
  Robert (ca.1551–1601) 39
  Samuel (1704–1784) 223
  Sarah (1670–1710) 166
  Sir John (1561–1612) 39, 114
  Susanna (1649–1694) 166
  Thomas (1665–1712) 166
Harrison
  Dorothy (1620–1666) 70, 111
  Ellen (1630–1666) 70, 111
Hart
  Abigail (1762–1852) 264
Harwood
  Anne (1630–) 73
  Elizabeth (1676–1737) 114
  Elizabeth (1694–1735) 165, 222

Hannah (1625–1670) 72
James 114
John (1600–1652) 72, 113
John (1621–1685) 72
John (1664–) 113
Mary 114
Mary (1703–1748) 165
Nathaniel 114
Nathaniel (1626–1716) 72
Peter (1633–1675) 73, 113, 164
Peter (1668–1756) 113, 164, 222
Peter (1697–1734) 165
Peter (1721–1748) 165
Robert (1628–1678) 72
Robert (1709–1781) 165
Samuel (1692–1781) 165
Sarah (1700–1755) 165
Thomas (1623–1706) 72
William 114
William (1578–1603) 72

Haskell
Benjamin (1719–1778) 257
Bethiah (1681–1738) 204
Elizabeth (1672–1715) 204
John (1648–1706) 150, 203, 257
John (1670–1728) 203
Josiah (1686–1733) 204, 257
Josiah (1686–1745) 204
Mary (1684–1741) 204
Patience (1679–1705) 204
Roger (1613/14–1667) 150, 203
Susanna (1691–1723) 204
William (1573–1630) 150
William (1674–1740) 204

Hawkesworth
Sarah (1775–1877) 268

Hay
Margaret (1570–1659) 60, 100

Hayward
Catherine (1548–1614) 105

Heath
Patience (ca.1735–) 228

Heaton
Ann (1582–1622) 41

Henderson
Elizabeth (–1880) 254
Thomas 254

Herleve "of Falaise"
(–1050) 29

Higley
Delight (1767–1800) 265

Hill
Abigail (1651–1725) 107, 156

Hills
Frances (1605–1680) 166

Hobbs
Thomas (1632–) 222
William (1653–1755) 222
William (1674–1755) 222

Hodgson
Joan (1560–1625) 71, 113

Hopkins
Elizabeth (1642–1690) 161

Horner
Margaret 43

Houston
Elizabeth 230

Howard
Mary Anne (1614–1658) 106, 155, 213
Phillip (1557–1595) 31, 65, 106
Sir Henry (1510–1533) 31
Thomas (1585–1646) 66, 106, 155
Thomas (ca.1536–1572) 31, 65

Humphrevile
Samuel (ca.1666–1748) 162

Humphreville
Sarah (1695–1727) 162, 220

Hungerford
Lady Lucy (1560–1627) 33
Lucy (1560–1627) 67, 108
Walter (1503–1540) 33
Walter (1532–1596) 33, 67

Hussey
Elizabeth Baroness (1510–1554) 33

Hutchinson
John (1615–1664) 157, 216
John (1641–1677) 158, 216
John (ca.1665–1757) 216
Thomas (1588–1643) 157

Hyde
Hamnet (1491–1526) 40
Maria (1579–1642) 74, 115, 168
Robert (1522–1571) 40, 74
Robert JR (1543–1614) 40, 115

Irby
Olive (1547–1614) 105

Isabel
(ca.1152–) 4

Jackman
Mary Frances (–1689) 203, 256

Jackson
Mary (1644–1704) 213

Jeffrie
Frances (1575–1605) 112

Jewel
    Mary (1717–) 209
Johnson
    Alice (1618–1698) 168, 225
Jones
    Mary (–1714) 258
Jordan
    Capt Samuel Silas (1578–1632) 35, 110
    Elizabeth (1690–1755) 218
    James (1665–1732) 160, 218
    Robert (1562–1599) 35, 69
    Samuel Silas (1578–1632) 69
    Thomas (1529–1589) 35
    Thomas (1634–1699) 110, 159, 218
    Thomas Fleming (1600–1687) 69, 110, 159
Jowet
    Mary (1608–1658) 41, 75
Keayne
    Benjamin 206
Kellog
    Mary 207, 262
Kelly
    Mary (1640–1685) 35, 69
Kempe
    Judith Agnes (ca.1589–1632) 62, 63
Ker
    Lilias (1587–1659) 100, 149
Kerr
    Lady Mary Elizabeth (1633–1706) 149, 202
King
    Abigail (1701–) 152
    Hannah (1696–) 152
    Henry (1707–) 152
    Isaac (1709–) 152
    Jane Allen (1624–1721) 101, 150
    John 151
    Lydia (1702–) 152
    Mehitable (1705–) 152, 206, 259
    William (1669–1748) 151, 206
    William (1699–) 152
Knollys
    Francis (1514–1596) 66
    Robert (1481–1520) 32
    Sir Francis (1514–1596) 32
Knowles
    Andrew (1592–1660) 108
    John (1596–1685) 108, 157, 215, 216
    John (1625–1705) 157, 215
    John (1661–1733) 215
    Richard (1614–1682) 157, 216
    Samuel (1651–1737) 216
    Sir William (1544–1632) 33, 107
    William (1544–1632) 66

    William (1566–1598) 67, 107, 157
Lambard
    Mary (1619–1686) 75, 116
Lane
    John 210, 269
    Katherine (1632–1683) 69
    Susanna 210, 269
Langton
    Maria (1534–1591) 35
Lattimer
    Rebecca (1646–1734) 211
Lee
    Alexander (–1807) 199
    Sarah 260
Leete
    Abigail (ca.1648–1710) 257
Legge
    Barbara (1701–1765) 226
Leigh
    Margaret (1516–1538) 31
Leighton
    Elizabeth 61, 102
Lemoine
    Anne (1638–1725) 76
Leverett
    Mary 206
Leversedge
    Apolyn (1529–1553) 68
Lewis
    Hannah 267
Loomis
    Kegiah 266
    Mary (1723–1790) 248
    Rebecca 219
Lowell
    Joanna Percival (1619–1677) 109, 158, 217
    John (1527–) 68
    Percival (1571–) 68, 109, 158
    Richard (1547–1577) 68, 109
Luttrell
    Eleanor (1498–<1531) 34
    Eleanor (ca.1495–1531) 33
Lyon
    Hanna (1758–1842) 228
    Uriel (ca.1728–) 228
MacAdam
    Isabella 91
MacArthur
    Duncan 177

Mary (1682–) 188, 247
MacAulay
   Mary (ca.1775–) 249
Macdonald
   Catherine (1600–1660) 52, 91
MacDonald
   a daughter of John 93, 143
   a daughter of Samual 93, 143
   a daughter of William 143
   Alexander 130
   Anne 186
   Barbara (1640–) 130
   Donald 177
   Florence 90, 132, 137, 138, 139
   Florence (1610–) 90, 134, 137
   Isabel (1567–1615) 84
   John Dubh 183
   Margaret 191
   Marian 183
   Marian (1594–1606) 47, 77, 83, 86, 87, 88, 179
   Marion 56
   Mary (ca.1695–1779) 243
   Ronald 186
   Una (1565–) 44, 47, 48, 49, 50, 51, 85, 86, 89
MacDougal
   Isabel 126
Macdougall
   Katherine (1702–) 173, 237
MacDougall
   Duncan 179
   Isabelle (ca.1678–) 179, 237
MacDuffie
   Malcolm 133
MacFadyen
   Margaret 252
   Neil 252
MacGillivray
   Julia (ca.1581–) 52
   Una 176, 234, 235, 236
MacGillvray
   a daughter of 121, 134, 187
   Alexander 175, 176
   Alexander (–1765) 192
   Martin 134
   Una 192
MacIntosh
   Alexander 199
   Angus 147
   Malcolm 59
   Marjory (ca.1715–) 146, 198, 199
   Mary 199, 254
   William 99, 149
Mack
   Jennet 269

Mackaskill
   a daughter of 55, 56
Mackenzie
   Janet (1576–) 46, 84
MacKenzie
   Ann 54, 55
Mackinnon
   Eunice 247
MacKinnon
   Alexander 233
MacLachlan
   Alexander 125
   Allan 119, 171, 172
   Julian 125
   Margery (–1770) 119, 171, 172, 230
MacLaine
   Allan 46, 179, 237, 239
   Allan (–>1776) 180, 181, 239
   Allan (ca.1675–) 88, 126, 179, 229, 237, 238
   Anne 237
   Archibald (–1784) 229, 238
   Catherine 230, 238, 239
   Donald 180, 181
   Elizabeth 179, 237, 239
   Finvola 88, 179, 181, 238
   Flora 239
   Flora Ann 240
   Harriet 239
   Hector (ca.1640–>1707) 82, 125, 130, 178, 179, 180
   Hector (ca.1727–ca.1749) 237
   Hector Odhar (1575–1628) 43, 46, 82, 83
   Isabel 229, 238
   Isabella 179, 237
   Jane 239
   Jane Jarvis 239
   Janet 46, 83
   John 83, 126, 130, 180, 181, 239
   John (1724–1788) 88, 179, 229, 237
   John (1792–1818) 239
   John (ca.1670–) 126, 179, 237
   Julia 83, 130
   Julian (ca.1700–) 88, 179, 238, 240
   Katherine 83
   Lachlan 126, 180, 181, 238, 239
   Lachlan (1695–1744) 173, 179, 237
   Lachlan Mor (1614–1687) 46, 77, 82, 125, 126, 129
   Margaret 126, 179, 230, 236, 238, 239
   Margaret (ca.1612–) 46, 48, 83
   Mary 46, 83, 88, 126, 180, 239
   Mary (1651–1729) 77, 83, 118, 119, 126, 130
   Mary (1740–1831) 173, 231, 232, 237
   Murdoch (1730–1804) 180, 181, 238
   Murdoch (1791–1844) 239
   Murdock (–>1729) 126, 178, 236, 237
   Murdock Mor (–1663) 46, 82
   Murdock Og (ca.1635–ca.1662) 82, 126, 130
   Phoebe 239
   Sarah 43, 46, 83

William 239

Maclean

Alexander (1722–1765) 188, 246
Alexander (1791–1876) 234, 235
Alexander (–1818) 231
Alexander (ca.1705–) 120, 174, 232
Alexander (ca.1709–1800) 123, 176, 234, 235, 236
Alexander (ca.1756–) 175
Alice (ca.1760–1840) 175, 234, 235
Alicia 185, 245
Allan (1641–1674) 84, 127, 180
Allan (1792–1871) 234
Allan (ca.1564–>1620) 44, 47, 48, 49, 50, 51, 52, 85, 86, 89
Allan (ca.1585–) 48, 51
Allan (ca.1615–1651) 48
Allan (ca.1630–) 52, 91, 140
Allan (ca.1657–) 132
Allan (ca.1660–) 121, 134, 174, 187
Allan (ca.1662–) 79, 81
Allan (ca.1694–ca.1723) 78, 122
Allan (ca.1710–1746) 120
Allan (ca.1725–1797) 185, 244
Allan (ca.1732–1754) 175
Allan (ca.1748–) 175
Allan (ca.1749–) 172
Allan (ca.1797–1818) 231
Allan the elder (ca.1641–ca.1670) 44, 50, 78, 79, 121, 122
Allan the elder (ca.1700–) 123, 175
Allan the younger (ca.1643–ca.1720) 44, 50, 79, 122, 123, 124
Allan the younger (ca.1706–ca.1730) 123
Allan Thomas (1793–1868) 235
Andrew (1812–) 231
Angus (ca.1690–1735) 131, 171, 185, 186
Ann 177, 181, 229
Anne 44, 50, 123, 231
Anne (1707–) 188, 246
Anne (ca.1750–) 175, 233
Archibald 185, 231, 234, 245
Archibald (1758–1830) 175, 233
Archibald (1761–1830) 176, 234, 235
Archibald (ca.1620–) 44, 81
Archibald (ca.1714–) 123
Archibald Donald 235, 236
Beatrix 181
Betty 185
Catherine 48, 176, 235, 236
Catherine (1714–1772) 188, 246
Catherine (ca.1712–) 170, 182, 229, 242
Charles (1695–1746) 78, 119, 122, 172, 173, 230
Charles (1806–1872) 231
Charles (ca.1592–) 48, 83
Charles (ca.1598–) 44, 50, 78, 79, 80, 81
Charles (ca.1610–1664) 43
Charles (ca.1650–) 91, 140, 192
Charles (ca.1660–) 79, 81
Charles (ca.1672–ca.1741) 80, 122, 175, 176
Charles (ca.1700–) 120
Charles (ca.1730–1754) 175

Charles (ca.1735–) 174
Charles (ca.1754–) 173
Charles James (–1837) 235
Christianna (ca.1700–) 185, 244
Christina 198, 231
Colin (ca.1756–) 173, 232
Colquhoun (–1822) 231
Donald (ca.1635–) 87, 121, 134, 187
Donald (ca.1668–) 79, 121, 122
Donald (ca.1672–1748) 130, 174, 185, 244, 245
Donald (ca.1675–) 79, 120, 139, 174
Donald (ca.1676–) 80, 184
Donald (ca.1685–) 121, 174, 187, 232, 233, 244
Donald (ca.1695–) 187, 188
Donald (ca.1704–) 123, 176
Donald (ca.1727–) 120
Donald (ca.1752–) 173
Donald (ca.1760–) 246
Donald Roy (ca.1770–1853) 173, 231
Duncan 174
Elizabeth 185, 245
Ewen (–1651) 48
Ewen (ca.1649–) 44, 50, 81
Fitzroy Jeffries Grafton (1813–1858) 231
Florence 44, 50, 121, 187
George 174, 233, 244
Gillean (ca.1583–) 47, 50
Gillean (ca.1700–) 182
Hector 44, 48, 86, 187, 188
Hector (1703–1750) 181
Hector (–1818) 231
Hector (–1834) 235, 236
Hector (ca.1601–>1641) 51, 86, 131
Hector (ca.1610–1683) 42, 47, 51, 82, 85, 128, 129, 130, 131
Hector (ca.1647–) 44, 50, 80, 184
Hector (ca.1660–) 131, 132, 171, 185, 186
Hector (ca.1670–) 78, 87, 119, 142
Hector (ca.1692–1765) 185
Hector (ca.1700–ca.1784) 122, 174, 243
Hector (ca.1702–ca.1798) 123, 175, 233, 234, 235
Hector (ca.1715–1796) 174, 232, 244
Hector Mor (ca.1603–ca.1630) 47, 84
Isabel 181
Isabell 123
Isabella 48, 231
Isabella (ca.1645–) 86, 128, 131, 170, 182
Jabez (1750–) 190
James 44, 176
James (ca.1698–) 182, 238, 240
Jane (–1822) 231
Janet 43
Janet Kinlochlaine (ca.1627–1700) 87
Jannet 80, 124, 132
Jean 120
John 43, 121, 176, 187, 231, 234, 245
John (1666–1696) 78, 79, 119, 121
John (–1822) 235
John (ca.1625–1681) 51, 86, 131, 136, 186
John (ca.1628–) 87
John (ca.1642–) 86, 130, 185
John (ca.1670–) 134

John (ca.1673–) 130
John (ca.1675–) 80, 184
John (ca.1708–) 123
John (ca.1726–) 120, 173, 232
John (ca.1735–) 238, 240
John (ca.1754–) 175
John (ca.1757–) 246
John Diuriach (ca.1625–) 48, 77, 87, 119
Julia 235
Lachlan 51, 81, 83, 86, 88, 120, 121, 122, 184
Lachlan (–1830) 235, 236
Lachlan (ca.1600–) 52, 91
Lachlan (ca.1635–) 44, 50, 78, 81, 120, 121, 139
Lachlan (ca.1665–) 134, 187
Lachlan (ca.1670–ca.1751) 80, 122, 174, 175
Lachlan (ca.1710–1799) 185, 244
Lachlan (ca.1712–1762) 123
Lachlan (ca.1722–1746) 120, 172
Lachlan (ca.1728–1764) 120
Lachlan (ca.1762–) 247
Lachlan Catanach (–1651) 48
Lachlan Og (ca.1610–) 48, 87, 134
Lillian 231
Louisa 181
Margaret 44, 50, 80, 123, 231
Marian 79, 81, 121
Marianne (1765–1840) 244
Marion 174, 233, 244
Marion (ca.1678–) 131, 185
Mary 44, 50, 51, 86, 181, 185, 231, 235
Mary (ca.1678–) 80, 184
Mary (ca.1730–1826) 174, 243
Mary (ca.1752–) 175, 233
Mary the elder (ca.1594–) 47, 49
Mary the younger 48, 51
Neil 48, 83, 88
Peter 79, 81
Salome (–1858) 234
Sibella 177, 229
Una 122, 173, 175, 230

MacLean
a daughter of Archibald 125, 171, 178
a daughter of Lachlan 94
Aleander 200
Alexander 58, 96, 100, 140, 190, 192, 244, 247
Alexander (1628–1671) 59, 99
Alexander (1670–1736) 127
Alexander (1686–1715) 130
Alexander (1690–1739) 80, 124
Alexander (1720–ca.1780) 148, 200
Alexander (1753–1835) 242
Alexander (1764–1855) 230
Alexander (ca.1625–1671) 58
Alexander (ca.1685–ca.1736) 100, 148, 200
Alexander (ca.1700–) 94, 143
Alexander (ca.1705–) 246
Alexander (ca.1715–) 249
Alexander (ca.1737–) 177, 236
Allan .. 43, 54, 55, 58, 81, 82, 93, 97, 98, 125, 142, 143, 149, 171, 172, 175, 178, 202, 241, 242
Allan (1668–1756) 77, 118, 126, 170, 171
Allan (1715–1786) 138, 190, 248
Allan (1724–1792) 120, 172, 230, 231, 232
Allan (1790–1876) 199
Allan (1827–1902) 254
Allan (ca.1536–) 141
Allan (ca.1551–) 53
Allan (ca.1577–) 45
Allan (ca.1582–1649) 42, 43, 44, 45
Allan (ca.1631–) 45, 82, 125
Allan (ca.1655–1715) 132, 137, 186
Allan (ca.1660–) 45, 81, 124, 136
Allan (ca.1665–) 78, 87, 119, 172
Allan (ca.1670–) 246
Allan (ca.1678–) 90, 138, 190, 191
Allan (ca.1684–1722) 128, 131, 182, 241
Allan (ca.1695–) 142
Allan (ca.1700–) 125, 178
Allan (ca.1705–) 123
Allan (ca.1705–1753) 118
Allan (ca.1710–1783) 170, 177, 182, 229
Allan (ca.1760–) 196, 252
Allan Og (ca.1565–) 53
Angus 97, 144, 197, 198, 199, 253
Angus (758–1794) 147
Angus (ca.1657–) 53, 139, 191, 249
Angus (ca.1691–) 80, 124, 172
Ann 56, 94, 96, 144, 177, 252
Ann (ca.1652–) 45, 79, 81, 90, 121, 136
Ann (ca.1682–) 55, 95, 144
Ann (ca.1705–) 176, 236
Anna 119, 124, 172
Anna (1765–) 230
Anna (ca.1595–) 48
Anne 54, 140, 190, 192
Anne (ca.1690–) 174, 185, 232, 233, 244
Anne (ca.1720–ca.1755) 170, 173, 182, 230
Annie 59, 99, 100, 149, 254
Archibald 55, 118, 143, 190, 196, 249
Archibald (1761–1830) 192
Archibald (ca.1610–) 55, 56
Archibald (ca.1668–1739) 54, 93, 143
Archibald (ca.1685–) 55, 95, 144, 247
Archibald (ca.1735–1817) 144
Archibald Og (ca.1680–) 246
Barbara 94, 199
Barbara (1761–1849) 147
Barbara (ca.1732–) 95, 144, 247
Beathag (1579–) 43, 46, 82, 83
Beatrix (ca.1672–) 77, 127
Bridget. 59
Catherine 49, 55, 58, 87, 98, 134, 138, 146, 173, 174, 176, 183, 190, 191, 192, 232, 243, 248
Catherine (ca.1590–1651) 88, 132, 133, 141, 193
Catherine (ca.1630–) 85, 89, 127, 180, 181
Catherine (ca.1665–) 129, 135, 137, 183, 243
Catherine (ca.1700–) 93, 142
Catherine (ca.1705–) 144, 243
Catherine (ca.1718–) 123, 177
Charles .. 43, 53, 55, 57, 59, 93, 97, 100, 140, 142, 143, 145, 185, 188, 196, 198, 202, 252
Charles (–1704) 83
Charles (1718–1778) 99, 146, 198, 199

Charles (1760–)	191
Charles (ca.1570–)	53, 92
Charles (ca.1590–)	52
Charles (ca.1592–)	52
Charles (ca.1622–)	87, 132, 137, 186
Charles (ca.1647–)	55, 95, 96
Charles (ca.1655–)	133, 186, 194
Charles (ca.1665–)	82, 125, 171, 178
Charles (ca.1680–)	77, 127
Charles (ca.1692–)	80, 124, 177
Charles (ca.1700–)	94
Charles (ca.1705–)	138, 191
Charles (ca.1710–)	93, 95, 142, 144, 196
Charles (ca.1712–1778)	147, 199, 254
Charles (ca.1720–)	144, 196, 252
Charles (ca.1754–)	173, 230
Charles Maxwell (1791–1864)	199, 253
Charles-Durell	236
Charlotte Amelia (1824–1910)	253
Chriatina	236
Christina (1718–1808)	98, 182, 241
Christopher	176
Christy	197, 248
Christy (ca.1728–)	246
David	59
David (1692–1719)	100, 148, 200, 201
David (ca.1610–)	60
Don Andrew (ca.1720–)	124
Donald	56, 57, 58, 59, 87, 94, 96, 97, 98, 139, 144, 145, 146, 184, 191, 198, 236, 241, 248, 252, 253
Donald (1600–>1655)	47, 85, 128, 135
Donald (1656–1729)	129, 135, 174, 183, 229, 241, 242, 243
Donald (1671–1725)	128, 131, 170, 182, 229, 230, 238, 240
Donald (–1774)	242
Donald (ca.1575–)	57
Donald (ca.1585–)	60
Donald (ca.1618–)	52, 91
Donald (ca.1630–ca.1693)	59
Donald (ca.1640–)	57
Donald (ca.1645–)	44, 50, 54, 80, 94, 124, 172
Donald (ca.1657–)	128
Donald (ca.1660–1726)	100, 149, 202
Donald (ca.1670–)	77, 118, 127
Donald (ca.1675–)	55, 95, 143, 246
Donald (ca.1679–)	57
Donald (ca.1685–ca.1773)	181, 238, 245
Donald (ca.1695–)	100, 148, 201
Donald (ca.1696–1731)	118
Donald (ca.1698–)	246
Donald (ca.1700–)	91, 123, 140, 176, 192, 193, 236
Donald (ca.1721–)	143
Donald (ca.1725–)	143
Donald (ca.1725–1790)	243
Donald (ca.1736–)	177
Donald (ca.1745–)	202
Donald Cubair	252
Donald Og (ca.1645–)	53, 93
Donald Roy	142
Dugald (–1818)	98
Duncan	91, 139
Duncan (–1770)	249
Duncan (ca.1550–)	49
Duncan (ca.1690–1770)	191, 249
Eliza	254
Elizabeth	55, 198, 253, 254
Elizabeth (ca.1620–)	52, 91
Ewen	55, 119, 134, 136, 139
Ewen (ca.1604–)	45, 82
Ewen (ca.1633–)	91
Ewen (ca.1635–1694)	43, 77, 118, 119, 126
Ewen (ca.1673–)	54, 93, 119, 142
Ewen (ca.1698–1729)	118
Ewen or Hugh (–1651)	89
Ewen the elder (ca.1605–1691)	43, 83
Farquhar	59
Finvola (ca.1630–)	89
Finvola (ca.1780–)	146, 198
Finvola (Florence) (ca.1610–)	47, 84, 89, 127
Finvole (Florence) (ca.1630–)	85, 89, 128, 135
Flora	45, 192, 197
Flora (1660–1702)	133, 193
Flora (1784–1885)	233
Flora (ca.1735–)	192, 249
Florence	45, 55, 79, 90, 95, 96, 120, 122, 133, 136, 138, 139, 143, 144, 183, 187, 190, 191, 194
Florence (ca.1675–)	94
Florentia	96
Gabriel	236
Gillean	238
Gillespick Mor	253
Hector	45, 58, 77, 82, 100, 121, 124, 125, 132, 136, 137, 178, 192, 197, 202, 232, 242
Hector (1555–ca.1614)	46, 48
Hector (–1689)	90, 139, 191
Hector (–1818)	252
Hector (ca.1605–)	49, 50, 89, 136, 137, 184
Hector (ca.1610–ca.1650)	60, 100
Hector (ca.1625–)	57
Hector (ca.1630–)	87, 133, 146, 186, 187, 194
Hector (ca.1639–)	60
Hector (ca.1640–)	54, 93
Hector (ca.1645–)	50, 90, 137, 184, 243
Hector (ca.1656–)	52, 91, 140
Hector (ca.1665–)	189
Hector (ca.1672–)	137, 184, 243
Hector (ca.1680–1754)	95, 138, 144
Hector (ca.1686–1756)	183, 241
Hector (ca.1687–)	81, 124, 130
Hector (ca.1690–)	181, 238
Hector (ca.1697–)	243
Hector (ca.1710–)	94
Hector (ca.1715–)	58, 98, 146
Hector (ca.1720–)	124, 177
Hector (ca.1734–1799)	177
Hector (–ca.1828)	252
Hector Mor (ca.1627–)	85, 135
Hector Og (1583–1623)	46, 84, 85
Hector Og (ca.1631–)	85, 128, 135, 181, 238
Hector Roy (1534–1593)	48, 49
Hector Roy (ca.1625–<1676)	80, 89, 128, 135, 182, 183, 184
Hector Ruadh (1626–1651)	84

Helen	254	John (ca.1678–)	57
Henry (ca.1709–)	57	John (ca.1680–ca.1760)	57, 98
Hugh	50, 90, 94, 133, 138, 144, 192, 194, 200, 233	John (ca.1695–1746)	91, 140, 192
Hugh (1738–)	140, 192, 249	John (ca.1699–)	94
Hugh (ca.1692–1786)	183, 241	John (ca.1700–)	95, 143, 181, 191, 238, 246
Hugh (ca.1725–1784)	202, 255	John (ca.1700–1739)	118, 171, 172, 230
Hugh (ca.1735–)	200, 255	John (ca.1701–1746)	99
Hugh (ca.1736–1768)	171, 172, 230	John (ca.1709–)	246
Isabel	55, 84, 94, 96, 144, 236, 252	John (ca.1710–1746)	147
Isabel (1620–1657)	52	John (ca.1712–)	94
Isabel (ca.1683–)	188, 246	John (ca.1720–)	97, 145, 197
Isabel (ca.1715–)	170, 182, 229, 237	John (ca.1722–)	148, 201
Isabell	55	John (ca.1726–)	143
Isabella	241, 254	John (ca.1732–)	177
Isabella (ca.1695–)	118, 170, 182, 229, 230	John (ca.1735–)	142, 196, 252
Isabelle	47	John (ca.1740–1760)	95, 197, 252
James	94	John (ca.1742–)	171, 178
James (–1767)	118	John (ca.1745–)	178
James (ca.1707–)	57	John (ca.1755–)	98, 146, 198
James (–ca.1828)	252	John (ca.1770–)	192, 249
Jane	201	John (–ca.1830)	253
Janet	59, 78, 99, 119	John 4th. Baronet (ca.1670–1716)	127, 180, 240
Janet (ca.1575–)	48, 88	John Ardfinaig (1696–1756)	183, 242
Janet (ca.1670–)	133, 187, 194	John Diurach (ca.1616–)	52, 91
Janet (ca.1685–)	90, 138, 191	John Dubh	47
Janet (ca.1716–)	123, 177	John Dubh (ca.1540–1586)	48, 86
Janet (ca.1758–1836)	245	John Garbh (ca.1590–1662)	48, 86, 88, 132, 133, 134
Jannet	49, 59, 79, 87, 89, 90, 100, 130, 133, 139, 147, 149, 199	John Garbh (ca.1600–1678)	45, 49, 84, 85, 88, 127, 128, 132, 135, 136
Jannet (1600–1650)	47, 51, 86, 131	John Garbh (ca.1680–1698)	183
Jannet (1704–)	99	John Hector Og (ca.1660–)	128, 181, 238
Jannet (1756–)	147, 199	John Mor (ca.1743–1798)	145, 197
Jannet (ca.1620–)	42, 51, 82, 85, 128, 129	John Og	146, 197
Jannet (ca.1647–)	86, 131, 171, 185, 186	John Og (1657–1707)	60, 99, 147, 148, 149
Jannet (ca.1666–)	80, 129, 135, 184	John Og (ca.1626–ca.1715)	58, 99
Jennet (–1791)	189, 247	John Roy (ca.1632–)	45, 79, 81, 82, 89, 136
Jessie (1835–1870)	254	Joshua	236
John	54, 55, 56, 58, 59, 77, 78, 94, 96, 97, 119, 122, 127, 132, 133, 138, 140, 143, 145, 173, 174, 184, 187, 190, 191, 192, 193, 194, 197, 199, 202, 236, 249, 252, 253	Julian	48, 88, 137, 179, 184, 229, 237, 238
		Julian (ca.1595–)	50, 89, 136, 137, 184
		Julian (ca.1725–)	175, 233, 234, 235
		Lachalan Og	45
John (1673–1748)	58, 99, 146	Lachlan	56, 58, 77, 96, 97, 119, 127, 136, 138, 139, 140, 142, 145, 146, 178, 180, 187, 191, 196, 202, 243, 245, 247, 252
John (1683–1748)	100, 147, 199		
John (1707–1805)	93, 142		
John (1716–)	125, 171, 178	LachLan	198
John (1724–1808)	57, 98, 241	Lachlan (1606–1648)	47, 84, 127
John (1754–1826)	147	Lachlan (1618–1619)	52, 91
John (1787–1848)	252	Lachlan (1650–1686)	85, 128, 131, 135, 170, 182
John (1802–)	249	Lachlan (1693–1744)	183, 229, 242
John (ca.1580–)	49, 91	Lachlan (1730–1802)	138, 191
John (ca.1600–>1671)	58, 59	Lachlan (–1752)	55, 96
John (ca.1610–)	53	Lachlan (ca.1582–1642)	49, 84, 88, 89, 90
John (ca.1620–)	56	Lachlan (ca.1596–)	56
John (ca.1630–)	56, 97	Lachlan (ca.1635–)	50, 90, 136, 189
John (ca.1643–1723)	54, 93, 94	Lachlan (ca.1640–1687)	86, 130
John (ca.1645–)	94	Lachlan (ca.1650–)	56
John (ca.1651–)	57	Lachlan (ca.1652–1687)	129, 135, 182
John (ca.1652–)	57	Lachlan (ca.1669–)	60
John (ca.1660–)	136, 189, 247	Lachlan (ca.1670–1744)	137, 184, 243
John (ca.1670–)	54, 94	Lachlan (ca.1675–)	176
John (ca.1674–)	80, 123, 176, 177, 229	Lachlan (ca.1680–)	54, 93, 142
John (ca.1675–)	57, 98	Lachlan (ca.1685–)	187

Lachlan (ca.1690–) 91, 190
Lachlan (ca.1690–1756) 149, 202, 255
Lachlan (ca.1705–) 57
Lachlan (ca.1715–) 57, 98, 146
Lachlan (ca.1720–) 148, 201
Lachlan (ca.1730–) 176, 236
Lachlan Ban (1750–1819) 233
Lachlan Mor (1558–1598) 46, 47, 48, 83
Lachlan Og (ca.1584–1642) ...47, 77, 83, 85, 86, 87, 88, 179
Laclhlan (ca.1635–) 60, 100, 149
Louisa 173
Malcolm 248
Malcolm (ca.1770–) 255
Margaret 45, 59, 77, 90, 96, 97, 119, 124, 127, 129, 135, 136, 139, 143, 145, 146, 171, 172, 177, 184, 197, 241
Margaret (ca.1590–) 53, 92, 140
Margaret (ca.1620–) 49, 88, 134, 193
Margaret (ca.1635–) 51, 77, 82, 86, 125, 126, 129
Margaret (ca.1655–) 90, 134, 137, 189
Margaret (ca.1665–) 79, 121, 174, 187
Margaret (ca.1702–) 118, 171, 185
Margory 178
Maria (ca.1750–) 177, 229
Marian 84, 122, 175, 176, 242, 243
Marian (1837–1909) 254
Marian (ca.1635–) 90, 132, 137, 186
Marion 56, 77, 98, 127, 143, 192, 197, 241
Marion (1560–) 48, 49
Marion (ca.1622–) 45, 79, 81, 82, 136
Marion (ca.1625–ca.1680) 42, 51, 80, 85, 128, 135, 182, 183, 184
Marion (ca.1650–) 44, 81
Marion (ca.1744–) 197
Marjory 119, 172, 191, 199
Marjory (1763–1820) 147, 199
Mary ... 43, 50, 57, 77, 78, 79, 80, 81, 84, 132, 138, 140, 142, 144, 146, 147, 173, 174, 176, 177, 191, 192, 193, 232, 241, 243, 248, 249, 252
Mary (1603–1665) 47, 86, 132, 133, 134
Mary (1707–) 99
Mary (1709–) 188, 246
Mary (1715–) 118, 171, 178
Mary (–1838) 197
Mary (ca.1660–) 91, 140
Mary (ca.1690–) 189, 247
Mary (ca.1700–) 55, 96
Mary (ca.1702–) 93, 119, 142
Mary Ann 236
Murdoch (–1867) 146, 198
Murdoch Mor 197
Murdock 97, 197, 202
Neil .. 54, 55, 56, 58, 94, 96, 97, 138, 145, 183, 197, 252
Neil (ca.1615–1651) 49, 90, 132, 134, 137, 138, 139
Neil (ca.1670–) 54, 93, 142
Neil (–ca.1830) 253
Neil Ban (ca.1695–>1760) 94, 143
Neil Ban (ca.1700–) 95, 144, 196
Nial Ban (ca.1610–) 54, 55
Niel 55
Norman 242

Patrick (ca.1610–) 49, 91, 139
Peter 255
Peter (ca.1715–1752) 92
Phineas 199
Phineas (1759–) 147
Robert 201, 255
Robert (ca.1710–) 148, 200, 255
Roderick 125, 242
Roderick (ca.1623–) 56, 97
Rory 56, 97
Rory Mor 145, 197, 252
Sarah 171, 172
Sibella 241
Susan 236
Susanna (ca.1735–) 191
Thomas Henderson 254
Una 129, 135, 184, 241
Una (ca.1640–) 89, 132, 136
Una (ca.1714–) 123, 177, 229
William 143
William (1706–1753) 99
William (–1759) 199, 254
William (1762–1841) 147, 198, 253, 254
William (1793–1872) 199, 254
William (ca.1712–) 148, 200
William (ca.1714–1753) 147
William Thomas Henderson (1826–1892) 254
Zeiretta 124

Macleod
Florence (ca.1580–) 49, 84, 88, 89, 90
Julian (1636–1650) 127, 180
Roderick Ruairidh (1562–1626) 84

MacLeod
Catherine 81, 124
Isabel (ca.1660–) 183, 241
Janet 122, 174, 175
Jannet (1731–1780) 241
John 122, 127
Margaret 84
Marian 174, 183, 229, 241, 242, 243
Mary (1605–) 84, 127
Norman 183
Roderick 81
Rory 183
Tormod 49

MacNeil
Flora 53

MacPherson
Mary (1670–1719) 180

MacQuarrie
a daughter of Hector 186
Catherime 80, 124, 172
Donald 80
Flora 127, 180, 181, 238, 239
Hector (ca.1630–) 186
John 54
Lachlan 127, 180, 181, 245
Marion 54, 93, 177
Una 80, 122, 123, 124

MacQueen
   Angus 59
   Marion 140, 192

Madison
   Elizabeth (1522–1624) 37

Manby
   Elizabeth (1580–1612) 74, 115

Manett
   Joane (1506–1567) 67

Manicol
   ? 255

Markham
   Isabella (1527–1579) 38, 73
   Sir John (1500–1564) 38

Marsh
   Benjamin (1704–) 206, 259
   Ebenezer (1674–1722) 206
   Margaret (1537–1563) 37, 71
   Mehitable (1731–) 206, 259
   Thomas (1520–1561) 37

Marshall
   Maud (1192–1248) 4
   Rebecca (1648–) 221
   Sarah Amelia (–1837) 253
   William (1146–1219) 4

Martin
   Katherine (1706–1787) 160

Matthews
   Elizabeth 57

Mauchline
   Margaret (1645–) 56, 97

Mc Lean
   Robert (1748–1828) 201

McDongal
   Agnes 196

McHutcheon
   Elizabeth (1709–1769) 194, 250
   William (1681–1763) 194

Mckinnon
   Mary (1715–1820) 240

McLane
   Andrew Francis (1710–1772) 246

Mclean
   Allan (1751–) 189
   Donald Watson (1765–) 232
   Florence (1747–) 189, 247
   John (1680–1756) 134, 188, 246
   Malcolm (ca.1750–1815) 240
   Margaret (1745–<1752) 189, 247
   Mary 250
   William (1702–1785) 148, 200, 254

McLean
   Alexander (1747–1806) 190, 248
   Alexander (1772–1843) 248
   Alexander (1781–) 196
   Alister (ca.1592–) 53
   Allan 172
   Allan (–1709) 43, 78
   Allan (1776–1864) 232
   Allen (1781–1861) 248
   Ann (1747–) 195
   Anne (1762–) 201
   Archibald 43
   Archibald (1658–) 133, 193
   Archibald (1767–) 195
   Barbara (1740–1803) 232
   Beatrix 43
   Catherine (1625–1660) 87, 132, 193
   Catherine (1730–) 194
   Catherine (1778–) 251
   Catherine (1779–) 196
   Catherine (1794–ca.1816) 251
   Catherine (ca.1696–1762) 242
   Charles (1630–) 87
   Charles (ca.1613–) 53
   Cornelius (1701–1762) 98, 145, 198
   Daniel (1736–1813) 240
   David (1760–) 201
   Donald 43, 78
   Donald (1654–) 133, 193
   Donald (1702–1795) 92, 141, 195, 196
   Donald (1737–) 194, 250
   Donald (1769–) 195
   Donald (1771–) 201
   Donald (1780–) 251
   Donald A. (1735–1809) 174, 232
   Dudley E. (>1748–1749) 190
   Duncan (1733–) 194
   Duncan (ca.1617–) 53, 92, 191
   Duncan (ca.1656–) 53, 92, 141
   Duncan (ca.1739–) 142, 196
   Elizabeth (1771–) 195
   Ewen (ca.1610–1651) 88, 92, 132, 133, 140, 193
   Ewen (ca.1655–1702) 88, 134, 137, 188, 189, 193
   Farquhar (1743–1822) 194, 249
   Farquhar (ca.1676–) 92, 141, 194
   Farquhar (ca.1701–) 141, 194, 249
   Florence (ca.1635–) 133, 141, 186, 187, 193
   Francis (1777–1861) 248
   Hannah (1769–1841) 248
   Harvey (1797–1869) 253
   Hector (–1654) 83
   Hector (1696–1775) 134, 137, 189, 247
   Hector (1750–) 195
   Hector (1765–1847) 250
   Hector (ca.1630–1693) 88, 132, 134, 141, 193
   Hector (ca.1706–ca.1796) 141, 194, 250
   Helen (1743–) 195
   Hugh (1715–1784) 188, 247
   Hugh (ca.1730–) 144, 189, 247
   Jabez (1746–1747) 190
   Janet (1658–) 133, 193
   Janet (1765–) 201

Jannet	43, 77, 87, 119
John	92
John (1727–1785)	146, 198, 253
John (1737–)	142
John (1746–)	195, 250
John (1749–1815)	240
John (1756–1821)	247
John (1765–1844)	195, 251
John (1796–ca.1826)	251
John (ca.1585–)	92, 140
John (ca.1633–1647)	53
John (ca.1655–)	43, 129
John (ca.1674–1723)	57, 97, 145
John (ca.1692–1787)	180, 240
John (ca.1699–)	135, 137, 189, 247
John (ca.1704–)	188
John Ban (ca.1655–1723)	53, 92, 141
John Crubach (ca.1603–1702)	42, 77, 78, 129
John Og (ca.1616–)	92
Jonas (1772–)	198, 253
Lachlan	92, 247
Lachlan (1652–)	133, 193
Lachlan (1714–1799)	242
Lachlan (1735–1819)	141, 195, 251
Lachlan (1774–)	195
Lachlan (1798–ca.1823)	251
Lachlan (ca.1636–)	43, 77
Lachlan (ca.1685–1755)	134, 188, 247
Laughlan (1744–1819)	171, 178
Malcolm (1771–1860)	250
Margaret (1752–)	189
Margaret (1767–)	201
Margaret (1776–)	251
Margaret (1783–)	196
Margaret (ca.1626–1660)	87
Mary	43, 78, 119, 121
Mary (>1744–1819)	190
Mary (1771–)	196
Mary (1773–)	251
Mary (1774–1776)	248
Mary (1785–1805)	249
Moses (1737–1810)	200, 254
Murdock (1774–)	250
Neil	189
Patrick (1776–)	196
Peter (1802–1877)	251
Robert (1735–)	194
Robert (1748–1828)	201
Rosannah (1789–1808)	249
Samuel D. (ca.1780–)	255
Sarah (1756–)	195
Susanna (1747–1748)	190
William (1670–1752)	132, 186, 245
William (1690–1718)	186, 245
William (1741–)	195
William (1769–)	201
Willian (ca.1768–1852)	250

McMalvay
Janet (ca.1675–)	92, 141

McNeil
Janet	128, 181, 238

McPherson
Mary (ca.1769–>1841)	251

McQuarrie
Elizabeth	249
Lachlan	180, 250

Mean
Mary	176

Meriam
William (1506–1566)	71

Merriam
John (1671–1754)	163, 221
Joseph (1599–1641)	71, 112, 163
William (1564–1635)	71, 112
William (1628–1689)	112, 163, 221
William (1700–1751)	221

Merrill
Achsa (1791–1817)	264
Allison (1793–)	265
Andrew (1792–1826)	268
Ashbel (1762–1793)	207, 264
Ashbel (1786–1867)	264
Betty (<1761–)	208
Bildad (<1750–1815)	208, 267
Bildad (1777–1851)	267
Charles (1768–)	266
Chester (1789–)	264
Diadama (<1778–)	261
Edwin (1795–1816)	263
Eli (<1772–)	261
Eliakim (<1714–)	152, 208, 266, 267, 268
Eliakim (<1742–1812)	208, 266
Elias (<1744–)	208, 266
Elias (1773–)	267
Emily (1802–1863)	265
Enos (1768–1858)	208, 265
Enos (1785–1858)	263
Erastus (1790–1809)	263
Esther (<1721–)	153, 209
Esther (<1730–1778)	206, 261
Esther (<1758–)	208
Esther (1765–)	261
Ferrand (1792–1809)	263
George (<1746–)	208
Hannah (<1766–)	267
Hervey (1793–1858)	264
Ichabod (<1728–)	206, 260
Ira (1779–1849)	267
Irene (1784–1813)	267
Irene (ca.1774–1776)	267
Isaac (<1728–<1749)	153
Isaac (<1760–)	208
Isaac (<1780–)	261
Isaac (1682–1742)	152, 206, 207, 208, 209
Isaac (1712–<1715)	152
Isaac (1748–>1817)	207, 262
Isaac (1770–)	266
Isaac (1781–1860)	267
James (1751–1807)	207, 262

James (ca.1789–) 264
James Seymour (1786–1816) 263
Jane Eliza (1818–1899) 265
Jeremiah (<1764–) 261
John (1636–1712) 152
Jonathan (1760–1836) 207, 263
Joseph (<1716–<1749) 153, 208
Joseph (<1732–1817) 207, 261
Joseph (1707–1788) 260
Laura (1799–1838) 265
Lewis (1799–1823) 268
Lucas Guernsey (1804–1890) 265
Lucy (1746–1752) 207
Lucy (1760–) 261
Lucy (1763–) 207
Lucy (1791–1873) 265
Lydia (1768–) 267
Malachi (ca.1787–ca.1850) 264
Margaret (ca.1793–) 264
Martin (<1754–1812) 208, 268
Martin (1801–1881) 268
Mary 261
Mary (<1747–) 208
Mary (<1775–) 261
Mary (1743–) 260
Mary (1743–1810) 207, 262
Mary (1777–) 266
Mary G. (ca.1795–) 264
Mehitable (<1734–1810) 207, 261
Nancy (1780–) 266
Nathaniel (1688–1749) 260
Nelson (1799–1875) 268
Noah (<1765–) 261
Noah (1707–1739) 152, 206, 260, 261
Noah (ca.1726–1739) 206, 260
Olive (1771–) 267
Orsamus Cook (1775–1869) 262
Rhoda (1758–) 207, 263
Rhoda (ca.1791–1870) 264
Ruby (1765–1845) 208, 264
Sabra (1785–) 266
Salmon (1773–) 266
Sarah (<1719–) 153, 209
Sarah (1752–) 208
Sarah (1794–1794) 268
Selah Higley (1796–) 266
Timothy (1709–1788) 152, 207, 262, 263, 264, 265
Timothy (1741–) 207, 262
Timothy (1781–1836) 263
Timothy Noble (1825–1899) 266
Titus (1771–) 266
Uel (1779–1811) 263
Unknown (1739–) 207
Zelinda (<1755–) 208
Zelinda (1765–) 266
Zelinda (1786–1863) 267

Merriton
Anne (1605–1670) 108, 158, 216
George (1567–1624) 108, 158

Messier
Francois Michel (1679–1749) 76, 117
Francois Michel (1707–1749) 76, 117, 169
Marie Judith (1737–1805) 117, 169, 228
Michel (1640–1725) 76

Milbury
Henry (1625–1695) 104
Mary (1651–1735) 104, 154, 159

Miville dit le Suisse
Marie Catherine (1632–1702) 41

Mix
Damaris (1757–1795) 267

Molyneux
Alice (1531–1581) 39, 74
Richard (1510–1569) 39

Molyns
Agnes Ann (1508–1552) 37

Montgomery
Elizabeth (1606–1684) 42, 76

Moores
Joshua (1680–) 110
Zipporah (1710–1783) 110, 160

Morley
Aaron (1779–1863) 227
Ann (1773–) 227
Christopher (1775–) 227
David (1710–) 227
David (1739–1815) 227
David (1764–1822) 227
George (1767–) 227
Hannah (1781–) 228
Isaac (1773–) 227
John (1759–1849) 227
Mary (1785–) 228
Moses (1777–) 227

Moton
Elizabeth (1503–1554) 38

Mottrom
Anne (1639–1707) 216

Munro
Christian (1547–) 34

Needham
Alice (1616–1690) 31
Anne (1574–) 30
Dorothy (1570–1629) 30, 65, 105
Edmond (1575–1677) 30
Elizabeth (1578–1617) 31
Jane (1542–) 30
Mary Margaret (1568–) 30
Maud (1550–1635) 30
Robert (1535–1603) 30, 65
Robert (1555–1631) 30
Robert (1572–1627) 30
Thomas (1510–1570) 30
Thomas (1566–) 30

Neville
  Margaret (1515–1559) 40, 75
Neville 4th Earl of Westmorland
  Ralph (1497–1549) 40
Newell
  Esther (1652–) 224
Newgate
  Mary (1615–1692) 42
Nicholls
  Elizabeth (ca.1573–) 62
Nikeich
  Christian (ca.1630–) 53, 92, 191
Noble
  Hannah (1664–1741) 226
  James (1677–1711) 226
  John (1662–1714) 226
  Mark (1677–1741) 226
  Matthew (1668–1744) 226
  Thomas (1580–1636) 168
  Thomas (1606–1632) 168, 225
  Thomas (1632–1704) 168, 225
  Thomas (1665–1727) 226
Norton
  Lot 209, 261
Notman
  Bessie (1645–) 202, 255
Ocington
  Mary (1669–1725) 223
Pantry
  Mary (ca.1632–1677) 258
Parke
  James 245
  James Allan 245
Parker
  Elizabeth (Ann) (1598–1623) 159
  Sarah (ca.1583–1683) 205
Parr
  Elizabeth (1652–1727) 218
Pawley
  Honora (1580–1658) 115
Peele
  Anne (1674–1754) 117, 169
Penman
  Elizabeth (1680–) 110
Pennyston
  Lettice (1485–1558) 32
Perceval
  Christian (1540–1589) 34, 68, 109
  Edmund (1493–1551) 34, 68
  James (1468–1536) 34

Pierce
  Alice (1600–1647) 113, 164
  Anne Alice (1660–1710) 222
Pittman
  Della Dolla (1690–) 245
Plumb
  ? 262
Prescott
  Abigail (1679–1779) 167
  Abram (1728–1733) 225
  Annie (1719–1799) 225
  Edward (1717–1804) 224
  James (1529–1582) 39, 74
  James (1607–1639) 74, 115, 167
  James (1671–1746) 167
  James Sr (1643–1728) 115, 167, 224
  John (1576–1607) 39, 74, 115
  John (1726–1785) 225
  Joshua (1669–1769) 167, 224
  Joshua (1713–1785) 224
  Mary (1677–1740) 167
  Nathan (1711–1764) 224
  Nathaniel (1683–1771) 167
  Patience (1724–1793) 225
  Rebecca (1673–1704) 167
  Reuben (1721–) 225
  Samuel (1697–1759) 168
Provost
  Marguerite (1706–1736) 169
Purefoy
  Mary 102
Quaint
  Anne (1610–1671) 164, 222
Radcliffe
  Eleanore (1512–1612) 39
Randes
  Henry Holbeach (1520–1551) 67
  Mary (1571–1632) 68, 108, 158
  Thomas (1546–1609) 67, 108
Ratcliffe
  Elizabeth (1668–1695) 218
  Richard (1642–1686) 218
Read
  Elizabeth 153, 210
  Margaret (1500–1548) 109
Robert
  I (1000 AD–1035) 29
Robertson
  Janet (1740–ca.1773) 250
Robinson
  Barzilla 219
  Mary Ann (1779–1845) 219

Rogers
  Martha (ca.1661–) 259
  Mary (1565–1634) 73, 114
  Thomas George (1541–1587) 73

Rose
  Hannah (ca.1622–) 225

Ross
  James 99, 149
  Mary (1768–1855) 232

Ruggles
  Samuel 259
  Samuel (1658–1715) 259

Rule
  Elizabeth (1707–1784) 200, 254

Salesbury
  Jane (1650–1695) 116, 169

Sanderson
  Barbara (1584–) 34, 69

Sargent
  Joanna (1607–1649) 154, 210

Saunders
  Elizabeth (1584–1655) 73, 114
  Emma 61
  Thomas (1559–1609) 73

Schoonmaker
  Sarah (1707–1764) 145, 198

Scott
  Grissel (1543–1604) 60

Scroyne
  John 237

Seymour
  Jerusha (1754–1827) 262
  William (1728–1782) 262

Sharp
  Rebecca (1671–1751) 221

Sharpe
  Nathaniel (1644–) 221

Shelley
  Elizabeth (1564–1610) 108

Sibley
  Hannah (1695–1731) 259

Sinclair
  Alexander 235

Skelton
  Alice (1535–1605) 61

Smith
  Elizabeth (1675–1743) 111, 161
  Isabell Bland (1602–1699) 215
  Johannah (1748–1822) 248
  Margaret 244

Soule
  Patience (1648–1706) 203, 257

Spalding
  Benjamin 104, 154
  Edward 104, 154, 210
  Ephraim 154, 210, 269
  Erastus 210, 269
  Martha Ann 269

St John
  John (1560–1594) 67, 108

St. John
  Elizabeth (1604–1677) 63, 104
  Elizabeth Lucy (1580–1658) 67, 108, 157
  Oliver (1575–1626) 63

Stafford Westmorland
  Countess Catherine (1499–1555) 40

Stanley
  Abraham (1705–1788) 224
  John (1647–1729) 224
  Samuel (1677–) 224

Starkes
  Katherine (1605–1656) 32, 66

Stevens
  Esther (1715–1813) 161, 220

Stewart
  Catherine 186
  Catherine (ca.1717–) 141, 195, 196
  Margaret 47
  Mary 255

Stiles
  Edmond (1520–<1565) 68, 109, 158
  Francis (1602–1662) 158, 217
  Hannah (1631–1677) 217
  Humphrey (1506–1557) 34, 68, 109
  Thomas (1550–1614) 109, 158, 217

Stone
  Abigail 260

Strelly
  Anne (1508–1527) 38

Stuart
  Jannet 49, 91

Styles
  Humphrey (ca.1487–1558) 33, 68

Sutton
  Mary (1509–1574) 33, 67
  Simon (1474–1567) 33

Swift
  Esther Susanna (1622–1691) 66, 107

Talbot
- Alethea (1581–1654) 106, 155
- Anne (1523–1565) 30

Talcott
- Rachel 213

Taylor
- Elizabeth (1669–1756) 164, 222

Thomas
- Benjamin (1584–1609) 37, 70, 112
- Daniel (1644–1694) 111, 112, 161, 162, 163
- Gershom (1725–1792) 162
- Israel (1685–1767) 112, 162, 163, 220
- Israel (1720–1784) 162
- John (1547–1603) 37, 70
- John (1616–1671) 71, 111, 112, 163
- John (1672–1711) 112, 161, 163, 220
- Lois (1727–1788) 163, 220
- Moses (1721–1762) 162
- Recompense (1709–1793) 162, 220
- Recompense (1735–1797) 220
- Sarah (1716–1796) 162
- Tristram (1522–1624) 37

Thompson
- Ebenezer (1712–1775) 111, 161, 220
- John (1561–1626) 36
- John (1589–1679) 36, 70
- John (1620–1674) 36, 70, 111
- John (1736–1790) 161, 220
- John Jr. (1739–) 262
- Joseph (1664–1711) 70, 111, 161
- Rebecca (1651–1716) 70, 111, 161, 162, 163
- William (1760–1822) 220

Thorne
- Susannah (1560–>1588) 102, 151
- Thomas (ca.1521–1589) 102

Tillinghast
- Lydia (1708–1748) 170, 228

Tisdale
- Elizabeth (1530–1597) 37, 71

Tomlinson
- George (1575–1628) 115, 168
- Henry (1606–1681) 116, 168, 225
- John (1545–) 115
- Margaret (1642–1698) 168, 225

Toppen
- Elizabeth (1595–1636) 35

Totteshurst
- Ann (1540–1633) 37, 70
- Thomas (1511–1577) 37

Tow
- Anne (1635–1680) 216

Towlson
- Ann (ca.1710–1750) 227

Townsend
- John (1608–1668) 42, 76
- John (1635–1721) 42, 76, 117
- Solomon (1667–1717) 76, 117, 170
- Solomon (1701–1756) 118, 170, 228
- Thomas (1594–1677) 42
- William (1745–1781) 170, 228

Treat
- Catharine (1706–1778) 211
- Charles (1695–) 212
- Dorotheus (1704–) 212
- Dorothy (1704–) 212
- Isaac (1701–1763) 212
- James (1634–1709) 211
- Mary (1709–1735) 212
- Richard (1622–1693) 211
- Richard (1675–1713) 211
- Richard (1694–ca.1757) 212
- Sarah (1706–) 212
- Thomas (1668–1712) 211
- Thomas (1699–1780) 212

Trumpour
- Mary (1773–1774) 253

Tudor
- Margaret Elizabeth (1473–1519) 33

Tuttle
- John (1631–1683) 69
- Mary (1678–1727) 69, 110

Tweedie
- James (1675–1694) 256
- Mary (1698–1762) 256

Tyndall
- Margaret 205

Tyng
- Rebecca 206

Una: **91, 140**

unknown
- first wife 52

Usher
- Dorothy Elizabeth (1599–1620) 38, 72, 113
- Hezekiah (1567–1595) 38, 72
- Matthew (1540–) 38

Wagstaffe
- Frances (1697–1714) 169, 226

Waldron
- Elizabeth (1645–1724) 217

Walker
- George (1715–) 117, 169, 227
- John (1604–1669) 41, 75
- John (1702–1766) 117
- Margaret (1740–1821) 169, 227
- Robert (1572–1641) 41
- Robert (1706–1770) 117

Thomas (1668–1726) 76, 116, 169
Thomas (1698–1760) 117
William (1630–1672) 41, 75, 116
William (1699–1700) 117

Warburton
Blanch (1496–1541) 40

Ward
Mary (1649–1685) 257

Warren
Abigail (1676–) 258
Hinchey (1727–1803) 203, 256
John (1561–1612) 60
Josiah (1759–1806) 256
Margaret (1495–1516) 40
Robert (1667–1721) 101, 150, 202
Robert (1700–1793) 150, 202, 256
Thomas Warren (1624–1670) 61, 101, 150
William (1596–1635) 60, 101

Warriner
Hannah (1643–1721) 226

Watson
Sarah 208, 266, 267, 268
Sarah Margaret 152

Weeks
Ann (1562–1601) 72, 113
Christopher 72

Welby
Olive 64, 104
Richard 64

Wentworth
Ursella (1514–1611) 39

Wheeler
Elizabeth (1602–1637) 163
Joseph (1610–1676) 213, 214
Rebecca (1645–1718) 213, 214

White
Elizabeth (1564–1648) 116, 168
Lucy (1588–1604) 110

Whiting
Katherine 153, 154, 210, 269
Samuel 63, 64, 104, 153, 210

Willard
Susan Noble (1782–1864) 265

Willis
Elizabeth (1621–1684) 157, 216

Willoughby
Elizabeth (1514–1580) 37

Wilson
Abigail (1694–1736) 218
Alice (1588–1658) 61, 101

Winn
Ann (1626–1682) 155, 210
Edward (1599–1682) 105, 154, 210

Winter
Joan (1545–1634) 73
Sarah (1564–1664) 35, 69
Sir Knight William (1536–1589) 35

Winthrop
John (1588–1649) 205
Mary 205

Wolcott
Anna (1620–1704) 74, 114, 166
Henry (1578–1655) 39, 73, 114
John (1516–1571) 39
John (1545–1623) 39, 73
Mehitabel (1689–1709) 162

woman
an unknown 56, 82, 97, 119, 134, 136, 172, 182, 188
an unknown (ca.1700–) 182, 238, 240

Woodbridge
Anne (ca 1653–1700) 205
Ashbel (ca.1704–1758) 259
Benjamin (1645–1709) 205, 257
Dorothy (1649–) 205, 258
John (1613–1695) 205, 257, 258, 259
John (1644–1691) 205, 257
John (ca.1590–1637) 205
John (ca.1697–1697) 258
Joseph (ca.1657–1726) 205, 259
Lucy (1641–) 205, 257
Martha (ca.1660–1738) 205, 259
Mary (1662–1712) 205, 259
Mary (ca.1692–1766) 258
Ruth (ca.1695–1731) 258
Sarah (1640–ca.1690) 205
Susanna (ca.1703–) 258
Theodore (ca.1717–ca.1747) 259
Thomas (1648–1681) 205, 258
Timothy (1656–1732) 205, 258
Timothy (ca.1686–1742) 258

Woodruff
Darius (–1841) 264

Wright
Francis (ca.1570–ca.1651) 158
Francis (ca.1601–1655) 158, 216
Francis (ca.1660–1713) 217
Richard Whittington (1633–1663) 158, 216

Wyatt
Margaret (1569–1642) 32

Wyllis
Hezekiah 258
Mehitabel 258

Wynne
Edward (1570–1645) 65, 105, 154
George (1550–1610) 29, 64, 105

Maurice (1529–1580) 29, 64

York
Edmund 151

Yorke
Dorothy (–1643) 151, 204, 205, 206
Elizabeth (1515–1601) 34, 68

Mary (1540–1596) 33, 67, 108
Roger (1497–1535) 33
Sir Richard (ca.1494–) 34
Thomas (1520–1574) 33, 67

Yuill
Margaret (ca.1712–) 250

About the Author

Ronald W. Collins, is the Chair of the Hebron, NH Historic District Commission, and served as the President of the Hebron Historical Society for fourteen years. He has written a number of histories, genealogies and literary books. His works include:

The Genealogy of the Clan MacLean;

The McLanes – The Origin of the Clan;

The McLanes – A New Hampshire Clan;

The History of Governor Nathaniel Berry;

Sergeant John Ordway, A History with his Genealogy;

A History of Newfound Lake;

The History of Hebron, NH;

The Genealogies of Hebron, NH;

The Collins Family History, and many other genealogies available on Amazon.

Ron is also a recognized poet. His collected work has been published under the title *Found There*. He has also edited four anthologies of poetry and prose: *Shadows of Water, Hills of Light, Valley of Ice*, and *Angles of Life*.

All of Ron's historical and genealogical works were published after he retired from a successful business career as a Fortune 500 vice president, and CEO of an international high-tech company. He lives in Hebron, NH. He is a member of the New England Historic Genealogical Society, the Scottish Genealogical Society and the Mull Museum.

Collins Publishing

Collins Publishing specializes in books of high quality by experienced, new and undiscovered authors. See our website at www.ColPub.com.

Collins Publishing started in 1994 as a publisher of family genealogies. In the last decade Collins Publishing has branched out into publishing novels, literary books, histories, novels, and cookbooks. We publish for writers, companies, as well as for towns, non-profits, and individuals.

Collins Publishing is a partner with Amazon, which sells all Collins Publishing books worldwide. Collins Publishing also e-publishes with Kindle.

Books Published by Collins Publishing

History and Genealogy Books
- The Ancestral History of Winfield Shaw Clark
- The McLanes - A New Hampshire Clan
- The McLanes - Origin of the Clan
- The Genealogy of the Clan MacLean
- The History of Hebron, NH
- The Genealogies of Hebron, NH
- Noted Women of Hebron, NH
- The History of Sergeant John Ordway
- The Ancestors of Anne Marie Boyce
- The Collins Family History
- A History of Newfound Lake
- The Ancestral History of the Constance Lee Cummings Family
- The Ancestral History of the William Bura Nobles Family
- The Ancestral History of Mary Andrews Smith

Literary works
- Newfound Poets 2011 - Shadows of Water, a collection of Poems and drawings
- Newfound Writers 2012 - Angles of Life, collection of poems, prose and drawings

- Newfound Writers 2013 - <u>Hills of Light</u>, poems, short stories, legends and historical sketches
- Newfound Writers 2014 - <u>Valley of Ice</u>, a collection of poems and essays
- <u>Found There</u> the collected poetical works of R. W. Collins.
- <u>Letters to Ezra</u> by Guy B. Stiles
- <u>Walking on the World</u> the collected poetical works of Guy B. Stiles
- <u>Myself and Others and the World</u> poetical works of Guy B. Stiles
- <u>Between Two Worlds</u> poetical works of Guy B. Stiles

Sci Fi, Fantasy and Novels
- <u>Isgalduin</u> by R.C. Setarcos
- <u>Tales of Isgalduin</u> edited by R.C. Setarcos
- <u>Hayden's War</u> by David Nash
- <u>Scythe of Chronos</u> by David Nash
- <u>Scenic Drive</u> by Ajeeb Prince
- <u>Ben's War</u> by David Nash
- <u>From Ash and Ruin</u> by David Nash

Cook Books
- <u>The Lakes Region Culinary Institute Cookbook</u>
- <u>Eat Well and Stay Healthy</u> by the Lakes Region Culinary Institute

North East Genealogical Research (NEGenRes)
(Established 1994)

All of the genealogies published by Collins Publishing were researched and written by NEGenRes. Since 1994 NEGenRes has researched the following families among many others:

A

Abel, Adams, Alexander, Alford, Aplington, Arcand

B

Baldwin, Ball, Ballard, Barlow, Bartlett, Barton, Beausoliel, Becker, Beeston, Bennett, Bidwell, Blevins, Blood, Bousque, Bowers, Boyce, Braley, Breland (Breichling), Brereton, Bronk, Brooks, Brown, Bryan, Bulkeley, Burton, Butler

C

Cane, Charlton, Chartier, Chauncey, Cheney, Chevalier, Clark, Colburn, Coleman, Collins, Converse, Cooley, Cook, Coon, Costello, Crawford, Crete, Crosby, Cummings

D

D'Arcy, Danieland, Dedrick, Denslow. Dibble, Dodd, Dolbere, Dorr, Doucet, Drace, Drury, Dudley

E

Ebenezer, Elliot, Ellmers, Eno, Ephraim, Esty, Eyre

F

Fabbri, Forbis, Forcier, Fordred, Foster, Fowler, Frederick, Frye, Funk, Funston

G

Gardner, Gauthier, Gay, Gaylord, Getman, Gibson, Giddings, Gilbert, Gillette, Goetschius, Goodale, Goodhue, Goodrich, Gould, Gregory, Grimwood, Grosvenor, Gugel

H

Haight, Hall, Hallock, Hammond, Hansen, Hanson, Hardy, Harper, Haskell, Haskins, Haas, Hay, Hazelton, Henry, Hobart, Hobart, Hobbs, Holland, Holmes, Holton, Hopkins, Hough, Hubert, Huntington, Hus

I

Ingram

Descendants of Duke of Normandy, King of England William The Conqueror

J

Jackson, Jacob, James, Johnson, Jonas

K

Keet, Kelsey, Kendall, Kilmer, Kimmel, Klingler, Knowles, Kuhn (Coon)

L

LaFarr, LaFontaine, Lamphere, Leggett, Leigh, Leland, Leppard (LaPort), Littlefield, Lockhart, Loescher, Lovejoy

M

MacLean, Mahaffey, Marcot, Marvin, Mathieu, Matteson, McCullum, McLane, McLaughlin, McLean, Melvin, Miller, Morgan, Morse, Mudge

N

Nevens, Newhall, Nichols, Nobles, Noyes

O

Ordway, Osgood

P

Perkins, Persinger, Phelps, Philbrook, Phillips, Pickering, Pike, Pittsley, Platt, Potter, Powers, Prescott, Prichard

R

Reynolds, Robinson, Robitaille, Runnels, Russell

S

Samuel, Sanger, Saraceno, Schilling, Schneider, Seeley, Shattuck, Shaw, Simeon, Simonson. Skinner, Slaten, Smith, Spencer, Sturges, Sutphen, Swartout

T

Tate, Taylor, Thurber, Treat, Trice, Tuck, Turner, Tuttle

V

Vacher, Verts, Voltz, Vore

W

Walfield, Walton, Ward, Warren, Webster, Weisinger, Weller, Westgate, Wharton, White, Whitten, Wies, Wiley, Williams, Wilson, Winegar, Wise, Walbolt, Woodbridge, Wright.

Contact NEGenRes at www.NEGenRes@ColPub.com

Printed in Great Britain
by Amazon